PRAISE FOR
SINCE I LOST MY BABY

"Selimah's life has been filled with both the bliss and the blisters of growing up in Los Angeles in the 1960s. Moving on throughout the decades, Selimah has an almost Zelig-like life story that put her in the middle of many historical events. She is a writer of great integrity and creativity, and her life story is a compelling read."

- TOM VICKERS
Former Record Executive and
Minister of Information for Parliament-Funkadelic

"Selimah Nemoy's memoir, *Since I Lost My Baby*, is more than the recounting of some portion of a human being's life story. It is also the weaving of that story within the context of history. With searing honesty and remarkable insight, she reveals a young woman who has earned every right to have her story read widely. I cannot think of another memoir so genuinely candid about the drive to love and to be loved, and the price a young woman is forced to pay to follow her heart. She is adept at shining a light on a culture that pretends to love a lover but instead punishes her free spirit at every turn. This is no confession; it is a skillfully crafted tale of love in all its forms."

- CORIE SKOLNICK
Author, *Orfan* and *America's Most Eligible*;
Blogger, Desto3.com

"Selimah Nemoy's writing is so transformative in its descriptions, her story so honestly told from her gut-wrenching reality, that the journey becomes a cinematic roller coaster, which makes me grapple for the words to compel you to strap in and take the ride. Reading *Since I Lost My Baby*, you may see the world whirling from another perspective than from the ground you are used to walking on, or it may take you back to familiar territory, like the track of your favorite song. Whatever your experience, you'll be glad you took the ride."

— AKOSUA BUSIA
Author / Actress

"In *Since I Lost My Baby*, Selimah Nemoy captures the cultural essence and exuberance of the 1970s, and the profound influence that era's music spoke into our lives. As The Emotions, my sisters and I are proud to have been part of that influence, and Selimah's got the best of our love for telling her story."

— WANDA VAUGHN
Singer and Songwriter, The Emotions

"Captivating! With elegance and wit, Selimah Nemoy artfully weaves the tempo and beat of a generation into an inspiring tale. While uncovering her truths, she leads us on a journey of loss, discovery, and redemption of self. *Since I Lost My Baby* is a glorious celebration of life itself. Brava!"

— ALEXIA LaFORTUNE
Author, *Sex, Love and Spirit*

"Great storytelling. Its raw sweetness pulls you in and takes you on a ride with one 'wow' after another."

— GLORIA WEINSTOCK
Actor, Director;
Professor, Chair (Retired), Theatre Department,
City College of San Francisco

SINCE I LOST MY BABY

Copyright © 2020 by Selimah Nemoy

All rights reserved. No part of this publication or photographs contained within it may be reproduced, distributed, or transmitted in any form or by any means, including photocopying, recording, digital scanning, or other electronic or mechanical methods, without the prior written permission of the publisher, except in the case of brief quotations embodied in critical reviews and certain other noncommercial uses permitted by copyright law. For permission requests, please address OGPressPublishing@gmail.com

> FREE CULTURAL DECODER – Get a free Decoder to the multicultural tapestry of music, people, and historical events referenced in *Since I Lost My Baby*; listen to the author's curated playlist, and get a free Book Club Reading Guide at selimahnemoy.com

Printed in the United States of America

ISBN 978-1-7341547-0-2 (Paperback)

ISBN 978-1-7341547-2-6 (Hardcover)

ISBN 978-1-7341547-1-9 (Ebook)

Library of Congress Control Number: 2019916407

For permission requests and inquiries, contact OGPressPublishing@gmail.com

selimahnemoy.com

SINCE I LOST MY BABY

A Memoir of Temptations, Trouble & Truth

SELIMAH NEMOY

OG PRESS • LOS ANGELES, CALIFORNIA

CONTENTS

Prologue | vii

PART ONE

Prisoner of Love | 1

PART TWO

You Can't Always Get What You Want | 79

PART THREE

Signed, Sealed, Delivered, I'm Yours | 177

PART FOUR

My Girl | 239

Epilogue | 293

With Love | 297

Author's Note | 299

About The Author | 301

Resources | 303

PROLOGUE

Los Angeles, 1967

For What It's Worth

I'd paid my dues, big time, the ultimate price for committing the unpardonable sin. After five months of humiliating incarceration, with the stroke of a ballpoint pen I agreed to the life sentence that had been handed down: I was walking out of there alone.

Early morning fog met me on the landing outside, and the whiff of budding flowers on a weedy Scotch Broom in the alley caught me by surprise. I wondered if it was heralding my freedom or mourning my loss. My father, shoulders sagging with resignation and relief, went first, carrying my suitcase to the car, where my mother, eyes forward but looking at nothing, was waiting inside with the doors locked.

I took one look back at the hideous institution from which I was being released. Behind its windows, like dark condemning eyes, were generations of secrets and shame—where the wanton and wayward were imprisoned by wicked old witches who had been born with their ugly gray hair in a bun and never been loved by a man in their whole life.

Across the street behind a chain link fence, a dirty Chihuahua yapped and barked as, for the last time, I descended the wide concrete steps of the Florence Crittenton Home for Unwed Mothers, a relic of last-century history to which teenage girls like me were banished for the crime of falling in love.

Halfway down the steps I heard someone call my name. The Director had forgotten to give me her farewell speech: those tired, fake words of wisdom that unimaginative old people hand to young ones as if they were tools or money or the Bible. Standing on the step above me, she put one lizard-like paw on my shoulder.

"Now dear, you're only seventeen years old. Your whole life is ahead of you. We've taken care of everything."

I held my breath, along with the urge to slap her and watch those withered old legs go tumbling down the stairs.

And then, just like everyone else who had ever inflicted damage on me, she poured on the perma-seal.

"Just go home and pretend it never happened."

PART ONE

PRISONER OF LOVE

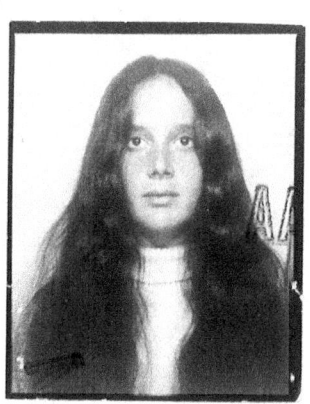

CHAPTER ONE

Los Angeles, 1971

The wide metal doors of the service elevator, creaking and worn from the strain of carrying so many lost souls, moved toward one another to close shut and take me to my assigned cellblock. I was twenty years old and had just finished being interrogated and booked at the Sybil Brand Institute for Women, a miserable facility on the eastern rim of downtown Los Angeles. It was my first time going to jail but not my maiden voyage of being locked up.

As the grimy panels of the elevator were about to meet, a voice from down the hall shouted, "Stop! Wait!" and the guard escorting me shoved a stubby palm between them, causing the doors to pop back open, allowing in three women and their jailor returning from the day's proceedings in court. It was late, about seven o'clock, and before going to our cells, we were all herded to the dining hall to be fed.

The two guards were faceless female forms stuffed into khaki; leather and metal jangling about their waists like a belly dancer's hip scarf. The three women prisoners joining us were the same age as I was and looked exactly like me: jail-issued denim dresses, dark blue varsity sweaters, and flip flops, although I noticed one was shod in clunky, orthopedic-type shoes. With our long dark hair and matching outfits, the four of us looked like repeating mirror images of one another.

The elevator doors finally closed, and a distinct tension began to fill the cabin. As it rose, the vibration escalated, making me scared the elevator was going to crash. I glanced toward the girls riding with me and saw an all-knowing smirk curling from the mouth of the one in the clunky shoes.

Her head was angled so that the guard wouldn't notice, and her eyes turned barely but quite deliberately in my direction, as if to make the point that although we were all in handcuffs, she harnessed a power that was beyond theirs. Then I realized that the distress in the elevator was cosmic, not mechanical, and I noticed the pale scar of an "x" between her brows and on the foreheads of the other two.

And finally I recognized who I was in the elevator with.

Like me, and like so many of us in the 1960s, Susan Atkins, Patricia Krenwinkel, and Leslie Van Houten arrived at the end of their teenage years damaged, vulnerable, desperate for love, and searching for the Big Truth. Certainly there were other less obvious, perhaps even pathological things that set us apart. But from my perspective in 1971, there was only one distinction between us.

I'd never crossed paths with Charles Manson.

Mindful of the guards, I studied the three hippie girls as if I were looking at myself. They had just been convicted of the 1969 murders of pregnant actress Sharon Tate and four others in Benedict Canyon; and that of a Los Feliz couple, Leno and Rosemary LaBianca, and were now in the sentencing phase of their trial, facing the death penalty. Ever since their arrest, sensational stories about the so-called Manson family had filled the newspapers. But standing face-to-face with them in the jail elevator that night, it was as difficult to imagine these three girls my age stabbing their victims to death and writing on the walls with their blood as it was to imagine myself doing that.

And yet, though it was merely a cliché to me in 1971, there was little else I could think of that had kept me from becoming one of them.

"There but for the grace of God go I."

Hitting The Wall

"Up against the wall!" we used to say out there in the quad of San Fernando Valley State College in Northridge, California, where I'd spent most of the four years prior to getting busted raising my voice and shaking my fist at the sky. "Up against the wall . . . !" followed by a colorful twelve-letter epithet beginning with the word "mother" that substituted for the name of any and all Establishment lackeys.

Swirling untethered in the Kennedy-Oswald-Ruby triangle, enraged by the war in Vietnam, and pumped on the boiling anger that had exploded in Watts and Newark and Detroit, we were the Alienation Generation: true believers in the idea that there was nothing left to believe in, and that a new order, by any means necessary, had to be forged. Back then it was a clear-cut Us against Them affair: the People vs. the Man. If you weren't part of the solution, you were part of the problem. And as the curtain fell on the peace-love contingent of the 1960s, courtesy of Susan, Patricia, and Leslie, we ended the decade suspicious, cynical, and hating everything.

But here at Sybil Brand Jail, "the wall" became something else: something to become like; something flat and dull, without anxiety or feelings; something without fear or hope; something without life. We all had to go there. Eventually every prisoner was forced to transit the arc of arrest frenzy and jailhouse denial, and to don the glaze of nothingness just to get through each hour. To become blank, like the mush-colored walls that held us in. There wasn't a doggone thing I could do about all the stuff that worried me like, *What am I doing here?* or *Who's going to water my Coleus?*

After dinner, where there was no talking allowed, the Manson girls and I went our separate ways, and I landed in a cell with Liz, a chunky lesbian who seemed to have some pull around the cellblock. When she saw I came in there with nothing, Liz handed me a Hershey bar and showed me a stash of candy, tampons, and cigarettes, which she used for barter and also sold at a mark-up when there was no commissary. Liz was tough, but for no apparent reason, she was nicer to me than I expected anyone to be. Word got around that I had no money, and as other women made bail, several of them left behind for me the little denim drawstring bags they'd been issued to keep their coins and wadded-up dollar bills in.

"Here, girl, you take this," said one sister, pushing her small bag through the bars. She had long fingernails, choppy jet black hair, and a huge cursive tattoo peeking out of the neckline of her dress.

"I got stuff on the outside." She smiled. "You be okay now."

I was surprised by the unexpected kindness. But Sybil's wasn't without class distinctions.

"What's your rap?" we were always being asked. That answer was far more important than your name; it established your identity, rank, and status. Although I appeared to be a *la-de-dah* flower child, with my look-alike hippie jail-mates convicted of murder, prisoners were now cautious about judging one another on appearance only. While the charges against me weren't capital murder, they were serious enough to raise plucked eyebrows and keep the bullies at bay.

For my part, it was felony dumbness that I wound up in jail. That day I'd been hanging out with a golden-haired hippie named John who suggested we stop by his pal Wally's place for something to drink. We'd only been there for five minutes when undercover cops wearing Hawaiian shirts came to the door. Holding a lit joint in his hand, Wally, who was dealing pot and pills, opened up and let them in. After the cops tore up Wally's bungalow, the three of us were handcuffed, shackled together, and taken to jail, where we were all charged with felony sales and possession.

I spent my first night at Sybil's huddled in my bunk, staring at the wall, and commanding my soul to shut down every emotion. At five o'clock in the morning, the guards shuffled us bleary-eyed toward the dining hall, where we were lined up single file with prisoners from the other cellblocks. At nearly every meal, I found myself sitting across from at least one pasty-faced girl with stringy hair and an "x" carved in between her eyebrows. You might think that the Manson family was composed only of the infamous handful involved in the Tate-La Bianca murders. But every movement has its doers and its followers—minor league groupies and wannabes who hang out on the fringe and talk the talk but somehow miss the Big Moment.

The inmates at Sybil's were of every age and background, including a shy, soft-spoken woman named Frankie who loved being in a place where she had her own bed, got fed three squares a day, and where people cared about what she did, even if they were guards. Frankie made no secret about the fact that as soon as they let her out, she would do something else so she could come back to jail. And then there was the elderly black lady who had gotten her wig in a tizzle for the last time at her abusive old husband, finally taking matters, and a pistol, into her own hands.

Our individual cell doors, which faced the narrow caged hallway of our cellblock, were opened during the day, and we were allowed to walk the length of the hallway within our block. A few days into my stay, I noticed a Latina woman who, despite the ban on going back to bed, was curled up in a fetal position on her bunk, her waist-length black hair wiping grime on the floor. Her head came up slowly when she saw me, and the two of us stared at one another for a long time. She wasn't that old, but she was a total wreck. Face mottled from acne, raccoon circles around her eyes, her scrawny brown body folded up like a lawn chair. She was a junkie, and she was going through withdrawal.

"You okay?" I asked.

She nodded her head and sat up.

"Why don't you tell the guard you need to go to the infirmary?"

"Cause I'm just in here for kiting. I can't get sent to a program. I got kids."

And suddenly we knew.

Her name was Marguerite, and we'd been locked up together four years earlier at the Florence Crittenton Home for Unwed Mothers, where she had been exotic, beautiful, and friendly. The two of us used to go for walks together, cutting through the alley where the Scotch Broom grew.

"You kept your baby?"

"Of course," she said, as if anything else was unthinkable.

I stepped back. No one—not the social worker, the Director, or my parents—had told me that keeping my baby was an option.

A pained smile crossed Marguerite's face. She reached out toward me from her bed.

"And now I got two more," she said proudly.

I didn't want to hear it. I fumbled in the pocket of my dress, handing over the Hershey bar Liz had given me; maybe it would help her get through the pain. Without saying goodbye, I turned and went back to my cell to stare at the wall.

Let Me Go The Right Way

Just my luck, I got arrested on the Thursday night before the four-day President Abraham Lincoln holiday weekend, so the clock wouldn't start ticking on my arraignment, which someone told me was required within seventy-two court hours, until Tuesday. Monday was the day Liz had waited for, banked on; the day when, after a long weekend in which the commissary was closed, everyone was out of everything, and she could mark up her prices accordingly.

I did my best to count the court hours, but I didn't know if they took off an hour for lunch breaks or what, and the days dragged on until I'd been there without going before a judge for seven days. Finally a guard came and told me, "The District Attorney has reviewed your case and determined there is not enough evidence to press charges."

Like duh, I could have told him that.

I pushed the little drawstring bag I'd carried since the night I arrived, a few coins still left, into Marguerite's hands as the guard escorted me past her cell and out of the block. They let me use the phone to call my father, who'd picked up my impounded Dodge Lancer the day I was arrested, and a few hours later he arrived at the jail. I would rather have taken the bus to my apartment in Hollywood, but my dad wanted to give me the heads-up that he'd told my mom I'd spent the weekend in San Diego. I was ashamed at having gotten into such awful trouble and agreed with him that not telling my mother the truth was for the best.

Having come so close to losing my freedom, I was desperately grateful to get home to my apartment on La Mirada Avenue, where my Coleus had died. That night I vowed to become a reformed citizen with appropriate fear of authority, and never to do anything wrong again.

CHAPTER TWO

Los Angeles, 1958-1960

A Very Cold War

The recess monitor checked her wristwatch, then blew her whistle twice, and all of us out there on the schoolyard blacktop froze in our tracks, just as we'd been taught to do. Flabby dodgeballs bounced away from their painted boundaries. Tetherballs orbited around their poles with no kids to punch them back. Petticoats up, girls were caught midway on the turnover rails, while boys dangled from the monkey bars, a few dropping to their feet in the sand.

And then we heard it begin: the low, ominous moan building up to a terrifying howl. It was the Civil Defense air raid siren going off. Even the teachers seemed to stiffen when they heard it blaring from the yellow bullhorn mounted on a tall pole at the corner.

Think fast! Is today The End? After all, Khrushchev said he was going to bury us.

It was useless to scan the blacktop for a friend; no one in elementary school liked me. I tried to reel myself back in with the one fact I knew.

It's Friday. It's twelve o'clock noon. It's just The Test.

Still, I couldn't help looking up at the sky, expecting to hear the faint roar of bombers overhead and see them descending upon my North Hollywood neighborhood like a hateful flock of birds. The siren blared for its assigned number of seconds as we all stood suspended in mid-play. Then I began to worry, as I did every week.

What if the Soviets know that Friday at noon is when we do The Test? What a perfect time for them to catch us off guard and attack! They know we'll think it's only The Test!

I considered telling a teacher, but when the siren's screaming wail faded and I saw other kids returning to play, I sighed and thought better of it. No one listened to me or cared what I thought, and what difference would it make anyway. The End was hanging over us, and there was no hope for the future.

It's Only Make Believe

When I was little, my mother used to tell me a bedtime story about what happened on the steamship that brought her and her sister Miriam to the New World from Poland in the late 1920s. We both thought it was such a funny story that I made her tell it to me every night.

"They gave us bananas to eat, but we had never seen a banana before," she would say. "And we didn't know any better what to do, so we peeled it, and we ate the peel, and then we threw away the banana."

I could just see my mom and my Aunt Mary as little girls, standing on the deck of a big honking steamship, tossing bananas overboard into the roiling, foggy sea.

Like all the stories my mother told me, I didn't question the veracity of having a tropical fruit for a mainstay on a ship huddled with terrified Jewish refugees. Or that any adult would let two children stand on the deck of a ship and toss food overboard. Each and every one of us is born a true believer: irresistibly, humanly hardwired to accept that everything our parents tell us is true, no matter how preposterous, confusing, or out of touch with what we will shortly—and perhaps shockingly—discover is the way the "real" world works.

For my mother, whose parents died in Poland when she was a toddler, reality was a frightening monster, and truth a do-it-yourself improvement project. After the United States enacted restrictive immigration quotas in 1924, it was impossible for Jews to get visas. So my mother and her sister Miriam, the youngest of fourteen children, were put on a ship to Canada by their adult siblings in Poland. Upon their arrival, the little girls were met by cousins who then hid them under blankets in the backseat of a car and drove them to New York, where two of their adult sisters had managed to legally emigrate years earlier. The rest of my mother's family, who were in possession of steamship tickets to the United States but couldn't obtain visas, were forced to remain in Poland and eventually perished in the Holocaust.

There was never talk about the "old country" in our house. My mother's fractured childhood was as well buried as a body in the basement, but the stench of that undealt-with horror pervaded everything. As if to ensure that my passage in life, unlike hers, would be on the good ship *Lollipop*, she dyed my hair blond like Shirley Temple's when I was three years old.

Lonely Teardrops

Life for me was always different.

From the day I'd entered kindergarten wearing my brother's hand-me-down, zipper-up-the-front jeans, instead of the kind girls were supposed to wear with the zipper on the side, I knew I was in for it. Even the food I brought to school made me an outsider.

"Jews don't eat that kind of *dreck*," my mother said when I asked her to make me a single-slice baloney-on-white-bread sandwich like I saw other kids pull out of their lunchboxes. I'm not sure how being Jewish got into the mix, but my mother's idea of a sandwich was four inches thick on coarse, dark bread, unlike anything I'd ever seen on TV or at school. I yearned for that refined, squishy-soft white bread that came in a blue gingham bag and was guaranteed to build strong bodies twelve ways, but there was no way in *Sheol* my mother would ever let that into our house.

By the time I was ten, I had reached my full adult height, needed Kotex and a bra, and had clocked in at 160 on my fifth-grade IQ test. That resulted in a conference in which the school counselor told my parents that I consistently tested at the genius level; she urged them to let the school skip me to the seventh grade, where I would be academically stimulated and fit in better.

My mother wouldn't hear of it; she wanted me to have a "normal" life.

Are you blind? The other kids don't even reach my elbow. They make fun of me in the bathroom. I'm not like them. I'm not even like you.

Normal or not, my parents decided I would stay where I was.

The way I see it, along with being born true believers, we are also equipped with an intuitive antenna to discern truth from lies, and that which is life-giving from that which is not. All of us arrive in this world with a functioning antenna until it's bent, broken, or hacked off altogether by people in authority who tell you that what you see isn't what you think it is; that what you feel isn't real; and that when anything hurts you, the best thing to do is just pretend it never happened.

Los Angeles, 1964-1965

Turned Out

By the time I was fourteen, I'd grown into my too-big-for-childhood body; my horsey overbite had been corrected with braces, and as long as I didn't say too many sentences in a row, you might have mistaken me for anyone else.

Junior high had put some welcome distance between me and my elementary school tormentors. I was in awe of the so-called "cheap" girls from ninth grade with their tight skirts and confident swagger. Yet despite my aching emptiness, I remained true to what I thought my parents wanted me to believe about being a "good" girl, though if asked, I could not have explained what that was. It didn't add up to substance or motivation, but having no other frame of reference, I accepted this irrelevance as how things probably were for everybody. Life was a random series of meaningless events, and then you die. *Just passin' through. Why bother? What, me worry?*

In the fall of 1964 however, the transformative moment of my young life took place.

The kid across the street, Richard, and I used to play ball and do stuff like ride our bikes in the dirt, collect old cans, and play store. He was three years older than me, and while he was my most consistent playmate, I can't say I thought of him as my friend. Being friends seemed to involve sharing secrets and emotions and other things that Richard and I never talked about. Maybe it was because he was a boy. I'd just ring the front doorbell, and he'd come out and we'd play.

It was October, and Richard had gotten hold of free tickets to a taping at the Santa Monica Civic Auditorium: a live concert for teenagers showcasing popular and emerging American and British artists like the Beach Boys and the Rolling Stones. Filmed in a new technology called Electronovision, the concert was to be shown later that year in movie theaters. It was called Teen Age Music International, or the TAMI show. My parents liked Richard and knew it wasn't, heaven forbid, a date or anything like that, so they let me go. Richard borrowed his dad's two-tone Buick, and we drove to Santa Monica, parked in the lot, and took our seats with thousands of other teenage kids in the cavernous auditorium.

Screaming comes naturally when you're young, hormone-fueled, and prevented by social taboos from expressing yourself any other way. In 1964 kids were still clean-cut, and skirts were still knee-length. So it's no surprise that the ear-splitting sound of screaming teenagers attended every moment of the TAMI show taping.

It was in the midst of this great human outpouring that I was baptized in what would become the litany and gospel of my teenage life: *Motown*. I had never before seen performers like the Miracles or Marvin Gaye, with their sultry, slick moves; or girls like the Supremes, all pouty, hair-sprayed, and glamorous. Something began to resonate inside me, not only to the rhythms of their music but also to the words celebrating heartbreak, betrayal, and suffering.

I didn't understand it, but I *felt* it. Out of the meaningless void with which I'd tried to come to terms, Motown exposed me to another world in which there *was* a place for passion—a world in which love was both the thing that saved you, and the thing that sent you to hell.

But when a compact black tornado in a checkered jacket with a mile-high pompadour took the stage, skating across on one foot, screeching and howling like a trapped coyote, and then, microphone stand and all, crashed to his knees—only to be comforted, caped, and brought to his feet by two lanky, conked brothers in shiny suits—and then break loose, stomping and wailing and busting through every inhibition known to man, I knew I had stumbled upon the threshold to heaven, and nothing would ever be the same. I had just encountered Mr. Dynamite himself, James Brown, and the Famous Flames.

It was the first time I'd ever witnessed anyone acting out all the madness and fury that I felt, having been rejected by kids, shut down by my parents, and made to think that nobody else in the world was like me. In soul singer James Brown, I saw a man who wasn't embarrassed or afraid to express all the exuberance and emotions that I had always been forced to restrain in myself.

I'd come to the Santa Monica Civic Auditorium believing that life was just a series of random, meaningless events and left a born-again convert to the power that exploded from its stage. Something got ahold of me, and as if revived from the dead, my antenna began to regrow. My previously pointless existence now honed in on that long-denied feeling and the uninhibited expression of it: SOUL. *Where does it come from? What does it mean?* Those two questions began to influence every choice I made and compelled my life's most imperative quest: To make direct contact with, and be validated by, something that was *really real*.

My first stop was KGFJ, Los Angeles's soul music radio station. Here disc jockeys like the Magnificent Montague (whose on-air catchphrase, "Burn, baby, burn!" would become the anthem of the Watts riots ten months later) kept me fed on a rich diet of soul music from artists like Bo Diddley, the Isley Brothers, and Ike and Tina Turner.

I didn't know anything about race or its implications. With my transistor radio now my lifeline and permanently stuck to my ear, all I knew was that soul music was the first thing that had ever moved me. Even if there was something unholy going on in the relationships the artists sang about, something sacred was going on inside of that music; something that filled up more

than my ears. I was irresistibly drawn by an intangible presence in the wailing music and desperate lyrics that begged for love, glorified its union, or brokenheartedly mourned its loss.

After the TAMI show, I started going to dances at the Valley Teen Center, a flat-roofed shoebox of building on Victory Boulevard in Van Nuys. Unlike all-white North Hollywood, kids at the Teen Center came from the black and Mexican neighborhoods of Pacoima and San Fernando. Although I had been klutzy and unathletic in school, I happily discovered I was a good dancer. It was a form of communication that, unlike words, could not be misunderstood.

I fell in love with dancing and discovered who I could be through it. Sweaty Saturday nights at the Teen Center were like tribal rituals; sometimes with a partner or all of us together, thumbs out for Marvin Gaye's "Hitch Hike." Or going down the middle of the room in between two lines of other dancers to Jr. Walker & the All Stars's "Shotgun."

It was soul music and seductive mayhem, flaunting our indestructible young flesh with confidence. Nothing less than the real thing would do. When the lights went down, we paired off into couples, tempting fate in the slow dances and whispering our terminal love to one another. Only the tambourine of Martha and the Vandellas's "Nowhere To Run" could shake us out of our trance.

I was hooked.

I started taking the bus after school to Hollywood, where I would head for the KTLA Studios on Sunset and Van Ness to dance on Casey Kasem's TV show *Shebang*. Patterned stockings were the rage, and I got the idea to cut the letters S-H-E-B-A-N-G out of felt fabric, then carefully place them on my calf, under the stocking on my left leg, where the camera would see it when I danced. It was a kick to watch myself on our TV at home, prancing around with the show's regulars, like Famous Hooks and June Strode, as well as artists like Little Stevie Wonder who came to lip-sync their hits. Though I never went to the show with a partner, the cameraman always photographed me dancing in a way that looked like I was with someone. It was one of the few frauds I could take pride in.

Between KGFJ, the Teen Center, and dancing on *Shebang*, I found my place in the universe, and for the first time I felt like I belonged. I was no longer the oddball; the music and songs spoke to my inner being, and in turn I could make people respond to me through dance.

I expected my parents to be overjoyed when I told them that I had finally made friends with kids who liked me and who thought about the same things that I did, including one boy from the Teen Center who'd become my regular Saturday dance partner. Assuming they would want to meet my new friends, I asked to invite them to our house for lunch.

I was floored when my parents told me no because my friends were black.

Like most Jews, my parents claimed to be liberals, voted Democrat, and nodded their endorsement of the civil rights movement. Assuming that meant they were open-minded, I had dismissed my mother's antagonism toward Gentiles, whom she called *goyim* or "heathens," as simply her peculiar landscape, never imagining that Negroes might be included in that category.

"You're not inviting them here," my father said. "Don't give them our address."

"What are you talking about?" I said. "Aren't you happy for me? Aren't all men created equal? That's what they teach in school. That's what you taught me."

"We can't have them over here. Not at our home."

"Please," I begged. "These are the first real friends I've ever had. I just want you to meet them."

"There will be other friends," said my mother.

"You're hypocrites!"

"Enough!" said my father. "You'll do what we say. You're too young to understand."

And with that, the case was closed.

My trust in my parents was shattered, and at that moment my world split from theirs. With no greater truth to hang onto, I'd been a true believer in the irrelevance their fears had wrought in me. But now that I knew what it felt like to be happy, there was no turning back. I wasn't going to give up my friends in favor of their prejudice.

It was the breach that invalidated everything my parents had ever taught me. That's the thing about being a true believer: It's all or nothing. There isn't any dimmer switch. Nothing my parents said could dampen the flame that'd been ignited in my heart. I'd become part of a community in which people questioned their place in the world, as I did. And the soul-wrenching, exhilarating depth of the music drew us together into what I'd been searching for my whole life: something that was *really real*. Dancing was our perfectly understood, wordless, rhetoric-free language.

For the first time I felt like I mattered, and on Saturday nights and at the TV studio I was free to discover, express, and be all that I really was. I loved my parents, but they turned my happiness into a racial issue in which all of us lost our identities and were divided by things over which we had no control.

So I abandoned their authority and became a star pupil to the raspy, tortured treatises of David Ruffin, lead singer of the Temptations; and a diehard disciple of the Gospel of Gordy, Saint Stax, and Master Motown. The message my musical teachers taught me was that being loved was the only thing worth living for. Whether it was ecstasy or agony didn't matter, as long you were committed to a lovesick drama powerful enough to kill you.

The wounds of so much "love" were like tribal scarring: painful but necessary rites of passage into the depths of my soul. At fifteen years old, I had no idea how much deeper it would go.

A Sewer Full Of Diamonds

Once a week my mother dropped me off at the North Hollywood Public Library, a Spanish-style building set among a sheltering grove of eucalyptus trees. Their pungent smell registered deeply that season in which I was growing out of my childhood, and evoked a longing for something I didn't understand but knew that I wanted.

I loved the library. It was where I could go and lose my problems in the rows and rows of books about other people's lives. I set a goal to read every novel in the four bookcases of the fiction section. Had I been the sort of genius who does things in a methodical way, I would not have started in the W's. But that's where I met the next person to articulate the feelings I couldn't. His books opened the door to a world that, in its own brutal and chaotic way, made more sense than the whitewashed, bland one I was being forced to grow up in.

The words and ideas of author Richard Wright—the fixated meditations on being different; a stranger to the world and its hopes; an involuntary non-conformist with no identity except that triggered by chance, madness, and tyranny—transformed my disjointed teenage angst into an existential purpose unto itself. Vicariously I took on the doomed identities of Wright's protagonists. Through *Native Son*'s terrifying journey of Bigger Thomas, who comes to life by an act of murder, I saw, as if through a lens that magnified what I felt a million times over, the same conflicted emotions that I saw in myself. I sweated through the intrigue of *The Outsider*'s Cross Damon, a frustrated postal worker who loses his overcoat and ID in a bloody train crash and winds up being declared dead, giving him the chance to become somebody else.

But the story that most captivated me was *The Man Who Lived Underground*. A frantic suspect evading cops climbs down into the sewer, where he creates a dirt sanctuary decorated with diamonds he's stolen by tunneling into a jewelry store. He makes mocking and nihilistic observations of the people at whom he peers from his detritus-strewn refuge and ends up shot dead, floating away with the trash.

Wright's world was peopled with desperate, disenfranchised souls who found themselves thrown into horrifying circumstances that not only brought them face-to-face with death but also gave form and meaning to their lives. His stories were laced with pervading anxiety and guilt that could never be put right, dreams and nightmares that supplanted reality—and all of it resonated to a frightening place in my own mind that had never been spoken to before.

The alienated and victimized characters of Richard Wright, who found their truth in violence and madness, fed what my intellectual mind longed for; while the throbbing rhythm of soul music, the raw passion that flushed out of James Brown, and the rattlesnake tambourine and long-suffering lyrics of Motown gave me flesh and bones so I could dance instead of explode.

Later, when I went to college, I read the works of writers like Ralph Ellison who gave further dimension and voice to the estrangement I had always felt, and the confusing rage I was beginning to harbor. The black writers in whose works I soaked confirmed the apocalyptic terror that had haunted me since elementary school: that The End was as imminently approaching as a hateful flock of birds.

I was too young to have any discernment so I took it all in. Once again I became a true believer, not knowing that a white girl from North Hollywood wasn't supposed to identify with the likes of Bigger Thomas. And that not everything Motown was telling me was true.

Rebel With A Clause

I want to make something clear before we go any farther. There aren't any bad guys in my story. I might say some bad things, but all the people I'm telling you about did what they did either because they were doing their jobs, like the cops, or because they didn't know any better, like my parents. Some meant well; others did not. It wasn't anyone's fault; not even the scoundrels who broke my heart. Not even Khrushchev.

Even the militant black students I met in college, who pontificated that I had no right to appropriate their writers and their pain to my life, were right in one sense: The alienation and disenfranchisement I experienced wasn't because of the color of my skin; I was an outsider because I was *different*. There are many kinds of different, but in the end, any one of us can become subject to the powerless terror of Bigger Thomas. Or the fractured fallout of a ride into the Promised Land under the backseat of a car.

When you cut through all the labels, excuses, and blame, I was born who I am and tossed like a Frisbee into the circle of life. And only God is responsible for that.

CHAPTER THREE

Los Angeles, 1966

It was only a matter of time before I crossed two boundaries. The first was, I became a liar.

In high school, the gene pool widened, and I found myself among more of the girls I'd watched from afar in junior high. I became friends with three stray cats who, like me, had no use for the sanitized suburbs and had initiated themselves into the alternate universe of soul music and dancing. All of them were older and wiser in the ways of the world. Antoinette was a meaty girl in a push-up bra, with a Miss Lady Clairol rust-colored mop, painted black eyebrows, and a gap between her front teeth big enough to float the Queen Mary. Iva had blue eyes and an alabaster complexion sprinkled with freckles. She was a dancing diva in mod rags and a beehive bubble and could outstep the best of them at our favorite nightclub, the Cinnamon Cinder. Fran was the one with a driver's license and a car.

It was simple enough. On a school night, Fran would come by my house in her turquoise and white Ford Fairlane, and my parents would wave goodbye to the four of us as we headed off to the "library"—a dance club, usually the Cinder, which was just minutes away on Ventura Boulevard in Studio City.

The Cinnamon Cinder was operated by a local deejay and had a live house band that played all the top hits. Sometimes we drove over the hill to Hollywood, where we flashed our fake ID's to inhabit another club called the Haunted House. To me, Hollywood was as exciting as legend had it. I never saw a movie star on Hollywood Boulevard, but it was where I felt like I was grown-up, out of my parents' radar, and could do anything. In contrast to the Valley's chloroform wasteland, the Boulevard, with its starry pink-and-bronze Walk of Fame, was messy and intoxicating; bustling with wig stores, lingerie parlors, tourists, and transients. Hustlers congregated at every corner, enticing visitors to the Wax Museum or shouting at passing cars and waving maps to movie stars' homes.

A few blocks away on Sunset and Vine was Wallach's Music City, a huge emporium with a row of soundproof listening booths facing the street. You could ask for a copy of any record in the store and barricade yourself in one of the booths all afternoon.

On Saturdays the Girlfriends and I would hit the sidewalk of stars with our babysitting money and go shopping crazy: a pair of fishnet stockings at Albert's Hosiery, a cute dress from Lerner's, a tiny bottle of Ambush perfume and some plastic earrings from Newberry's. Every week we'd take a roll of pictures in the photo booth: four shots for a quarter, one for each of us.

Saturday shopping was merely a prelude to the night's rendezvous. Fran would park the Fairlane, and our hearts jumped at the sound of music blaring loudly from inside the club. One last check in the rearview mirror, each of us applying Max Factor Erase Stick to white-out our lips, and another thick coat of the extra-black eyeliner we weren't allowed to wear at home. We passed around a can of Aqua Net and lacquered our do's.

The brothers were into pompadours and purple ruffled shirts, and all of them knew how to do the splits. The girls wore tight skirts, butts and knees sticking out as they danced. Teenage tail feathers shaking, we formed a black-and-white, brown-and-beige, multi-ethnic stew of soul music and hot bodies. When the tambourine shaking stopped, the lights went dim, and the band started playing "My Girl." Couples slow danced in the shadows, knees and hips touching, belly rubs and bulges, feet barely moving—all Shalimar and sixteen years old, the breathy gasp of virginity just under the wire.

Back at the Teen Center, the deejay hadn't been allowed to play two slow songs in a row, otherwise, it was feared, those bulges could turn into babies. It was a theory about as useless as a ten o'clock curfew intended to safeguard virgins from getting into "trouble." Soon enough the naïve superintendents of my teenhood would be forced to admit that the ultimate act of going all the way did not have a built-in fail-safe for specific, agreed-upon, late-night hours.

In fact, the dirty deed could happen at such an innocent time as four o'clock in the afternoon.

Summer Of Love

Six, sixty-six. Might have been the address for Satan.

In June 1966, a roar filled my city's streets as puberty-stricken teenagers tore out of schoolyards: books flying, report cards and notebooks tossed into the trunks of Mustangs and forgotten. Punks and eggheads, surfers and greasers alike all took part in the ritual. Horns honking and hormones rocking, like caged lab rats suddenly set loose, they took off in every direction; filling the buses in noisy packs, or sneaking off to lonely sections of North Hollywood Park, where they drank in the scent of freshly mown grass and groped through fasteners and elastic, finding eucalyptus seed buttons and gravel in their underwear later that night.

School was out! We were free!

All those trips to the "library," as well as my dialed-down yet still workable IQ, had garnered acceptable grades, and I had nothing on the planet to be worried about. Stepping into the bus, I dropped my coins to freedom in the fare box and watched the Valley disappear as we rumbled over the hill to Hollywood.

Today I'd left the Girlfriends behind for a very special reason: I had a date.

The bus driver let me out at Hollywood and Highland; I walked past Lee Drugs toward Hollywood High, where that school's end-of-term chaos was also in full swing: malts, burgers, and hot rods at the drive-in on Sunset; Mexican girls with Ronnie Spector hair and cigarettes dangling from their lips, waiting for their prince to come; and "Mustang Sally" by the Wicked Wilson Pickett blasting through an open window from somebody's car radio.

Then I saw him, right where we agreed to meet.

Douglas was suave, handsome, and full of life, with skin the color of toasted spice and a Kirk Douglas dimple in his chin. His eyes gleamed with mischief and hilarity. We were both sixteen years old and had met at a dance contest at Hollywood High, winning first prize.

Douglas was the most fascinating guy I'd ever met. He came from a different world than the kids at the Teen Center and lived in a glamorous apartment in Hollywood with his mother, Ena, who was an actress and drove a sporty Jaguar. Douglas was a good-natured rascal living a charmed life between his movie star mom and his family on the East Coast. He loved to have fun. We spent the day walking the streets of Hollywood, meaning to catch the bus but talking and laughing our way along Santa Monica Boulevard until we wound up at his mother's apartment. Ena was out, and we were alone.

"Come on, let's go in my room and listen to music."

"What's wrong with the stereo out here?" I asked.

"It's broken," he said, taking my arm.

The afternoon sun was shining in dreamily through Douglas' bedroom window. We talked some more and laughed some more. He put on a record album by the Miracles, and the liquid heat of Smokey's voice on "Oooh, Baby, Baby" met the warmth of the room and our bodies. The music was hypnotizing and matched the way we slow danced.

"Let me show you how much I love you," he said.

The sound of his voice sent shivers down my body.

"No, we can't."

"Why not? Aren't I good enough for you?"

"No, that's not it and you know it."

I pushed him away, even as I asked myself, *Okay then, why can't we?* I'd already fumbled away my virginity in the back of a car to my Saturday night dance partner from the Teen Center. But with Douglas, it felt like I was falling in love. He ran his fingers through my hair and gently kissed me on the neck. Then my forehead, finally my lips. The warm afternoon sun and his sweet-talkin' charm were melting my resolve.

"What could be so wrong when it feels so right?" he whispered, running his hands down my body.

For that I had no answer. I felt more wonderful and alive than ever; I was sharing something profoundly important with someone who loved me. Every move I made with him brought an adoring response that was even greater than what I'd given. It was what I'd dreamed of all my life. Love really was bliss, just like all the songs said.

"But what about . . . "

"Don't worry," he said as we sank into the bed, and whatever last restraint I had was abandoned.

"Trust me."

(I'm A) Road Runner

A week later Douglas left Los Angeles to spend the summer with his East Coast family. I pulled off a big victory and got permission from my parents to take a summer school class at Hollywood High and an after-school job as a telephone solicitor for a magazine subscription company on Cherokee Avenue. Every morning I rode with my father into Hollywood, where he dropped me off at school. After class let out, I walked to a little food stand on Selma and Cherokee for a chili dog and chocolate milk, then joined my coworkers in an upstairs boiler room full of telephones. It was my first job, and I was to be paid $1.50 an hour for signing up subscribers to *Look* magazine.

The best part of my job was that by five o'clock, I was already out of the house with my parents' approval. It made connecting the lies I had to tell about what I did every evening after work a lot easier. Usually Fran and the girls would pick me up, and we'd go to the Haunted House. By this time, lying had just become a way of life. In order to do what I wanted to do—what I felt I should be allowed to do—I just had to tell my parents what they wanted to hear. Having established a solid campground on the banks of that old River, the one nicknamed "Denial," the plan worked for them, too.

It was near the end of July when I found myself retching over the toilet in the wee hours of the morning, the water faucet going full blast, and a wash rag clumsily in my hand to muffle the sound from my parents, whose bedroom was just on the other side of the wall. It must have worked, because when I came into the kitchen, my mom was fixing breakfast for my dad and me, and neither of them said anything about it, which was how things usually went at our house anyway. My two older brothers had both gotten married and were long gone; it was just the three of us, plus a thick cloud that never seemed to lift.

My peculiar illness appeared to be under control until one morning when I was riding in my dad's car to school and felt my stomach flip upside down as we reached the intersection of Hollywood and Highland. We still had to cross the Boulevard to get to the front of Hollywood High, but I couldn't hold back the inevitable. Just as my father pulled up to the curb next to Lee Drugs, I opened the car door and aimed my head at the gutter. My cinnamon toast and orange juice went next.

"Bye Daddy, see you later!" I gurgled, jumping from the car and running away.

Neither he nor my mom ever spoke to me about it.

I spent my summer school mornings with my head on the desk, but by the time I went to work pitching magazine subscriptions, I felt good enough to chow down my chili dog and chocolate milk. It would be romantic to say that I dreamed about Douglas, but when summer ended, he stayed on the East Coast, and I was on my own. There was no one but the Girlfriends for support, and I refused to believe I was pregnant since Douglas had said I could trust him.

Antoinette, Fran, and Iva nodded affirmatively when I told them I was sure it was just a tumor. After all, anybody's period can be almost three months late. Still, just before summer ended, I decided to see a doctor, finding an ob-gyn in the *Yellow Pages* who was just a bus ride away in Burbank. But I had no money; my paychecks from the telephone soliciting job had all bounced. I made an appointment anyway and then applied my talent for lying, telling the elderly, white-haired doctor I was nineteen years old and married. He agreed to send his bill in the mail, and for his kindness, I provided a fake name and address. It was a shock but no surprise when, beaming like a benevolent old Santa Claus, the verdict fell from his lips.

"Good news, Mrs. Smith. You and your husband are going to have a baby."

Suddenly I heard the tinkling of a music box and saw miles of ruffled white eyelet. A little life was growing inside of me! In a split second I became a baby's adoring mother, encouraging my child to dance and to dream. I was buoyant, joyful, and filled with love. Then, just as quickly, I fell back to Earth with a thud.

Snap out of it! Who do you think you are to be glad about this? It's a disaster! What will your parents do? You are in so much trouble!

The old doctor stuck out his hand to shake mine, and I stared at him stupidly, wondering if he knew I'd faked my age and lied about being married. On my way out, his nurse handed me a little white bag filled with pink pre-natal vitamins that looked like Good 'N Plenty candies. I rode the bus home in a daze and stuffed the paper bag in the bottom of my dresser drawer.

A few days later, the fall semester started up, and there I was, back at North Hollywood High School. As if summer and nothing had ever happened.

Will You Still Love Me Tomorrow?

I saw my father's big red Mercury parked across the street when I got out of school that blustery October afternoon and knew it was a bad sign. I always walked home from school, and at three o'clock he should have been at work. The Girlfriends and I had been planning our Halloween hijinks when, through the Mercury's windshield, my father's eyes made contact with mine. I heard him rev up the engine as he motioned for me to get in. I told Antoinette to call me later and headed for my unavoidable date with destiny.

My father and I rode the twelve blocks to our house in silence. The loving twinkle I'd always seen in his eyes was replaced with anger. My mother was waiting for us, stretched out across the bed with a wet rag on her forehead. Her face was swollen and red. She'd been snooping around in my room and found the bag of pink pills.

"How could you do this to us?" she pleaded.

To YOU? Why was it always about them?

"It's the colored fellow, isn't it?"

They assumed it was the boy I had told them I danced with at the Teen Center, one of my new friends whom they wouldn't let me invite to our house. They knew nothing about Douglas.

"No! Not him! Somebody else . . ."

I made a feeble attempt at telling them it was a surfer from North Hollywood High. *Maybe it would be less horrible if they thought I was pregnant by a white guy.* But when I couldn't even think of a boy's name to blame it on, that strategy unraveled.

My parents' worst nightmare had come true. Their sixteen-year-old daughter, whom they had loved, protected, and groomed to be like Shirley Temple, was pregnant by a Negro. Having raised me blindfolded, they didn't have the vision to look at what had gone on inside of my heart and mind; instead they took my mistake and misfortune as a personal assault upon themselves.

I tried to tell them what soul music, dancing, and feeling loved meant to me, but the rest of the afternoon became little more than accusations and tears.

"We trusted you," said my father.

"Then why wouldn't you let me have the friends I wanted?" I said.

The three of us ate our dinner in silence. I couldn't bear to see the pain on my mother's face. With thoughts too heavy to bear, my father propped one elbow on the table and sadly rested his chin on his fist. Each tasteless bite fought its way down my throat with lumps of sorrow. I went to my room filled with shame, wondering if they would try to suggest an abortion. The fleeting moment of joy that I'd had in the doctor's office wafted across me, and then the awfulness returned. I laid both of my palms on my belly. There was a life inside of me; it was both incomprehensibly wonderful and terrifying.

The telephone rang, and I heard my father tell Antoinette that I couldn't talk. I knew the word would spread to Iva and Fran.

As the autumn winds whipped through the patio outside my bedroom, sending my mother's flower pots crashing to the ground, that carefree, school's-out afternoon in Hollywood seemed like a million years ago.

Society's Child

Since no one had ever disgraced our family so badly, my parents had little idea what to do. They weren't going to ask anyone whom they knew for advice, because that would mean having to reveal the family secret.

At nearly four months pregnant, I was too far along for an illegal abortion, not that my parents would have wanted that anyway. So the first thing they did was make an appointment for the three of us to meet with somebody at a Jewish adoption agency. But once the caseworker learned that my baby's father was black, she ended the interview, telling us the agency would never be able to place a Negro baby in a Jewish home. It was a stinging rejection for my parents, who had assumed that fellow Jews would stand by them.

Confused and hurt, they turned to the Los Angeles County Department of Social Services who assured them that if I were sent away to live in a home for unwed mothers, I could be quietly rehabilitated and returned to North Hollywood as if nothing had ever happened. To my parents, it must have sounded like a solution that would safeguard the family reputation and redeem their errant daughter's future.

I, on the other hand, was becoming increasingly detached as these plans, in which I was given zero say-so, were being made.

Like a convicted criminal, I knew that my fate, be it gallows, guillotine, or gurney, would usher me to the certain death of my happiness, self-worth, and sense of belonging. Everything I'd claimed for myself since the TAMI show was about to be taken away.

One of my father's friends worked at a research library in the Georgetown district of Washington, D.C. Even though it wasn't a high school, and even though it was the middle of October, my parents told everyone in our family that I had been accepted into an exclusive academic study program there. My father's friend sent me a fake welcome letter on the library's stationery as proof for any skeptics in the family. It was astonishing to see such a web of deceit being constructed by my parents in order to cover my disappearance for the next five months. Still, I accepted it, just like I was going to have to accept everything that was about to happen, whether I liked it or not.

Things moved quickly, and on Halloween I said goodbye to the Girlfriends. They were on their way to the Cinder's costume party. We sat in Fran's car, parked in front of my house.

"Come with us tonight. Who's gonna know? What the hell, you're already in trouble."

Fran was dressed as a Playboy bunny. She had great legs but needed a pair of sweat socks to fill out her bra.

"My parents won't let me."

"So what?" Fran insisted, folding a stick of Juicy Fruit gum into her mouth. "That's never stopped you before."

It was true. I'd lied about my age and done what I wanted to do for two years. But now the fact that I was pregnant and a minor could not be ignored; my parents were in control.

Fran clicked her tongue and shifted her attention to her hair, which had been ratted into a lacquered tower. She stabbed a pair of rabbit ears into it.

"Tough for you, then. Everyone's gonna be there."

Antoinette and Iva looked at me sadly.

"I'll come visit you," Iva promised.

"I'd like that," I said, not believing I'd ever see any of them again.

"Hey, you're not going to die there."

I felt like I was.

Antoinette was wordless. She sat in her corner of the front seat, smelling of Intimate perfume, mascara running in black rivers down her face. She licked a puddle of tears from her lip and struggled to smile with that gaping hole between her two front teeth.

"Don't cry," I told her. "Anyway, you're not the one being locked up."

I had a Kleenex in my pocket and handed it to her, but I tried to look away so I wouldn't start crying, too.

"We love you," said Iva, giving me a hug.

"We'll tell everybody at the Cinder you said hi," said Fran, starting the car.

"Bye," gulped Antoinette, wiping her eyes with the Kleenex and reaching over into the backseat where I'd been sitting with Iva.

I got out of the Fairlane and watched them drive away. The moon hung like a cantaloupe slice in the sky, and I thought about how this was the last night I would be free to stand out here in front of my own house. Tomorrow I would be shuffled off to a jail-like home for unwed mothers stashed in an obscure pocket of East Los Angeles, stuck there for all the holidays from Thanksgiving to my seventeenth birthday next year in March.

Even though the maternity home was only twenty miles from North Hollywood, I felt like I was being shipped to Mars. My parents had been assured by a social worker that no one we knew would ever run into me on the streets of this ragtag Mexican neighborhood. I would spend the next five months writing phony letters on stolen stationery and stuffing them into a big manila envelope addressed to Washington, D.C. to be mailed from there with the fake boarding school's postmark.

There was never any question that the baby I was carrying would not be returning home with me. To my parents and the social workers, my baby was as unreal and disposable as a paper doll. To me, my baby was the only person who couldn't reject me or place any conditions on our love. As long as I was pregnant we would be there for each other.

We headed into exile together, along with my transistor radio.

WELCOME

The Florence Crittenton Home

LOS ANGELES, CALIFORNIA

KEY SERVICES FOR PROBLEMS OF UNWED MOTHERHOOD

CHAPTER FOUR

Los Angeles, 1966-1967

From Here to Maternity

As a memorial to his daughter Florence who died at the age of four, Charles Crittenton established a safe haven in New York in 1883 to hide unmarried pregnant girls from disgrace and public scorn. Over time, Florence Crittenton Homes popped up all over the United States, including one in Los Angeles at 234 East Avenue 33. Built in 1914, the Los Angeles Home was where, in 1966, my parents decided to send me.

November first arrived like any other morning, but I knew it wasn't. This would be the last time in five months that I would wake up in my own bedroom, or hear the sound of gray doves cooing outside my window.

While the Girlfriends had partied it up at the Cinder the night before, I'd packed my suitcase. After an awkward breakfast, my parents and I got in the car and headed toward Lincoln Heights. I sat in the backseat. Busted or not, at sixteen I wouldn't have been caught dead riding three in the front with my parents, and they knew it. I watched my familiar neighborhood go by and pretended I was on my way to Paris.

My father pulled onto the Hollywood Freeway, and as we passed the Highland exit I wondered if I should have called Douglas' mother, Ena. But as the freeway exits came and went—Cahuenga, Vine Street, Gower—I let the thought evaporate without conclusion. Like a lot of things, it was too late to do anything different.

Near downtown we transitioned to the Pasadena Freeway and got off at Avenue 43. Following directions he'd written on a slip of paper, my father headed up the hill and took a right turn onto Griffin.

My new home was safely tucked away in a district that had premiered sixty years earlier as the pride of Los Angeles. Its curving boulevard was lined with once-charming bungalows that now sported peeling front porches and tired dry lawns. Gathered on every corner were brown men with shiny black hair. Over the years this neighborhood, with its Mexican *carniceria* and penchant for loud music and low cars, had become like a foreign country to most white people. That made it perfectly suited for hiding their defiled daughters.

Less than three blocks from the Florence Crittenton Home, "Flossie's" as it was nicknamed, was Booth Memorial, a Salvation Army Home also for unwed mothers. A few miles away was St. Anne's, Los Angeles's third refuge/reformatory. Reputation had it (though not officially) that the limited spaces at Flossie's were reserved for upstanding white girls who'd made a tragic mistake. Booth Memorial, which was larger, was for Mexicans, Negroes, and trashy whites but not the hardened sexpots who wound up at St. Anne's. There were slip-ups, however, as in the case of Marguerite, the Latina whom I encountered at Sybil Brand Jail four years after we'd been locked up together at Flossie's.

In 1966 the demand for these secret asylums was at its peak, and all three were filled to capacity. Flossie's was even fundraising to add a new wing, unaware that the entire stealthy system was but one graduating class and hippie love-in from extinction.

An afternoon stroll of Lincoln Heights would reveal clusters of pregnant girls headed for Five Points: a bustling intersection which tied together a Safeway, Thrifty Drug Store, Jack-In-The-Box, and a Woolworth's which was popular for its extensive selection of pastel-colored baby yarn and knitting needles. The Crittenton girls were free to walk openly in Lincoln Heights; there'd be no need to hide anyone's pregnant condition here. A few blocks from Five Points was the Lincoln Heights Jail, another solid institution of reckoning for violators. Indeed, my new neighborhood was a cohesive community of prisoners—ethnic, moral, and civil.

My father's car wound around Griffin Boulevard to Avenue 33, where he turned the corner into a narrow cul-de-sac, and I gasped at the sight of the behemoth Crittenton Home. It rose ominously above the smaller houses on a dead-end street, its bleak windows reminding me of the Vincent Price movie, *The House on Haunted Hill*. As my father lifted my suitcase out of the trunk, I wanted to beg him not to leave me in this place; I was certain I would never get out alive.

Prisoner Of Love

The three of us sat in the Director's cramped office. The windowless room sighed with the weight of human burden, but no relief for that seemed apparent despite the piles of evidence at hand. A credenza covered with stacks of messy folders filled half a wall. The files, some so thick they were bound with rubber bands, held the anguish of young women forced out of childhood yet denied admittance into the sacred arena of motherhood.

The Director was a prune-faced, old spinster with short, oily hair combed flatly behind her ears. She spouted off a litany of rules and regulations, and it soon became clear to me that according to the Crittenton code, nothing could be more abnormal than to be a hormone-driven teenage girl wanting to be loved.

Flossie's was equipped to provide the "appropriate correction" needed for fifty girls at a time, she told my parents. No complication of this trial would be overlooked. Not only were doctors and nurses on duty but also psychologists and social workers. It was assumed that each new resident came with a smudged past fueled by rebellious confusion. For this, she said, the Crittenton team was well prepared. The caseworkers prided themselves on their aggressive approach to reforming the behavior of their charges to prevent, as she described it, a repetition of the "crisis" that had brought girls like me to the Home.

I had no idea what she was talking about.

Making love wasn't a crisis; it was a direct route to the acceptance and love I had always wanted. It was romantic and beautiful; it made me happy, and sharing love that way with another person was even better than dancing. There was no way I would submit to "correcting" that.

I bit my lip to keep quiet while the old lady yammered on. From the way she talked, it sounded as if the Crittenton goal was to make girls like me feel worthless so they could wear down our rebellion and then brainwash us into becoming dried-up, loveless hags like they were. She continued her pitch to my parents.

"Along with regular Tuesday clinic check-ups by the doctor, your daughter will be required to see a psychologist three times a week, as well as assigned to an adoption worker to make plans for the immediate relinquishment of the newborn at the hospital."

Panic seized me. *Were they not even going to let me see or hold my baby?*

I glanced at my mother. Her shoulders dropped from under her ears to their normal slope, and she nodded faintly. The news of my baby's instant disappearance was a big relief to her.

Barring medical complications, the Director said, I would be released from the hospital to Flossie's infirmary and could expect to go back home within ten days. She smiled at my parents as if that were the end of it.

Once delivered of both baby and sin, it seemed I would be deemed fit to rejoin the unforgiving society which had cast me out.

The bottom line was, I had no rights, and there were no options. I was a minor, and nothing was going to happen without my parents' permission. My father had made that clear. Making this child a part of our family had been so utterly unthinkable to my parents that we'd never even talked about it. And not wanting not to lose their love on top of everything else, the true believer in me had to agree that giving up my baby for adoption was the best thing to do.

Then there was the matter of school. When the North Hollywood High girls' vice-principal found out I was pregnant, I was suspended and told I would not be welcome back, even though I'd be un-pregnant by the time of graduation. Flossie's offered benevolent sanctuary in its third-floor schoolroom of manual typewriters, sewing machines, and carved-up wooden desks; all of us from every grade in the same classroom at the same time. Though I had only completed half the eleventh grade when I arrived, as long as I showed up every day at Flossie's Hideaway High, I would be marched along the paper trail, ultimately culminating in an early diploma issued from a school for handicapped children.

At least I finally made that promotion they wanted to give me in the fifth grade, I thought.

"Now we strongly advise," the Director said to my parents, "that your daughter not mention to anyone here that the father of her baby is a Nee-grow."

The word fell from her lips like the diagnosis of a terminal disease. Finally I'd had it with this horrible woman. I fought the urge to put both my palms on the underneath side of her desk and flip it over onto her smug, oily head. Instead, I stuffed a handful of fingers into my mouth. My mother nudged me to take them out.

If you only knew what major catastrophe this minor sin is substituting. I dumped my hands into my lap and clasped my swollen fingers like a pile of fat worms.

The old gasbag waited for a response from my parents, but my dad just coughed, and so she barreled on.

"Privacy is the golden rule here at Florence Crittenton Home. The girls are allowed to call one another only by their first names, and we invite them, if they like, to make up a 'special' name during their stay with us."

She lowered her voice as if offering privileged information. "We find it puts more distance between the crisis that brought them here and their healthy return to normal life."

I could not imagine what this unpleasant woman thought was normal. All this time she had been speaking about me in the third person as if I weren't even there. At last she leaned forward and looked at me.

"Now dear, is there some other name you'd like to be called?"

I thought of a billboard I'd passed by on my bus rides home from Hollywood. It hung alongside the freeway near the Pilgrimage, a rustic outdoor amphitheater that had been carved into a hillside opposite the Hollywood Bowl. Every year the Pilgrimage held a big pageant about an Indian maiden named Ramona, and a rendering of the tragic Ramona with her long black braids was plastered on the billboard.

"Ramona," I told the Director.

My parents looked uncertainly at one another for my having picked such an ethnic alias.

Be glad it's not Aretha, I thought.

Don't Let Me Be Misunderstood

My parents probably hated to leave me there at Flossie's even more than I hated to stay. At least by living somewhere else, I could stop thinking about them for a while, but they weren't going to stop thinking about me. I'd been the only child in their house since I was ten, and now my mother and father were going home to an empty house for the first time in twenty-six years with nothing left to call family, not even a shameful, rebellious daughter. Nothing says failure like having to send your kid away for someone else to rehabilitate.

We lingered outside on the wide cement porch, the chilly autumn breeze making it irresistible for my mother to try to button my bulky knit sweater over my too-fat front. I felt their agony and hugged my parents with more affection than I had in a long time. Looking into their sad faces, all I could think about was how much I'd hurt them. It was too late for me to pull together my unraveling destiny or undo the trouble I'd caused. A wave of terror swept through me that my parents might never love me again.

I'll change. I won't lie anymore. I'll do everything I'm told. I promise. I'll become the daughter you want me to be.

We said goodbye, and I watched them lumber down the steps, my father's arm wound protectively around my mother. He opened the door of the car and tucked her safely inside before getting into the driver's seat. I could tell my mother was crying. My dad glanced back up at me as he pulled out from the curb and drove away.

A pair of pregnant girls passed me by on the steps, swayback madonnas balancing basketball bellies on spindly legs. Whispers buzzed between them as they checked me out from head to foot. I was standing dumbly on the landing, as if I didn't know where to go. One was a drippy-looking mod about nineteen; her long blond hair had been ironed straight and hung in two stiff sheets down the front of her face. The other had short brown hair in a flip, the top of her bangs embellished with a white clip-on bow. Both were in their last months of pregnancy, a form of status, I would learn. Just like how you were defined by your rap in jail, here at Flossie's it was your due date. That meant a newbie like me, only four months along and barely showing, was the bottom of the barrel.

The two girls paused at the front door, trying to appear lighthearted, but they were gasping for breath from climbing up the stairs. Each dangled a shopping bag full of yarn; a pair of deadly ice blue needles poked out of the blonde's bag.

"You the new girl?" accused the brunette, as her companion pulled open the heavy front door. Giggling, they both disappeared before I could form the words to answer. I followed them into my new home, weighted with the baggage of confusion and loss. In the lobby, the tail end of the day's sunlight was streaming through a transom above the door. It had been cold out there on the steps, and the warmth inside felt good. I hoisted my broken spirit on the crutches of repentance and took a look around.

To my left, a visitors' room boasted a sagging loveseat, two straight-back chairs, and a coffee table topped with a box of Kleenex. To my right was the reception area and a beat-up counter upon which sat a page of rules entombed in a yellowing plastic sheet next to a sign-out book. Residents could smoke cigarettes but not wear slacks; only below-the-knee skirts were allowed. We could leave Flossie's for an hour and a half every day, twice a week for eight hours, but never stay out overnight. And since I was under eighteen, no one could visit me without my parents' permission. *Well, I guess that eliminates everyone but them*, I thought.

Next to the sign-out book and bolted to the wall was an outgoing mailbox bearing the dandy Mr. Zip, all ready to deliver my phony letters from private school. Had my parents known that Crittenton had a vast network of out-of-state addresses for its residents' fake correspondence and invented boarding school postmarks, they could have been spared the trouble of concocting their customized story about me going to private school in Washington, D.C.

A wooden sign hung over the reception area. It had been painted long ago, and little flecks were missing from some of the letters, but the command it required we obey was loud and clear. You couldn't enter Flossie's without heeding it, and you surely weren't getting out without having it tattooed on your brain: *To Get Along You Have To Go Along*.

Something like the nauseating rush of anesthetic hit me as I sensed what came next. There was no ducking the cosmic machete that was about to slice through my tender, freshly regrown antenna. Once again, the high frequency radar of my being was severed, putting out of commission that part of my soul I'd learned to count on for discerning what was real from what was fake. Just as I'd been an outsider in school, I expected to be mocked and rejected here at Flossie's. With my antenna back in cold storage, I braced myself for another season in the wilderness by shutting down all hope. If I didn't expect much, I wasn't as likely to be disappointed. I would try to go along, but I was certain I would never get along, no matter what I did.

Ain't That Peculiar

"Anybody talked to the new girl?"

"Claims she's a virgin."

"Says she passed out at a party and then missed her period."

"Oh, I just don't know what happened!"

"Too bad! Missed all the fun!"

The room full of fat pregnant hens cackled at the tired joke they'd already told to one another a million times.

"Get this. Doctors agree that aspirin is an effective method of birth control."

"Yeah, just put one between your knees."

These were the ladies-in-waiting of the Florence Crittenton Home For Unwed Mothers, sitting around the sunroom smoking cigarettes and talking about nothing, just like they did every day. Between housekeeping chores, which everyone was assigned, counseling appointments, medical exams, and craft-making sessions organized by thin-lipped charity matrons, the click-clack of knitting needles played rhythm section to their bitchy solos of speculation, mockery, and gossip.

The ignorance they flaunted was truly remarkable. My first week I sat among a small group engaged in trash-talking about Sue Ann, a squat blonde who, at the slightest hint of friendliness, would pull out a tattered snapshot of her baby's black father and flash it quickly for only you to see. Everyone in household had made it their mission to get Sue Ann to show them the photo so they could laugh at her behind her back.

"You can always tell a girl who hangs around with colored guys, can't you, Ramona?" one of the ringleaders said to me.

Since each girl was there to hide her shameful condition and ultimately be restored to the outside world as if nothing ever happened, there was little to cultivate and even less to bind us together. Friendship would only make the inevitable goal of our collective amnesia even more difficult: *I won't remember I saw you here if you promise to forget you saw me.* Mean-spiritedness was the safest release for the hurt, frustration, and anger we all felt, and most of the girls acted like hormonal shrews.

The sunroom was on the main floor and named as such for its tall windows and glass doors opening out to a short concrete terrace and cinder block wall. Besides the reception area and visiting rooms, downstairs was also home to the counselors' offices, the dining area, and a single pay telephone that we could line up to use after dinner. To keep the queue moving, calls were limited to ten minutes, although not everyone obeyed that rule until somebody made a fuss.

There was also a formal living room with the Home's only television set; we weren't allowed in there until after school hours. The night of my arrival I watched myself dancing on TV for the last time, but no one else in the living room realized the girl with S-H-E-B-A-N-G on her leg was me. The second floor housed the infirmary, and the third floor was the schoolroom, but both floors also served as dormitory residences, each with a high school-style lavatory and showers. And all of it was painted Pepto-Bismol pink.

The only personal space each girl had was a small nightstand beside her bed, which most converted into a holy shrine with memorabilia such as a dog-eared valentine, a matchbook cover, and a snapshot of some pimply-faced guy or square-jawed soldier. No one ever used the term "boyfriend" at Flossie's, and you would have been laughed at all the way to Five Points if you tried to call anyone your fiancé. The acceptable term of endearment was FOB, otherwise known as Father of the Baby.

After a skirmish with one of my roommates in the six-bed dormitory, and the serendipitous vacancy of the only single room at Flossie's by reason of its previous resident's delivery, I wound up in a room by myself. It was the most I could have asked for in that Pepto-Abysmal place. My room had a small bed, a dresser, and a closet, as well as a window facing the fire escape. The room next to mine belonged to the night nurse, whose starched uniform and liver-colored sweater hung by the door, ever ready for the broken water bag at two A.M. and a fifteen-minute drive to the hospital in the Home's trusty station wagon.

There was no shortage of characters with stranger-than-fiction backstories who took refuge at Flossie's that winter. Probably the oddest resident was Binky, a twenty-two-year-old midget with hands as small as a doll's and the gravelly voice of a pack-a-day smoker. I'd first seen her in the basement laundry room. Amid the steamy hot air and stench of Clorox, Binky was perched on a stool behind a pile of folded wash cloths. She wore a pair of small eyeglasses with clear-blue frames, like the kind children wear, and I assumed she was the daughter of someone who worked there. That night in the dining room I was astonished to see little Binky waddling across the floor with a huge platter of meat in her freckled matchstick arms, a checkered monitor's apron pulled around her oversized belly. She claimed to have been a prostitute with an exclusive clientele of San Diego sailors.

Next to my room, at the end of the third-floor hallway, a door opened onto the fire escape, where I could contemplate a view of downtown Los Angeles beyond the tops of neglected palm trees. At night, when no one was watching, I would sneak outside to sit in the moonlight, wrapped in a blanket with my transistor radio and a contraband jar of peanut butter, looking at the far-off city lights and wondering what I was missing, what my baby would be like, if I'd ever be happy again, and whether anyone cared.

My parents came faithfully every Sunday for the eight-hour visit, and I looked forward to that. My father would drive us to Pasadena, where nobody knew our family, and we'd have lunch and go to Vroman's bookstore or to a movie or the park. The meals we ate and the places we visited gave us things to talk about that had nothing to do with the anguish and distress that each of us felt. When they dropped me off back at Flossie's, these visits seemed to register as painfully satisfying.

The psychologist assigned to my case was a middle-aged Jewish woman whose fleshy face and watery eyes bespoke sympathy but who nonetheless was charged with getting to the root of my problem and straightening me out. She asked me a lot of stupid questions and, like most adults, was convinced I'd be happier if I were more like her. We wrangled for weeks about why I had Negro friends, why I liked soul music, and whether I got pregnant in order to hurt my parents.

When she couldn't wring the answers she wanted out of me, the psychologist reviewed my school records, noting the odd decline in my IQ from 160 in the fourth and fifth grades to 140 in junior high, and ordered me re-tested. The new test was a combination of identifying words from a choice of definitions and putting together a series of pictures to form a sequence of events, like a cartoon panel. I got all the words right. But I failed every one of the picture-stories, producing a new score of barely above moron. The psychologist heaved a deep sigh of disappointment; she still had nothing to show for all her hard work on my case and wearily pronounced the verdict:

"You are a smart girl, Ramona, but you have a warped perception of society."

Love Child

In February 1967, about one month before my due date, I received in the mail a large manila envelope with no return address, out of which dropped two unfamiliar items: a copy of the *Los Angeles Free Press* and a hand-rolled marijuana cigarette (which I immediately flushed down the toilet). The headline story on the front page of the *Free Press* was about a protest on the Sunset Strip by three thousand "flower children" against "police manhandling and verbal abuse." The photos were of crazy-looking girls and geeky white boys. It was like reading about life on another planet. I folded the newspaper and put it away, having no clue how much sense it would make after I left Flossie's and gained enough perspective on what had happened to me there to join their angry ranks.

When my time came, the night nurse donned her uniform and sweater, and it was my turn to ride in the station wagon as my predecessors had. I don't know what led me to expect better treatment from them, but the hospital staff wasn't nice to us fallen Flossie girls, leaving me to endure the agony of hard labor without so much as a kind touch or word. Maybe the nurses thought it was their duty to punish teen mothers. After sixteen hours of labor, I gave birth to a baby girl. They let me hold her one time and then, as promised, she was whisked away.

By then (and minus a functioning antenna), I had convinced myself that what all the adults told me was true: I was too young to be a mother, and my baby would have a better life with somebody else. I secured that deadbolt of fake rationale by vowing that when I became an adult, I would never look back or wish I'd kept her. I committed myself to this decision with dogged, true-believer blindness, hoping the power of that would forever shut the door on my feeling bad about what I'd done.

Finally, like the rest of them, I too set up camp on the River Denial.

After a week's recuperation in Flossie's infirmary, in March 1967 I returned home to North Hollywood, where I spent the rest of that spring waiting for my courtesy diploma. A telephone, minus the rotary dial so you couldn't call out, was installed in my bedroom to receive conference calls from the handicapped kids' school and complete my last semester without contaminating others in a public setting. The phone was only supposed to be used for the school to call me, but one day my telephone teacher accidently recited the number, allowing me to give it to friends and to field clandestine telephone calls from Douglas, who had also returned from exile. I told him what happened, and though I still longed to be around him, he was seeing other girls, and my heart was too broken and bound up in fear to fall in love again.

Or so I thought.

Soul Man

He was earthy and raw, as big and powerful as the V8 engine on a Cadillac Eldorado. He could out-plead and out-rasp David Ruffin, and there was something about the gruffness in Otis Redding's voice that brought out the woman in me like no smooth slickster from Motown ever had.

On stage he worked himself into a magnetic frenzy, but Otis didn't lose control or need the mop-up crew like James Brown. There were no Famous Flames to cape, carry, and console him, even though his desperation-ridden cries of "Ple-eeze . . . ple-eeze . . . ple-hee-hee-heeze . . . " tore your heart out. There were just the horn players: egging him on, punctuating his stricken body on "I Been Loving You Too Long," and heaving their mournful sighs on "Pain in My Heart." He roughed up "My Girl" and may have sent the Tempts in their shiny suits fleeing for cover with his chaotic stuttering in the vamp. Otis plowed his way through every song with full force and came out smiling from a heart as big and bright as the Georgia sun.

And all of that propelled me toward the next place that soul music would take root in my life: a place where strong gruff men would articulate the growing well of hurt in my soul and provide the perfect antithesis to my blossoming womanhood.

I was discovering The Blues.

Just as the untamed fervor of James Brown had turned me out, Otis Redding got deep down and personal in that part of me that was so bottomless and so hungry, and those same feelings that had been unleashed at the TAMI show rose again to the surface; this time seasoned with the anguish and alienation of Bigger Thomas and Cross Damon.

When I heard that Otis Redding was going to perform at a pop festival in Monterey three months after I got out of Flossie's, I knew I had to go. My precious but clueless parents wanted to reward my "graduation from high school," so I put in my request. My dad reserved a motel room for the three of us and purchased tickets for the Saturday night show. We drove up there in his big red Mercury.

My conscience was still smoldering from the punishment I'd undergone at Flossie's, and I'd been trying to walk the straight and narrow path of obedience and do what I was told. But now, in June 1967, my skirts were too long; the rules I'd just agreed to follow were being broken by everyone else; and the draft cards, bras, and minds of all the other kids my age were going up in smoke. The Monterey Pop Festival would be my first face-to-face encounter with that strange bunch I'd read about in the *Free Press*.

My parents and I arrived in Monterey; my mom bundled up in a warm coat, my father protective of us both in the midst of all its counterculture strangeness. I coiffed half of my long hair into a huge bouffant, leaving the rest to hang down my back, and wore a pair of striped bell-bottom hip huggers with a vintage 1940s jacket. I thought I looked cool in a Carnaby Street sort of way. Prior to the concert we strolled the long green expanse of the Fairgrounds looking at the booths of stoner stuff on display. The crowd ran the gamut from shorthairs and paisley mod-types to hippie potheads and fresh-faced flower children with no underwear. Mine was a generation in transition.

The concert, as history would document, was the undisputed transformative moment of Otis Redding's career, just as James Brown's performance at the TAMI show had been for him. None of us there in Monterey had any idea of how privileged we were to experience this phenomenal old soul of so few years—Otis was only twenty-five—who that night bridged the gap between the broken-hearted blues of black folks and the starry-eyed abandon of the flower children. How could anyone know that we were about to lose him just a few months later when his plane plunged into an icy Wisconsin lake two weeks before Christmas.

The Monterey Pop Festival was a unique and profound moment of history that wove together a diverse group of people into a remarkable tapestry of peace and love. There were no bad trips, no uprisings, no baton-wielding enforcers, no angry epithet-spouting herds. That would come the next summer in Chicago at the Democratic Convention. And the summer after that—in the same week as Woodstock—it would all come to an end on the orders of Charles Manson.

But for that one sweet weekend during the Summer of Love, straights and stoners, mods and hippies, even cops and counterculturists got happily and peacefully along with one another (and drugs). Before any of us realized the hellish turn things would take, we abandoned all the rules with awe and wonder, calling it freedom. That and the music fused us into a force which, for better or worse, would overwhelm the next decade and change the world.

I tried my best to be a good daughter, but I knew in my heart that eventually I'd go the way of the hippies, and not long after Monterey, I transited out of my parents' orbit and did just that. Yet the anger, cynicism, and resentment I'd taken with me from

Flossie's would quickly speed-dial me from the innocence of blowing bubbles, to the in-your-face of wanting to blow up a whole lot more than that.

CHAPTER FIVE

Los Angeles, 1967-1971

Get Off Of My Cloud

It really was more than anyone ought to have hoped for. To expect that at Flossie's I could be rehabilitated from moral failure, only to then enter my generation's "Hell, No!" college years and not be swept into its unruly fray, was like smashing a champagne bottle at the launch of the Titanic.

Fact was, after I left the Florence Crittenton Home, they began to have a hard time filling those precious fifty slots. The populations went down at Booth Memorial and St. Anne's, too. With the Sunset Strip riots and the sexual revolution firmly underway, being an unwed mother wasn't so shameful anymore, and soon the market for fake boarding schools collapsed.

In the fall of 1967, I became a freshman at San Fernando Valley State College, a modest institution set among citrus groves at the north end of the Valley. With my formal education stalled by years of self-imposed dumb-down and my detour out of high school, going to college provided the great hope for a high-functioning intellectual renaissance.

But after a sincere effort to actually attend classes that first semester, I spent the rest of my three years at Valley State sounding off in the cafeteria and shaking my fist in the air yelling "F*&# you!" out in the quad. I cheered the fiery rhetoric of the Black Students Union, Students for a Democratic Society, and visiting radicals like Angela Davis. Three months before he was assassinated, Robert Kennedy paid a campaign visit to our college, and we welcomed him with merciless heckling.

Deep in my heart, however, I was still stuck in the theology of Motown and believed that romantic love was the answer to everything. Yet the colossal tide of anger that my generation was riding was irresistible. By 1969 I'd joined a clan of nihilist yippie comrades veering off Revolutionary Road and headed for a direct hit with theatre of the absurd. If everything was nothing, none of it mattered anyway; the fun was just in stirring things up. It picked up a thread from my end-of-the-world, why-bother, what-me-worry days in elementary school, with the added knife to society's gut of becoming sexually liberated. I also started smoking pot and taking LSD.

Undoubtedly LSD finished off the job I'd begun years earlier to rid myself of excess brains cells. But there was also something healing about the way I could physically watch myself, like having an out-of-body experience, while on acid. Often the clan took our trips in somebody's living room, listening to Jimi Hendrix brutalize "The Star Spangled Banner" while staring fascinated at things that were invisible when we weren't high, such as the time-lapse trails of image and light left behind by moving your hand across your face. On other occasions, we'd travel to the beach or local mountains, or the deserts of Palm Springs and Yucaipa, where we'd cavort and commune with nature.

My first magic carpet ride happened in the forest, where an army of sky-high old trees encircled me like protective soldiers, and cold, smooth boulders punctuated a splashing crystal stream. The air was green and smelled like rain. For some reason

I had on a red denim shirt and jeans, while my companions wore the traditional blue work shirts of our day. As the crescendo of our hallucinogenic glory reached its peak, I saw the figure of a lovely girl in red flitting from rock to rock, laughing, smiling, her long brown hair flying as she moved as if it were wings. She was beautiful, and I admired her so much. Then suddenly I realized it was me. My entire life I'd seen myself as ugly, oversized, not good enough. Counterfeit as it may have been, the drug-induced vision I had out there in the woods in 1969 may have been the first time in which I saw myself as attractive and a person that somebody might want to know.

At nineteen I hooked up with Marvin, a member of our tribe, and moved out of my parents' house to live in sin with him. We called ourselves Mr. and Mrs. Freak. Marvin was a thirty-two-year-old former capitalist and ex-husband from the suburbs who was now living out his second childhood as a faux radical college student. Marvin was Jewish, which ought to have been a plus with my parents, but with his full beard, wild Semitic hair, and rimless rose-colored glasses (not to mention the fact that he was thirteen years older than me and defiling their daughter on a nightly basis), they hated him even more than they'd hated my black FOB.

Being provocateurs, lunatics, and outlaws was intoxicating to both of us but eventually, like the drugs we took, that thrill wore off. So when President Richard Nixon's second-in-command, Spiro Agnew, issued his challenge, "America: Love It or Leave It," Marvin and I decided we'd leave. For the summer anyway.

In June 1970 we flew to Amsterdam. As soon as we arrived, we stashed our rucksacks at the train station and began walking the streets. Eager as I was to take the advice of a million car bumper stickers that'd told me to shape up as an American or ship out, it didn't take long before I began to have second thoughts. Everything in Amsterdam smelled weird. Exhaust fumes belched rudely at us from all sides. There weren't any drinking fountains. The sidewalks weren't flat, and my feet hurt from tromping the cobblestone streets in heeled boots. I wanted a hamburger, but what the Dutch had to offer, a "Wimpy," was totally unacceptable.

Marvin took me to Paradiso, one of Amsterdam's nightclubs where you could buy and smoke hashish. Later that night we landed at a youth hostel and paid a couple of guilders to crash on the floor of a giant loft with a bunch of other hippie trekkers. When we saw sunlight streaming through the windows the next morning, we got up and resumed our troll of the streets. I was hungry, but nothing was open and all the clocks seemed to have stopped at four. The city was deserted, and it took us a while to figure out that at that time of year, in that part of the hemisphere, the sun goes down at midnight and comes up at three A.M. The arrogant defiance that had prompted me to "leave it" was now reduced to a whiney whimper as I stood outside a darkened Amsterdam gift shop and fixated on its display of imported Snickers candy bars. I would have done anything for a taste of something familiar but fell short of the guts needed to break the shop's window. With that, I had to admit that I was an American after all.

We took a train ride to Rotterdam, passing Holland's scenic tulip farms along the way, and purchased a used Citröen Deux Chevaux—a funky little French delivery van with sides made of corrugated metal and headlamps that looked like the bug-eyes of a startled cartoon character. We outfitted it with a foam mattress, sleeping bags, and provisions; then we began a three-month road trip.

First we toured Belgium and then Germany, where we stopped in the woodsy and unassuming hamlet that had been home to the Dachau death camp. Parking the Citröen, we trudged along gravel walkways, picking up small stones for souvenirs, as if Dachau were any other place we visited, and showing little regard for the horror and injustice that had taken place there. That was one of the ill side effects of the anti-everything agenda that Marvin and I pursued; it built neither character nor compassion, nor did it lend itself to genuine love, learning, or personal growth. At that time, I had not yet heard the backstory about my family's tragic history in Poland.

From Germany we passed through Austria, marveling at its picturesque scenery, then we headed down the coast of Tito's Yugoslavia where we found what we were looking for: the beach. I got a suntan and my first glimpse of a peasant woman draped in black with a wooden cart. At the town of Split, a ferry took us across the Adriatic to Italy, where we hightailed it to Rome, then Spain, intending to wind up on the sun-kissed island of Ibiza.

For most of our adventure, we relied on campgrounds with cold water, hot fires, and cozy nights spent in our makeshift bunk in the back of the Citröen. But when we got to Barcelona, it was cheap to rent a *pension* with a hot shower and a real bed, so we took a room near the great boulevard known as *La Rambla*. On one of our daily adventures, we found ourselves in *Plaça Reial*, a popular square where musicians, mostly African, hung out. There I met the next Teacher in my journey: a fellow American wanderer, storyteller, and blues singer who invited us up to where he was staying in La Floresta, a lush hillside neighborhood above Barcelona, reminiscent of Topanga and Laurel Canyons in Los Angeles.

Sometimes people enter our lives in order to lead us to other people. And those people lead us to someone else. It's that circle of life we boomerang around in until one day we find where we belong.

Day Tripper

It was a beautiful summer day in La Floresta: warm and fragrant, the sounds of crickets and flute music floating in and out of the colorfully tiled house. The place belonged to a friend of the Blues Man, and as was the custom of the day, travelers and crashers were welcome. So were drugs. Marvin offered a tab to the Blues Man, who declined. But he comfortably folded his large frame into a corner of the room, cradling his acoustic guitar in his arms like a woman to whom he was about to make love, and companioned with us for the duration of our acid trip.

Reliably the LSD started to take effect, and after chatting with us for a while, the Blues Man turned his attention to his guitar. Straight or stoned, I'd never heard anything like it. His deep voice and the sound emanating from his instrument filled the room with melodic, resonating waves. I could have fallen in love with him if I hadn't been there with Marvin. The unvarnished simplicity of his music spoke to my soul like an ancient language, and I wondered, as I had so many times before, *Where does it come from? What does it mean?* I watched the Blues Man, thinking maybe the answer wasn't as complicated as I'd thought.

The Blues Man was also watching me. He was a big, broad-chested man laden with the legacies of Africa and the Caribbean; both poured through his tapered brown fingers to the strings of his guitar. His music was captivating, joyful, and at the same time melancholy (or maybe I was). It transported us like a marvelous escalator to our destination of high.

When he sensed that we were beginning to peak (for me, the walls of La Floresta had begun melting like a Salvador Dali painting), the Blues Man set down his guitar and asked us what kind of food we ate. Back home Marvin and I lived on burgers, mac 'n cheese from the blue box, and midnight delivery from Pizza Man. Disapprovingly the Blues Man shook his head and growled at us.

"Yeah . . . that's what people in El Lay think is food."

Marvin and I shrugged off his verdict. Heck, we were why-bother hippies whose literary hero was the cartoonist R. Crumb. We did drugs, ate meat, and had been known to snack our way through the supermarket and then leave without paying. Occasionally we scavenged from dumpsters behind restaurants and markets. Nutrition was not high on our agenda.

The Blues Man started talking about "spiritual consciousness" (it wasn't hard to tell that these two acid-dropping freaks from L.A. had none) and how there was, as he put it, "more to life than the physical realm." No one had ever spoken to me about that. Even though I was stoned, his words struck an unexpected chord that didn't dissolve hours later like the usual spent pyrotechnics of a trip.

More to life than the physical realm. Marvin and I had made a religion out of living in the physical realm. We were brazen, bona fide heathens. Our truth was that there wasn't any. Purpose? We had none. What were we about? Living in the moment; sex, drugs, adventure, and making fun of things. What more could there be? To us, that was a rhetorical question.

Or maybe the answer was yet to come.

The Blues Man picked up his guitar and tried to restore a bit of the cosmic to our afternoon before launching into a dissertation about the benefits of fruit and vegetables: how beautiful their colors are and the life they impart to those who eat them. When Marvin had asked me once about making a salad for dinner, I'd replied, "What for?" I wasn't being a smart-mouth; I just didn't know why anyone would bother to eat vegetables.

Having captured our souls and imaginations with his music, the Blues Man moved in for the kill, literally. Aware we were whizzing on acid and how vulnerable our minds were, he began to tell us in calculated, horrifying detail how animals were slaughtered and how really disgusting eating them was. How badly those poor frightened cows and friendly little chickens suffered, and how that misery and their decaying flesh turned putrid inside your body. Our heads were spinning with movie reels of his gross-out graphics. Then the Blues Man asked his friend at whose house we were visiting to bring out the communal lunch: a huge salad bowl filled with a psychedelic swirl of bright purple onions, dark green lettuce and cucumbers, orange carrots, magenta radishes and shockingly red Murcia peaches. With that, he returned to his narrative about the sensual, colorful beauty of vegetables, weaving it over the dark and scary hole he'd created for us about eating meat, and turning me into a vegetarian.

We stayed in Barcelona a little longer, and the Blues Man took us to Gaudi's Park Güell, where he played a flute while I danced for him under a pavilion of mosaic tiles. Feet twirling, long hair swirling, arms in flight, dancing. *I was dancing.* Life with Marvin as a foul-mouthed, trouble-making prankster never inspired me to dance.

I might also have been falling in love, but I wasn't sure with what or who. I could feel the Music, now an entity unto itself, trying to break through the wall of negativity that I'd built around my soul. My fellowship with fury, outrage, and drugs had provided great insulation from the pain, but it had also separated me from the love and vulnerability that made me who I really was. I barely remembered that girl—the one ushered out of irrelevance by James Brown and tutored in the ways of life by Motown; the girl who could dance till delirious at the Teen Center and Cinnamon Cinder; and who laughed her way through the streets of Hollywood on the last day of school, letting herself be told she was everything he ever wanted by a dashing and handsome young man.

All Along The Watchtower

Our plane took off from Amsterdam on September 18, 1970, the same day that Jimi Hendrix died, and two things happened when Marvin and I got back to the United States. First, after having gained some perspective while away from college, it occurred to me that many of the students protesting how much they hated the government and their parents were free to do so because either the government or their parents were supporting them. In my no-dimmer-switch, true-believer mind, this hypocrisy could not be tolerated any more than the revolution could be televised. I concluded that to continue as I had at San Fernando Valley State College, never taking my education seriously and just tossing about in the quad, made me a phony game-player. So I quit school and became a worker.

The other thing that happened was that Marvin hooked up with his old mistress and went back to his old life as a middle-class Establishment capitalist pig. I moved into the apartment on La Mirada Avenue in Hollywood, and after my run-in with the LAPD and the Manson girls, decided to make a go at becoming an upstanding citizen.

Among the revelations I'd had during my summer in Europe was that my parents were getting old, and I wanted to know and love them better as people. No longer did I have to fight them for the right to make my own decisions, as I had when I was a teenager. Whatever mistakes they'd made, my mother and father had always loved me, and I didn't want to lose them before at least trying to repair the damage.

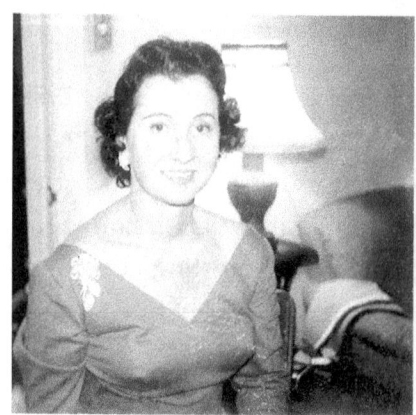

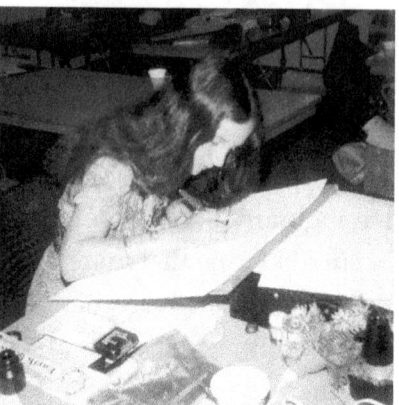

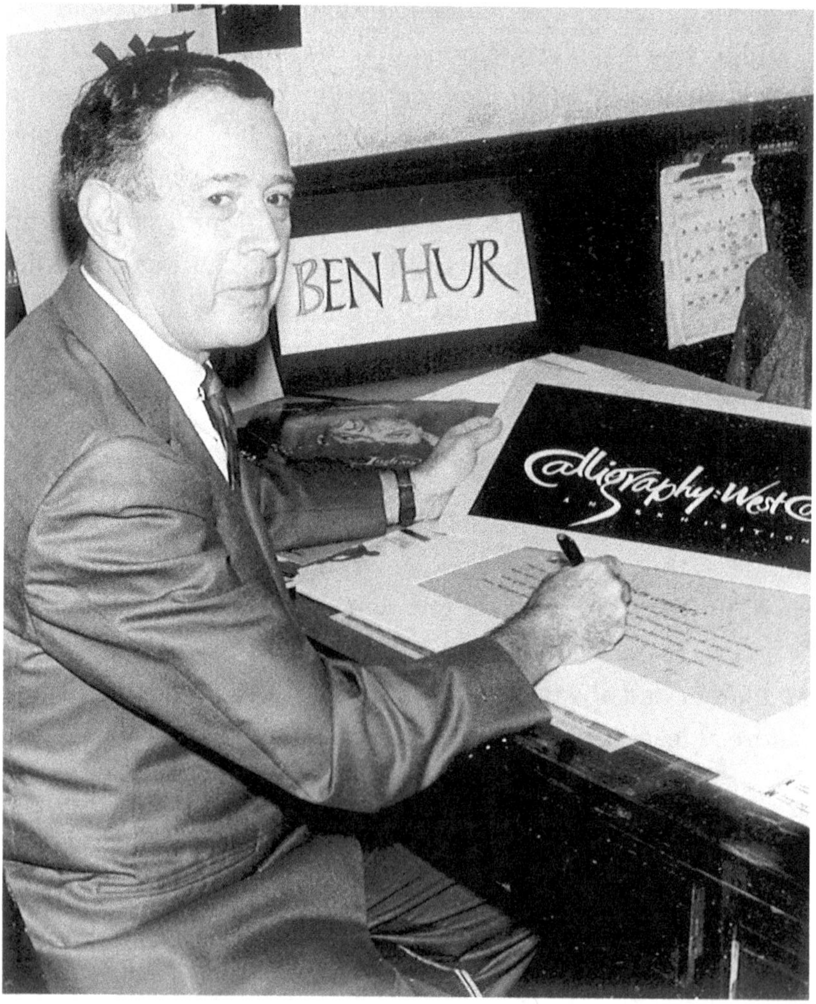
BEN HUR
Calligraphy:West

CHAPTER SIX

Los Angeles, 1971-1973

Respect

Not everything about my childhood was terrible.

I loved art, and since my parents were artists, it was an approved subject they could nurture and support in me. One of the few genuinely happy moments I had in elementary school was in first grade, when the teacher assigned us to create a self-portrait. Using construction paper and yarn wetted with starch, I twisted the yarn to make a head and face, adorning my image with a tiny purple hat and gobs of loopy brown hair. The caption I provided was typed out by my teacher and pasted at the bottom: "I want to be an artist when I grow up," I said. "I have to, or my Daddy will kill me."

My father, Maury Nemoy, was a fine arts painter, respected graphic artist in the film and record industries, and beloved teacher who pioneered the revival of calligraphy in Southern California in the 1950s. For thirty years he taught calligraphy at UCLA Extension, which was probably the most gratifying of his pursuits. He mostly worked freelance and had a studio behind our house, where he kept bottles of ink, all kinds of pens, sheets of exquisite paper in custom-made drawers, beautiful

Prismacolor pencils, pastel chalks, and watercolor paints from Germany—all of which he let me use. He and my mother never hesitated to encourage and equip me when it came to art, and on jaunts by ourselves, my dad and I frequented stationery and art supply stores in which we indulged our mutual fondness for sniffing pink rubber erasers and pencil lead.

The walls of our living room were lined floor to ceiling with books about philosophy, art, and film, and we had a huge collection of LP records: Frank Sinatra, pop, classical, and jazz, many of which were among the hundreds of album covers he designed for Capitol Records and became part of our listening collection. He also gave exclusive calligraphy lessons to a few celebrities, including actor Charlton Heston, whom our family jokingly referred to as Moses from his role in *The Ten Commandments*. My father did private commissions for kings and sultans, the Kennedy White House, the family of J. Paul Getty; and for iconic landmarks such as the Chapel of the Holy Cross in Sedona, Arizona and the Clock of Nations in Rochester, New York. Screen credit for title design was rarely given in those days, but later in his career, his work was recognized with a Primetime Emmy Award for *Ziegfeld: The Man and His Women*.

My mother found her artistic soul in gardening, pottery, and sculpture; she loved working with her hands, be it in soil or clay. When I was little, her sister Miriam (my Aunt Mary) sewed us matching aprons, and we took ceramics classes together at North Hollywood Park.

After my misadventures with Marvin, college, and the criminal justice system, I realized how much I missed being an artist. So I asked my dad if I could come with him to UCLA and take his calligraphy class. We entered a season of bonding that served us well and brought restoration and wholeness to our relationship.

Every Wednesday evening my father would pick me up from my apartment on La Mirada Avenue, and we'd go first to Ship's Coffee Shop in Westwood, where he'd buy me dinner, and then we'd head to class. My father was patient and kind with his students, never telling them their work was bad (even if it was) but rather giving them encouragement to improve. He invested the best of who he was in his students, inviting each class to a semester-end party at our home, for which my mother would show off her talent for hospitality and hors d'oeuvres.

Calligraphy added a new dimension to my search for the Big Truth. I sought high-minded quotations that spoke to my heart about eternal love, beauty, and hope—things I still believed in and wanted. Like a Medieval scribe, I sat for hours at my drafting table, almost in a trance, a lit candle nearby and music playing, immersed in perfecting my pen strokes and creating works of meaning and aspiration out of letterforms. I tried selling some of the pieces I made at hippie shops and craft fairs, and went with my father to the Menucha calligraphers' retreat in scenic Oregon.

At the beginning of his UCLA teaching career, it was all fingers crossed that my dad would get the necessary twelve students to hold class. Thirty years later, everyone in Southern California who did calligraphy either learned it from my father or from someone whom he'd taught. The offspring of public figures rarely have any idea who their parents are in the eyes of the world. After all of our family struggles and my declaration of independence from parental authority, I became whole enough to see more of who my father was, and to learn as so many others had from the undisputed master of the art.

After I'd done well in calligraphy, my father asked if I would like to become his apprentice. He was working for Columbia Pictures at their lot on Sunset and Gower in Hollywood designing movie titles, film trailers, and print advertising. Being the boss's daughter (he, not the studio, paid my salary) also meant a free lunch every day at the restaurant around the corner. My father showed me how to use rubber cement, single-edge razor blades, and a T-square (with which I gave myself the classic mark of a craft apprentice: a missing slice of my left index finger). I learned to carefully line up and place movie titles onto squares of black cardstock. The type was set in white letters on black photographic paper so that color and background could be added when they were shot. If my work wasn't perfectly straight, even a fraction of an inch would result in the title appearing crooked on screen.

Both of the arts my father taught me, calligraphy and paste-up—one revived from ancient times and one as modern as it got in the 1970s—would become obsolete when computers arrived. But that period of learning from and working with him provided us with our most special time together. While there were so many disappointments and failures I laid before him and my mother, for at least one season I shared in his life's work and made my father happy and proud of his daughter.

Into The Mystic

I have always lived in great places for absurdly low rent. The apartment on La Mirada Avenue was a completely furnished one-bedroom for which I paid ninety-five dollars a month. Then I met a woman who told me that she and her husband were moving out of a house in Mount Washington, a rustic enclave just north of downtown Los Angeles, and I could take over the place from them. It was my next circle-of-life encounter: like a relay race or treasure hunt in which a person you barely know leads you to something (or someone) important and then vanishes forever.

Mount Washington was a stone's throw from the Florence Crittenton Home, just on the other side of the same Pasadena Freeway exit, Avenue 43. You'd make a left instead of a right, and rather than circling the flatlands on Griffin, head across Figueroa, past the Lucky's supermarket, and then over the train tracks and right onto Marmion Way. Just beyond the entrance to the Southwest Museum, you'd downshift to first gear, then hang on and punch it straight up single-lane Crane Boulevard. A good clutch foot and brakes were mandatory, as well as a boatload of patience, because a formal minuet was required if you met another car going the opposite way.

The story goes that Mount Washington was one of the first residential neighborhoods in Los Angeles, developed in the early part of the twentieth century as a resort to attract visitors. The mountain was studded with humble wood cabin rentals, and a grand hotel was perched at the top. By the time I moved there in 1972, the Mount Washington community had become a pleasant mix of low-income folk and bohemians living in the cabins, and independent thinkers with cash who built startling modern homes that took advantage of the panoramic views: downtown Los Angeles from one side, green hillsides and the Arroyo Seco on the other.

The hotel and its manicured gardens had long since been transformed into the headquarters of the Self-Realization Fellowship, which I believe commissioned my father to do the cover lettering on an edition of founder Paramahansa Yogananda's book, *Autobiography of a Yogi*. A copy of it sat on the bookshelf in our living room throughout my teenage years, the author's calm brown face and Mona Lisa expression beckoning us to higher ground. But that, and any form of self-realization, would have required us leaving our family camp on the River Denial.

My season on Crane Boulevard was contemplative and lush. The cabin was pretty much just a shack; it had single plank walls that let in both the daylight and cold air, but it had also been refurbished by the previous tenants to include a second bedroom under the house, a chicken coop covered in grape vines in the back, and a rotting deck that I christened my moon-viewing platform. It was ideally located directly above the museum, right next to the fire road, and offered an expansive view of the city, not unlike the one I'd had up in my Rapunzel tower at Flossie's.

My neighbors on the other side of the fire road were a friendly couple with a yard full of children. The husband was caretaker for the Southwest Museum, which had opened in 1914, the same year as the Crittenton Home, and contained a stuffed grizzly bear and Native American artifacts. The museum's entrance at the bottom of the mountain was a tunnel that had been drilled straight through the rock and lined with backlit dioramas of Native American life. At the end of the tunnel visitors had to ride a rickety old elevator up to the museum proper, which poked out from the middle of the mountain.

The monthly rent for my house on Crane Boulevard was just five dollars more than the apartment in Hollywood had been, and I furnished it with items I'd liberated from La Mirada, along with other stuff scavenged on weekly runs through the neighborhood the night before the trash trucks came. I also acquired a second-hand waterbed that took up the whole downstairs. Bricks, boards, and wooden Seven-Up crates filled in for bookcases and end tables, and I acquired a yellow tabby cat (or maybe he acquired me) to whom I granted the self-determination of choosing his own name, a little clicking sound.

With my fireplace, cat, and moon-viewing platform, I was serenaded every afternoon by the warning bell of a guardrail coming down and the clanging thunder of the freight train that ran along Marmion Way. No sound apart from music has ever moved me the way a train does. It's that same yin-yang thing I feel about the blues: screeching steel meets lavender and lace.

The arrival of the afternoon train provided the opening act for the big finish of sunset, and dependably applauded my activities of the day. Mornings, upstairs in my studio, I ventured into Van Morrison's *Astral Weeks*, wrote cosmic poetry, and practiced my calligraphy at the funky wooden drafting table my father had given me. Later, outside in the sunshine with a glass of Mateus rosé in hand, I awaited the train's imminent arrival to the wails of my old friend Otis Redding bellowing "Lover's Prayer" from stereo speakers inside the house.

I wanted to go headfirst into my pursuit for something deeper, something beyond where I'd been. But I had no knowledge or understanding of what that might be, or what spirit made one "spiritual." So I embraced the earthly manifestation of things that seemed transcendent—the liturgies of love, poetry, art, and music—and made them my religion. Mount Washington was my temple, Van Morrison was the preacher, and Otis Redding led the worship.

Every now and then I paid homage to the carnal with a pilgrimage to Burrito King, a fast-food stand on the other side of the hill in Echo Park. The Dodge Lancer had been replaced by a tomato-colored 1968 Volkswagen Beetle in which I tore through back roads of Elysian Park with as much noise as a Harley, popping out into the bustling intersection of Sunset and Alvarado for my bean-and-cheese fix.

On the other side of my cabin lived Delilah, a ballet dancer who'd been raised by progressive parents and knew how to grow her own food. Delilah shared vegetables from her garden with me and a story that I took to heart regarding the priority of people over possessions. One bitterly cold winter, Delilah's family ran out of firewood, so her mother burned the furniture to keep them safe and warm. No one ever regretted it.

Life on Crane Boulevard was full of lessons. I learned them from my neighbors, from Van Morrison, from the celestial skies I watched atop the moon-viewing platform, in the walks I took up the mountain, and in one instance when I foolishly befriended a moody Jamaican from whom I learned about Joni Mitchell and Miles Davis, and also why you should shouldn't invite people to live with you.

Because it's really hard to get them to leave.

Ain't Nothing Like The Real Thing

Then there was the Blues Man.

With Marvin out of the picture, the Blues Man and I picked up where we'd left off under the pavilion in Barcelona. His soul was spectacular, hovering somewhere between the Southern fried gruffness of Stax and the silky polished charm of Motown. He could take me from one to the other on the sound of his voice, and his guitar spoke to a place inside me that was African and American and all the oceans in between. He introduced me to avocados, Howard Tate, and Kahlil Gibran. A laugh at "How Come My Bulldog Don't Bark, Baby?" might segue into an hour's worth of speechifying about the meaning and purpose of life.

Whatever he was talking about, I was now under the Blues Man's spell. His magic was deep and supernatural, and though he professed to teaching me about "more than the physical realm," the realm we found ourselves in was pretty doggone physical.

That I was in love with the Blues Man is an understatement; I was living out the lyrics of the Carpenters's song "Superstar" with all my true-believer heart; fantasizing, as women infatuated with artists are prone to do, that I was his muse. I blocked any thoughts about what (and who) he might be doing during the months that we were apart, months in which my soul would subsist on his music and the memories he'd left behind. Camped out on the banks of that Old Man River (by now you know which one), I patiently waited for his return, trying to grow myself as an artist and a woman in the ways I thought he wanted me to become.

The Blues Man promised nothing, but I was happy to fill in the gaps and imagine the perfect future of our love affair all on my own. He lived in Northern California, but his travels brought him to Los Angeles for gigs, sometimes at a folk music club on Melrose Avenue called the Ash Grove. I parlayed my calligraphy talent into a job at the Ash Grove in which every Monday I climbed a ladder outside the building and brush-lettered in calligraphy the names of the artists who were performing that week on three huge marquees. For this the owner, Ed Pearl, gave me five dollars a week and free admission to the club.

One weekend when the Blues Man came to town, I headed to the Ash Grove, expecting that after the show he would come back to Mount Washington with me, as he'd done the last time he was there. I arrived at the club and went to the greenroom, really just a little hole in the wall from which you could see people as they walked in. I was decked out in my finest 1972 hippie regalia: long peasant skirt, boots, something glittering and gaudy from India on top, and my hair down to my butt.

Then *she* arrived. First I noticed the shapely chocolate leg, exposed all the way up to her well-toned thigh, sticking out of the slit in her embroidered Chinese dress. Then the very high heel on her trim foot, and then the champagne-colored boa floating behind her. It was Ena, Douglas' mother! I couldn't imagine what she was doing there.

When the show ended the Blues Man walked me to my car, but he didn't get in.

"I'll see you tomorrow night," he said.

Ena was standing down the street, poised next to her Jag.

"You're going home with *her*?"

He kissed me lightly, then turned and walked away.

"How could you?" I yelled after him. "She's my daughter's GRANDMOTHER!"

I drove home in tears, barely able to see the road, and dumped myself face down on the waterbed, sobbing. The cat took one look and bolted outside to spend his night in peace under the stars. I couldn't believe what had just happened; how could he hurt me like that ... with *her* ... but neither did I have the self-respect to not want to see him again.

The next night the Blues Man came back to Mount Washington with me, and life was good once more. Everything was back to normal.

Dysfunction At The Junction

By this time, I'd been camped out on the River Denial for so long I hadn't noticed how much of my stuff had been hauled off by weasels. You might say I had no backbone, no self-esteem, but since I'd learned to accept the unacceptable just to stay in the game, I turned it into a noble character trait: *Please, allow me to apologize for your mistakes*. Never mind that he was my Teacher, the Blues Man was playing me, and I was grateful to be his anything, including his fool. I'd been taught well how to do that by Motown.

After the TAMI show, the Motown songbook became my encyclopedia, how-to guide, and bible, and even though other songwriters were behind so many of the lyrics that screwed up my thinking about how men and women were supposed to behave, I held Smokey Robinson responsible. The sharp-looking Miracle was out there in front, his vulnerable tenor sending me ecstatically to the go-go and then leaving me a tear-faced beggar. If it hadn't been for Smokey, I might never have fallen in love, but if hadn't been for the mantra delivered by the writers of "I Could Never Love Another (After Loving You)", I would not have cursed my future.

Looking back, it was a tragedy that nobody in my family or my schoolteachers ever taught me anything I could use when it came to relationships, sending me to my transistor radio for advice from Motown, Stax, and other purveyors of soul music. The songs I listened to over and over again laid a cracked foundation about how to carry on relationships. Along with cool dance moves and slick spins, they taught me that desperation, humiliation, and sadness were fundamental to the way men and women got along. And if a guy didn't want you, all you had to do was beg and plead and fall out crying, and he would come back. That gross act of self-abasement, the songs promised, would make him love you again.

It's not much of an excuse, but the truth is, I didn't know any better. I was still living on the fumes of James Brown's slobbering, "Please, Please, Please," and there was no one willing or wise enough to pull my coattail or teach me to respect myself. So I kept listening, I kept pleading, I kept wishing for rain, and believe me, I was never too proud to beg. The tattoo emerging on my forehead was evident to the scoundrels I fell for but not to me: *1-800-VICTIM. EVEN THE CALL IS FREE.*

This Old Heart Of Mine

In 1973 I decided to leave Los Angeles and move to San Francisco, telling myself it was to study Chinese painting at the De Young Museum, even though I knew it was really to be closer to the Blues Man's world. He and I had taken several road trips up to the Bay Area and points north, notably the mud bath and trailer park town of Calistoga in the Napa Valley, where he had friends. He neither welcomed nor discouraged my move, so I took that as a positive sign. My parents were sad to see me leave but generously offered to subsidize me until I found a job. I packed my stuff into a U-Haul, leaving the waterbed and its murky contents for the next occupant of Crane Boulevard. It was my way of giving back.

The night before my drive-off there was a knock on my door. Surprisingly it was Douglas. How he knew to show up that night is one of those cosmic mysteries. We'd stayed in touch, but I hadn't spoken to him for a long time or mentioned my plan to leave. The sparkle and mischief in his eyes, and the feelings that had brought us together as teenagers, were still there. We commissioned the waterbed for its last voyage and said goodbye in the morning.

I tried to find the cat, but he must have known about the cardboard box and eight-hour U-Haul ride waiting for him, and, free spirit that I'd raised him to be, he ran away. I left some cash and a bag of cat food with Delilah and rolled out to the next stop on my journey: Market and Castro Streets, San Francisco, California.

PART TWO

YOU CAN'T ALWAYS GET WHAT YOU WANT

CHAPTER SEVEN

San Francisco, 1973

Among other things, driving in San Francisco was nothing like it had been in Los Angeles. The year I arrived, Bay Area Rapid Transit, otherwise known as BART, was putting the finishing touches on its Market Street subway and had turned the once stately boulevard with its signature streetcars into a planked and riveted mess. Every San Franciscan with a lick of sense knew better than to try to drive on it. But I was a greenhorn, and according to the street map, it seemed like the most direct route to my new home.

The U-Haul bounced block by block as I dodged pedestrians, policemen, and Caltrans workers. I waited for lights that took forever to change and then waited some more as guys in orange vests held up traffic to make way for their beeping behemoths to cross the road. Finally I came to a beat-up intersection where, over a period of time, sign after sign had been nailed to wooden poles, but nobody had bothered to take down any of the previous ones.

"No Parking." *Well that makes sense. There's not much room here.*

"No U-Turn." *Yeah, those are always iffy.*

"No Left Turn." *I'm not going that way anyhow.*

"No Right Turn." *Okay whatever.*

"Do Not Enter." *What the hell?*

Was it a test? A philosophical enigma? A government conspiracy? It could have been any of those, but with a herd of drivers honking their horns behind me, I chose to make it the moment in which I learned the meaning of executive decision.

My new digs were located on 16th Street, at the three-way crossroads where it met Market and Noe, just a block from Castro. To enter, I had to go down some steps below street level, unlock a door, and walk through a dark alley beneath a Victorian flat, from which I'd emerge into a stark concrete patio. There in the back, a boxy two-story building with sliding glass doors for entry had been erected. I chose the upstairs unit because the ceilings downstairs were too low for anyone over five feet tall. My apartment had one bedroom with a window facing a tree, a living room in which I placed the holy shrine of my record player, a kitchen, and a small balcony where I sat in the sun and tried to imagine that I was happy and everything made sense.

Looking back there appear to be common themes to places I've lived, like underground tunnels leading to perches in the sky: atop the Southwest Museum and my moon-viewing platform on Mount Washington, or the third-floor fire escape at Flossie's. Over the next decade, all the places where I'd wind up living would have the same setup. Who knows how coincidences like that happen. Sometimes things just fall together in a pattern or that circle-of-life thing. I often heard it credited to "the universe," but as far as I could tell, planets and stars were just spinning globs of gas and dirt that couldn't even set themselves into orbit.

Yet, as a seeker of the Big Truth, I was open-minded to all possibilities, and San Francisco in the 1970s was the Wild West of Enlightenment—a New Age mecca for those with an oversized ego, convincing oratorical rhetoric, and a bucket to collect the cash. With Charles Manson in the can, the season was ripe for people with big personalities to lay claim to The Big Answer To Everything and reap the harvest of mixed up souls like myself. Like "est," Werner Erhard's Seminar Training. Definitely not my style. It cost a bundle, and I'd heard he wouldn't let participants go to the bathroom during a session. Or the Reverend Sun Myung Moon. I went to hear him speak on behalf of a friend who was shuttling weekly to the Moonie camp in Mendocino. Though his message was entirely in Korean, he affected a terrific impression of Hitler.

Then there were the swamis and mystics. I squirmed through meditation, but when the chanting was over and devotees raved about seeing the blue pearl, I bolted for the door, having nothing to report. There was Baba Ram Dass who told us to "Be here now" (like, where else were we?) and J. Krishnamurti who told us to "Think on these things" (a thought he himself lifted from the apostle Paul).

There was the Good Reverend Cecil Williams and his joyous Glide Memorial Church, where everyone was everything, and the Bad Reverend Jim Jones and Peoples Temple, where the dream of utopia became a nightmare from hell. The true believer in me was as prime a candidate for that piece of history, including its cataclysmic Kool-Aid ending, as it had been for some of the other Big Moments that I missed, notably the one that took out Manson followers Susan, Patricia, and Leslie. And while Peoples Temple was located on nearby Geary Boulevard, for whatever reason, I never visited it.

Then there was the Symbionese Liberation Army that kidnapped heiress Patty Hearst. Not even Ringling Brothers could compete with that. My friends at the time and I were hurtling across the Richmond Bridge in a beat-up old van when we heard the reinvented Tania call her wealthy parents "pigs" on the radio. We all cheered, as if our team had just won the Super Bowl, but we weren't about to engage in anything that heavy or dangerous. To be sure, we cared about social justice, but for us the emphasis was still on theatrics.

Special interest groups also dotted the landscape, like the feminists whose idea of fellowship was to have a nurse practitioner teach women how to use a speculum. There were potheads and Deadheads, iChing throwers and Edgar Cayce followers, save-the-whale and back-to-nature types, folkies and jazz buffs, free lovers and Free Huey supporters, Unitarians, vegetarians, goofballs and gurus—each more certain than the rest that theirs was The Way. And to keep the cosmic drama interesting, we also had the Zodiac Killer.

For me, the quest continued to be personal, not political. Wanting to prove that I had transited beyond the physical realm, I sought to appear mysterious and deep. With my ethereal looks and ability to seem profound by saying things that didn't actually make sense, I pulled it off. But inside, I believed people wouldn't like me if they knew who I really was. I could only pretend to be perfect, like they were.

Not knowing how to be (or love) myself, I embraced the identify of *Artist* and looked to women I admired, like Beatrice Wood, and fell in love with the writing of Maya Angelou. But it was the cloud of compulsion conjured up by Anaïs Nin that spoke most deeply to my conflicted soul. Like Nin, I began to carry around a journal so that when I found The Answer, I could write it down and then refer to it whenever I felt insecure. Which was often. The surge of confusion for me was constant, like a fast-moving tributary of that stinky old River. My antenna had grown back, but it was so waterlogged and warped I could hardly tell "Hello" from "Hell, No!"

And all that, combined with unrequited love, unreturned phone calls, an uncertain future, and unlimited marijuana made me one authentic head case.

Lookin' For A Love

San Francisco's Castro District was a colorful neighborhood inhabited by gypsies, playboys, and fabulous creatures of indeterminate gender. Soon I was outfitting myself in the same fashions I saw styled by my peacock-inspired neighbors. One of them gave me a flamboyant top with long draped sleeves that had been made out of a green and purple Indian bedspread. I especially liked wearing it to the airport when I went to visit my parents. The gawking gazes of buttoned-down businessmen were just what I'd intended to provoke.

I was no longer simply getting dressed; every day I costumed my body as art, a kind of living guerrilla theatre intended to define myself outside the boundaries of a place I'd never fit in or been welcome to anyway. I embraced being a stranger in this world as if it were my choice, convincing myself I had turned the tables on rejection.

On nearby Market Street, not far from my subterranean door, was Finilla's Finnish Baths, a funky throwback to the 1920s offering rock steam baths and therapeutic massages. (What actually went on in the massage rooms was anyone's guess.) For two dollars you could get a private room with a small cot and shower, an extravagance reserved for special occasions or a secret rendezvous. But for fifty cents less I could use the women's communal steam bath and locker room, where lively conversations ran the gamut from debate over whether Epsom salts or corn meal provided the best exfoliation to vociferous agreement that all men were rascals and you couldn't trust any of them.

I wasn't used to San Francisco's bone-chilling fog or the vertical landscape of its tall buildings. Going to Finilla's every night before bed became my evening ritual. It was hot. It was wet. It took the disturbance out of my system and left me supremely relaxed. There was plenty of interesting gossip bouncing off the tile walls, and when I finished schmoozing, steaming, scrubbing, showering, and slathering myself with coconut oil, my body felt as smooth as glass. Those first few months Finilla's provided a warm ending to my cold and rather purposeless days.

I was lonely. It was harder than I thought to make new friends. I didn't hear much from the Blues Man, and I was gravely deficient in the discernment necessary to distinguish friend from phony or to size up the potential value (or liability) of relationships. I tried (unsuccessfully) to get to know my fellow art students at the De Young Museum. I chatted (to little avail) with customers at the bank and the produce market on Castro. I met people in Golden Gate and Duboce Parks and invited them over for dinner, then never saw them again. Or worse, saw them again and got ripped off.

The only bright lights those first few months were my neighbors in the front Victorian, Craig and Penelope, roommates splitting the rent. Although we didn't hang out together, they were always friendly when I passed them going in or out of the underground tunnel. Craig was a peacock, and Penelope was a registered nurse. Both of them were looking for Mr. Right.

Love And Happiness

We were headed for a day's worth of sightseeing and *dim sum* in Chinatown, and we'd just found a parking space. But it was on one of those treacherous San Francisco hills, the kind that force you to crank up your handbrake, burning the heck out of it, while keeping one foot on the clutch and the other on the gas pedal at the same time so you don't roll backwards. I maneuvered the Beetle into the tight spot and turned my steering wheel as hard as I could to the left so my front tires would butt up against the curb. It was pointing nose up, and the sheer force of gravity had my companion and I pinned in our seats.

As I went to pull my key out of the ignition, we saw a wild-eyed man come running down the hill toward us, his jacket open and fluttering behind him like a cape. Then we saw a knife, a big scary one, sail past the window, and then we saw a woman, screaming obscenities, running after the knife, running after the man, her arms flapping like a rooster's wings. I quickly rolled up my window and locked the door. But my passenger had other ideas.

"Come on! Get out! Let's go follow them and see what happens!"

That was Rose.

Six feet tall and fearless, Rose had become my friend a year earlier on one of the trips I'd taken with the Blues Man to the Napa Valley. She and her lover, a big hunky guy, were caretakers at a shuttered dude ranch on picturesque Mount St. Helena, just up the road from Calistoga's 1950s trailer park and colon hydrotherapy clinics.

Five years older than me, Rose was a half-Sicilian, half-German goddess with waist-length blond hair and the superhero armor of wrist-to-elbow silver bracelets. She had the presence of a Nordic giant, the smile of an angel, and the soul of a Mafia enforcer. When she was angry, you knew it; her bracelets clanged together as loudly as a car crash. She drove a camouflaged, gutted-out Land Cruiser, her golden hair flying madly in the wind. A country girl from Michigan who grew up on a cattle ranch and could hold her own in the face of trouble, Rose's philosophy was simple: Let's have a party. Great food, music, and marijuana were the essentials, and she anointed herself queen of it all.

By the time I moved to San Francisco, Rose was done with the dude ranch and hunky boyfriend. At an otherwise festive celebration with dozens of party guests, things went, as they say, horribly wrong. Her lover got upset over some perceived disrespect on the dance floor and punched her in the face. Warrior and goddess that she was, Rose, with a broken jaw, drove herself one hundred miles in the Land Cruiser to San Francisco General Hospital. After multiple surgeries, she resettled in the hills above Calistoga, renting a two-bedroom cabin at the Triple S Ranch, next door to the Petrified Forest.

In summer, both of us flaunted our youthful bodies in styles we invented but never bothered taking credit for, like pairing skimpy sun dresses with kick-ass hiking boots. In the winter, we ripped open the pant legs of our jeans and overalls and made mini-skirts and dresses out of them, including a denim evening gown studded with rhinestones across the bust. We sewed these ourselves because in 1973 no one else was making them.

Rose and I also pooled our artistic talents, my calligraphy with her decoupage, to create one-of-a-kind artworks on weathered old pieces of barn wood, which we gave away as gifts. We made up recipes, embroidered our jeans, threw fabulous parties, and were so far ahead of our time that time never caught up with us. Full of ideas but without ambition, we never considered turning what we did into enterprise, and by the time the things we did became of commercial interest to others, we'd moved on.

When Calistoga's one block and two horses weren't enough for her, Rose would come to the City for adventures with me, like that day we witnessed the knife drama in Chinatown. And when my soul became overwhelmed by San Francisco's unfamiliar urban frequency, I'd run away to the Napa Valley and recalibrate.

At the Triple S, I discovered magic in the way silence bounced back at you from the mountains, the way light and shadow played tag across the valley in the afternoon, the sharp smell of walnut and Manzanita trees baking in the hot sun, and how you could hear the flapping of a hawk's wings from seventy feet in the sky. We gorged ourselves straight from the trees in the Triple S's plum and apple orchards and watched fish dance at a muddy little pond hidden by tall grass that met us at the end of Mountain Home Road.

We went for sunset rides in the Land Cruiser up the Oakville Grade after stopping at the Dairy Queen in Rutherford, tooled through Highway 29's canopy of trees linking the vineyards of Calistoga with the town of St. Helena, and spent lazy, mind-altered afternoons at her friend Robbie's, where we swam, sunbathed, smoked pot, and chased imaginary pink and purple Indians.

At night we sat by the fireplace in her cabin with a bottle of Mateus and talked story, laughing (and crying) at humiliations and injustices inflicted on us (and occasionally by us in retaliation), and affirming that whenever either of us wondered, "Is it me or is it them?" it would always be them.

Will It Go Round In Circles?

Taking Chinese brush painting classes five hours a week at the De Young Museum hadn't been as compelling a pursuit as I'd hoped, and my San Francisco days began to feel empty and worthless. The motivation to consider myself authentic by leaving college to become a worker had been in neutral since I left Los Angeles, but now I felt like it was time to let my dad off the hook from sending me a monthly check. So I decided to look for a job.

After researching the San Francisco telephone book for businesses I thought I might enjoy working for, I was interviewed, then hired as an editor by Reverend Hogen Fujimoto of the Buddhist Churches of America, or BCA. The office was on Octavia Street between Bush and Pine, right in the heart of San Francisco's Japantown. It might have seemed an unlikely post, since I was neither a Buddhist nor Japanese, but Reverend Fujimoto said they had been looking for someone with good English and writing skills to copyedit articles that had been roughly translated from Japanese for their monthly bilingual newspaper, *Wheel of Dharma*.

Working for Japanese Buddhists seemed like a great opportunity. I'd been infused with love for Asian art and culture by my parents, and being on a mission to find the Big Truth, I was certain to find it here.

The skills that my father taught me at Columbia Pictures were a big plus. BCA had just purchased a Selectric Composer, one of IBM's new typesetting machines that would store keystrokes and then print them out justified and camera ready. The Bishop was very proud of that machine, which had cost a lot of money, and he often brought visitors from Japan up to my third-floor office to meet the *hakujin* and get a live demonstration. I was also equipped with familiar tools: a drafting table, light box, razor blades, and rubber cement to lay out the work I did and get it ready for the printer.

In addition to *Wheel of Dharma*, I copyedited, typeset, and pasted up Buddhist tracts and books, which were then printed and sold in the bookstore that BCA operated on the ground floor. When a regular customer visited the bookstore one afternoon, and the manager mentioned that fugitive heiress-turned-bank-robber Patty Hearst had just been captured, the customer's eyebrows raised.

"I thought she worked upstairs," he said, referring to me.

Working in Japantown I was exposed to new tastes and experiences, like the gummy mystery of *mochi*, slurping one long, fat *udon* noodle from a cast iron pot of steaming hot soup, and going to see Japanese movies at the Kabuki Theatre after work. There I met Zatoichi, the blind swordsman, as well as the star-crossed lovers of *Double Suicide* who kill themselves in order to be together in the next life.

The tenets of Buddhism made sense, but I wasn't drawn to it emotionally. It seemed more like a way to understand life and be a good person than what I was looking for: the supernatural, cosmic connection to another realm.

I learned to value the profound kindness and humility of my Japanese-American coworkers, but I didn't believe I would ever have the capacity for respect that they did: turning everything from serving tea to flower arranging into a ceremony, and greeting one another with the gesture of gratitude and reverence called *gasshō*, palms together and a small nod or bow of the head. I couldn't relate to how they weren't up-in-arms angry about their internment during World War II, and I was certain I was too damaged to ever be that forgiving. But they never demanded that I be like them. They tolerated and embraced me, and even showed their own irreverent sense of humor on Amida Buddha's birthday, when we gathered in front of the shrine at noon, had cake, and then got the rest of the day off.

My residency in the Castro came to an end when a friend of Rose's offered me the bottom flat of her vintage Victorian at 729 Oak Street. The neighborhood was in transition; to the north were the dilapidated remains of the once high-flyin' Fillmore District; to the south, the beginnings of gentrification, a fancy word for people who have money taking over the neighborhoods of people who don't.

The Oak Street flat had high ceilings, two marble fireplaces, and a kitchen bigger than my entire La Mirada Avenue apartment. I stayed there long enough for the Blues Man to pay a few visits in which he schooled me about Paul Robeson, reggae, and Jimmy Cliff; and for Rose and I to throw a memorable party that lasted three days. Then the Victorian's owner decided to sell it, and I had to move out. Temporarily BCA let me stash my stuff in one of their garages, and I slept on the floor of my musician friend Ron's apartment.

It was time to reassess my situation. After living less than a year there, I decided that foggy, vertical San Francisco wasn't the place for me.

Sittin' On The Dock of the Bay

There was a certain way sunshine smiled on the City that you could only see from one place, and that was across the East Bay at the tip of a little pinky finger of land that stuck out into the water at the end of Ashby Avenue. I knew it as the fishin' place, where retired old men and dreamers who couldn't be tied to a desk sat out in the weeds and wildflowers with their poles to see what they could catch.

The spot was remarkably quiet, save the gentle splashing of water and the clinking you always hear in places like that, though bustling Highway 80 was right behind it and the Oakland-Bay Bridge just to the left. The Blues Man had first taken me there, and later it became a place I went to by myself to get away and find needed perspective. I could sit on a rock and write in my journal, looking at San Francisco from afar as if the whole city were just a single entity. Like Jonah looking at the whale from the safety of a harbor instead of from inside its churning guts.

An old friend from the tribe of my Marvin years in Los Angeles had relocated to Berkeley, where he'd opened a garage and fixed VW Beetles like mine. The Hippie Mechanic was on a slightly different track than the rest of us, having never been a college student, but he was filled with the same barrel-of-monkeys subversive mischief as we were.

One afternoon during my season of homelessness, I went by to shoot the breeze and have him change my car's oil. When he mentioned that he and his girlfriend were looking for a house to rent in sunny Oakland, I told him to get an extra bedroom for me, which they did. Sight unseen, I moved in with them.

CHAPTER EIGHT

Oakland, 1974-1977

People Get Ready

It was probably the Blues Man who introduced me to astrology, and back in those days I was ready to give whatever might explain things a try. Despite its cool symbols and mystical allure, however, astrology proved to be just another counterfeit in terms of fulfilling its celestial promises for my future here on Earth. But it did provide a name for the perpetual conflict that hammered my soul, leaving me indecisive, insecure, and exhausted with myself: Pisces, the two fish swimming in opposite directions.

Make that the two Piranhas.

Their conflict in me was likely amplified by the duality I'd grown up with in Los Angeles, where suspicion and cynicism were survival skills because nobody was ever really who they presented themselves to be. Like the undercover cops in their cheerful Hawaiian shirts. Like me as "Ramona" at the home for unwed mothers. Like the respected household I came from, where the closets were bulging with secrets and shame. Certainly those warring, cold-blooded Piranhian adversaries populated my River Denial, making it toxic with Fear and Doubt, their evil spawns.

But here in humble North Oakland, a micropolis of tidy homes, mom-and-pop grocery stores, "You Buy 'Em, We Fry 'Em" fish joints, a Wonder Bread/Twinkie bakery across the street, and the monstrous Judson Steel Mill nearby, I encountered for the first time unpretentious, straightforward humanity that was simply lived out. If you passed a man on the street, and he said, "Good morning," it wasn't to psyche you out or as the prelim to an abduction. It was just "Good morning," and nothing else was meant by it. This kind of uncomplicated interaction with people was a startling revelation to my jaded soul.

I moved into the house at 53rd and Market Street as wide-eyed as if I'd relocated to a foreign land. My neighbors included hardworking men who labored at the steel mill and spent Saturday night (and their paycheck) with their best girl and a bottle, turning out the arm of their record player so that Johnnie Taylor's "Who's Makin' Love to Your Old Lady?" would play over and over again all weekend; "Hey, hey, hey!" and drunken laughter (and an occasional gunshot) pouring out of their windows. There were also decent-minded parents trying to raise their kids right and Sunday morning churchgoers: fluttering pastel ladies, like butterflies, in big flowering hats, and sharp-looking gentlemen in freshly pressed suits.

Unlike its San Francisco namesake, this Market Street was a bustling little thoroughfare by day, quiet as a cemetery at night except for the Oakland Local, an arthritic, creaky old train that slowly clanged its way behind the Twinkie factory late at night. It was the route of confident young men making their way back home at midnight and talking about their exploits, and weekday office workers waiting in the morning sun for AC Transit buses that rumbled one after another, shuttling them to jobs in downtown Oakland and across the Bay Bridge to the City.

The neighborhood was dotted with houses of prayer: Church Of God In Christ, Apostolic, Baptist, A.M.E, and Pentecostal.

It also had its share of teenage punks who might replace the wheels on your diamond-in-the-back Ford LTD Brougham with cinder blocks, but they weren't conniving swindlers trying to cheat you out of your birthright.

Our house sat on a slope connected to a storefront, which we sublet to a collective of glass blowers to help with the rent. The storefront had the street entrance; to get into our space, my roommates and I had to walk up the driveway and enter through the rear, where a mudroom had been built on the porch between the kitchen and the back door. That was also where a crude shower had been installed, so besides the awkward moment when a visitor would show up while you were sudsing in the buff, in the winter you'd have to turn on the oven full blast to warm things up before hopping in. I didn't have any complaints about it, and neither did the Hippie Mechanic and his girlfriend, whose previous residence had been a former Helms Bakery van. We were all glad to call the place home.

From the kitchen, you entered the living room, which faced a patio hidden from the street; on the other side of the main floor was a bedroom with its own bathroom that was equipped with a temperamental toilet, small sink, and claw foot tub. Its window faced the driveway.

The patio side of our house was covered in serpentine vines of pink roses that twisted their way up to the second story. Upstairs was a loft with windows all the way around; the tangle of vines on the south side pressed so tightly against the glass you had the feeling you were underwater looking at seaweed from the porthole of a sunken ship. That was where I stayed.

The sights, sounds, and smells that rose up to my room on Market Street filled me with delight. On occasional Saturdays, a high school parade with drum corps and marching band would pass through. While school pride was unfamiliar to my history, I became choked up and close to tears when these parades went by.

At night, after the Oakland Local took its last labored gasp about midnight, The Quiet rolled in. You could feel it, especially upstairs. There was a palpable sense of something akin to fog blanketing my little neighborhood, and The Quiet seemed to absorb every bit of movement that had churned throughout the day. It was in that dark stillness, alone and safe, that I would write in my journal: questioning, dreaming, imagining, mourning, and celebrating through my pen; or typing stories and poetry on a used green Olivetti I'd bought for twenty dollars. It was in those wee hours that I'd sometimes hear the voice of a young man walking down the deserted street below, singing acapella, as if it were street opera, to no one but himself and God.

Unlike life in Hollywood or Mount Washington, Oakland was simple, ordinary, and reassuring. Once more the end of my day was heralded by a train, and after being tucked in by The Quiet, I fell asleep every night to the sweet, yeasty aroma of Twinkies and Wonder Bread that wafted in from across the street.

> *YOU . . . Oh, glorious you,*
> *with laughing eyes and sparkle of life.*
> *YES . . . We have touched.*
> *How very beautiful we are.*

The landlord who rented the house to the Hippie Mechanic and his girlfriend was Louis, a jolly older man whose wife had passed away. Louis was an engaging character, and with nothing much else to occupy him in retirement, he came by regularly to check on his property which included a three-unit apartment building next door with a street-facing storefront like ours. That building and our house were separated by a common driveway, and from the downstairs bedroom, we and our next-door neighbors could take stock of one another's comings and goings.

Directly across the driveway was Clarence, a steel mill worker whose Johnnie Taylor records and "Hey, hey, hey!" were our weekend soundtrack. The upstairs apartments were rented by James, a kind-hearted soul who worked nights at the General Motors plant in Fremont, and Medina, a Puerto Rican writer and activist. The storefront to their building was occupied by a man who sold vacuum cleaner parts.

Louis and his wife had lived in our house before she died, and he still kept a number of their things in the garage, where he'd go and piddle around on his visits. Sizing me up after we'd been there a few months, Louis pulled out a trunk of vintage clothes that had belonged to his dearly departed. They fit me perfectly: suits and dresses from the 1930s and 1940s, button top shoes, even a real fur coat.

Shortly after I began wearing them, my roommates and I agreed there was a problem with the downstairs bathroom. No matter how tightly we thought we'd shut it, the door would open, seemingly by itself, and there always seemed to be a freezing cold draft in there, even in the summer. Knowing what a presence she still was to Louis (and now my wardrobe), my roommates and I joked that maybe the bathroom was inhabited by his wife's ghost.

Land Of 1000 Dances

The setting of normalcy that life on Market Street provided was a salt-of-the-earth baseline from which to release my creative chaos. Having ordinary people around me—people on whom I could depend to remain ordinary—meant I could soar into the mystic with my poetry (and marijuana) and still find the lights of the airstrip when I needed to come down. I told myself I wanted to be free, but without something to pull away from, I would have just been adrift on my own.

Besides writing and art, I began taking African dance classes at two homegrown studios in my neighborhood: Full Spectrum on Telegraph Avenue and Everybody's Creative Arts Center at the corner of Broadway and 51st. I had been captivated by the drums and African dance ever since I was a kid and saw the 1959 movie, *Black Orpheus*. The classic Greek myth of doomed lovers Orpheus and Eurydice was reset in Rio during Carnival to the rhythms of samba and the netherworld of Afro-Brazilian spiritualism. I watched *Black Orpheus* so many times that every drumbeat, dance move, and nuance of the supernatural drama became embedded in my soul.

Something about the drums *moved* me. The power generated by a wall of live drummers at African dance classes in Oakland was intense, breathtaking, and reminiscent of what I'd felt at the TAMI show and all those years of sneaking into clubs to dance to soul music.

Oakland's African drummers had muscles like boulders; the dancers were festooned in swirls of colorful fabric: leaping, jumping, flying across the floor to ecstatic climax with the drums. There were blacks, whites, Latinos, Asians; all kinds and colors came to dance. Every class concluded with a circle in which each of us was encouraged to go into the center and do our own thing solo. As much as we admired technique and talent, what you did in the circle wasn't as important as the fact that you did it with your whole heart. The point was to be fearlessly yourself, and all who did were celebrated for that, no matter how awkward or out of step we might have been.

Money was always tight in those days, so I asked Boni Grove, who taught African dance at Full Spectrum and was also the studio's owner, if she would let me design some business cards in calligraphy in exchange for her classes. Boni was beautiful, elegant, and friendly. Off the dance floor she chain-smoked Marlboros and seemed to be holding back a secret storm, yet she never presented herself as anything but peaceful and calm. She was a single mom with two small boys. Outside of dance class I often ran into them at Lake Temescal, a swimming spot in the Oakland hills, or at the Co-op, a progressive supermarket in our neighborhood. From time to time Boni came by the house on Market Street to hang out with me. We became friends.

I also became friends with Halifu Osumare, one of my dance teachers at Everybody's Creative Arts Center. I was in awe of Halifu, an exquisite African-American woman with reddish hair and a face full of freckles. She had traveled the world and seemed far above it in many ways. Her influence went beyond the moves she taught and into the realm of transformation that dance could foster, both in seekers like me and in the community at large.

At Everybody's I was exposed to amazing teachers from different African countries, including Malonga Casquelord, a squat fireball who led us in hip-swiveling Congolese, darting across the floor ahead of us, and rolling his eyes with madness and laughter as he demonstrated the steps. Dancing with Malonga was a joyous, maniacal experience, after which we dancers were little more than exhausted puddles of sweat, our hearts beating so fast we joked about calling the paramedics.

African dance classes proved a safer outlet for my energy and emotions than romance had; they were sweaty, physical expressions of passion without the messy entanglements, confusion, and potential for disaster that came with relationships. Ninety minutes of uncensored, throbbing, collective intimacy and then, out the door and home to shower without all those unasked, unanswered questions, or any of that annoying next-day longing and wonder.

Just as when I'd first seen James Brown on stage, African dance spoke to the deepest part of me, a place complete in itself that didn't require anyone else's validation. It coaxed out the real-deal truth: unedited, unembarrassed, and unashamed; my body a calibrated instrument responding to the telegraphy of the drums, and then acting that out in front of everyone. Dance became life itself.

The confidence and strength African dance gave me by forcing me to be myself at raw and uncensored dimensions, and then to be celebrated for that in the circle, became a powerful, positive force in my life.

Everyday People

Once a week I filled my pockets with quarters and hauled my laundry and a box of Tide over to the Wash-O-Mat, the big one up on Telegraph, next to the barbeque joint. The place had enormous windows through which you could see the rows and rows of machines slopping duds and suds back and forth. It could almost make you seasick when they were all going at once. But there was also a degree of Zen to sitting there and watching clothes go round and round through the dryers' glass portholes, listening to the drone of the washers, and occasionally eavesdropping on other people's conversations. Sometimes I wrote poetry there.

> *Did you ever hang out in a laundromat*
> *And check out the people, both skinny and fat?*
> *Did you ever sit under the bright light waiting*
> *For your clothes to dry while contemplating*
> *On time and space and grocery stores*
> *And Hollywood parties where people are bores.*
> *And while I sit and watch them spin,*
> *I think of you and wish we were in*
> *Our cozy house, just digging each other—*
> *Yes, you are my laundromat lover.*

One afternoon, as hot sunshine poured in and dryer steam misted up the windows, a round, dark-skinned African-American woman wearing an indigo blue dress and matching head wrap walked in. Her clothing was long, and her hair was completely hidden by fabric, so all I could see was her face. It was a remarkable, lovely face, but I can't say what it was about her that struck me. When she saw me staring at her, she smiled.

"I like your colors," I said, pointing to the deep blue of her dress. I meant something else, but I couldn't put my finger on what it was or how to say it.

"I like yours, too," she said to me.

Aeeshah was a profoundly good-hearted woman who believed that the source of everyone's success or trouble in life was in their attitude, and that a conscious effort toward becoming forgiving, grateful, and loving could heal even the most difficult person or circumstance. As we got to know one another, Aeeshah introduced me to her cadre of women friends: Sharifah, Yusefa, Matina, Najila, and Munira. Wholeheartedly the women accepted me with friendship and affection. We came together regularly to discuss our issues, solve the world's problems, and on weekends we'd cook up a feast, everyone's kids running playfully around the house.

It was my first season of friendship with bright, provocative women who were expanding their minds and hearts in new personal, spiritual, and political directions. Like me, they were seekers of the Big Truth, open to wherever that might be found, including embracing me.

"You're the first white girl we ever made friends with."

"Yeah, we used to beat 'em up in the bathroom."

Danger: Heartbreak Dead Ahead

I should have known better when I first saw him at the Co-op checkstand, pulling a wadded-up handful of dollar bills out of his pocket to pay for a jumbo box of baby diapers.

Despite positive new developments in happy Oakland—sisterly girlfriends, African dance, a job I enjoyed, and a stable home life on Market Street—when it came to men, my radar had been fried like summer lightning, and my antenna wasn't picking up valid signals, just backwash chatter and Bobby Womack. I had a hole in my soul that no amount of positive energy, dancing, or sisterhood could plug. It had been jackhammered and excavated by all those long-suffering songs I'd believed in years earlier, leaving a giant fissure through which everything good now being poured into me was leaking out just as fast.

No man had ever wanted me in the way I so desperately yearned to be wanted. Even though I'd witnessed firsthand the terror of what happened to Rose—the broken jaw, the hiding for months from her ex-lover, the fear of more violence—secretly I believed there was something glamorous and exciting about being wanted so badly that it drove your pursuer to madness. Without a man, I had no value as a woman. The more I was wanted, I figured, the more I'd be worth.

No longer hearing from the Blues Man, and with my airstrip just a crash landing away, I convinced myself I was a cosmic being, not subject to gravity or the common sense rules that ordered everyone else's dull life such as: *Don't get mixed up with a married man*. Whatever progress it looked like I'd made, deep inside I was still hoping for the kind of tortured romance that my Motown mentors had taught me about.

Finally, in 1974 I got it.

The Piano Player was a handsome, charismatic jazz musician, and I was egged on by my desire to be the lover and muse of a great artist. In exchange for being his paramour, I evicted the glass blowers and gave him the key to the storefront downstairs, where he and his band could rehearse. He taught me about McCoy Tyner, and I agreeably ignored the fact that at his home around the corner, he had a wife and baby.

By this time, the Hippie Mechanic and his girlfriend had broken up and moved out, and apart from a short-lived series of revolving roommates, I had all of the Market Street house to myself.

At first the Piano Player built me up and made me feel like I was the most extraordinary woman in the world. But after he got me hooked, he would routinely back me into a corner, where he'd menace, interrogate, and berate me—not for anything I'd actually done, but for what he supposed I was *thinking*. Which might lead to *something*. It became a sick and diseased ritual between us. As I cowered under his fury, he would badger, threaten, and humiliate me for hours, smashing his fist into the wall next to my head until he could get me to admit to the thing he was looking for, my fatal flaw, to prove his point and justify his abuse. Powerless, broken, and exhausted, eventually I would come to agree with his conclusion that I was a stupid, worthless failure, handing him the jumbled confession he demanded just to end the torment.

It became impossible to stay close to Aeeshah and my new girlfriends. The bedrock of our gatherings had been accountability and fearless truth, both of which I had to bury by the River in order to keep my boyfriend.

By 1976, I had stopped eating, lost thirty pounds, and looked like what my mother called "death warmed over." A vegetarian since Barcelona, I became paranoid that, in one way or another, everything in the food chain was contaminated or unhealthy, and I was a bad person for eating it. Withered and anorexic,

I went to a doctor who took a blood test and told me that the answer to my problems was to eat liver.

Perhaps my saving grace was that I kept looking for help. Eventually I found myself in the hands of Dr. Ramamurti Mishra of the Yoga Society of San Francisco. Dr. Mishra had been trained in both Eastern and Western medicine, and prior to coming to San Francisco, he'd practiced in India and New York. He was a medical doctor as well as a spiritual teacher, and though I wasn't a yogi or a follower, Dr. Mishra robustly welcomed me into his care.

Several times a week I went to the Yoga Society where he treated me with acupuncture, hooking up the needles to a box that ran an electric current up and down my body. Then he'd have me relax for ten minutes in a steam cabinet, kind of like a hot refrigerator with an opening at the top for my head. As it had been at Finilla's, the wet warmth made me feel safe and whole.

After treatment, Dr. Mishra and his assistant, an older American woman named Sarasvati, would always invite me to stay for lunch. It wasn't just a courtesy; sharing a meal of chapattis and lentils with their ashram family, they said, was part of the cure to heal my broken soul.

"You need to be in a place where you are loved and accepted," said Dr. Mishra.

He was a kind, sweet man with a unforgettable smile.

I was welcome to attend their meditations but never obliged to. There were no lectures, no lessons, no telling me what I'd been doing wrong. Nor did Dr. Mishra or the Yoga Society ever ask me to pay for the treatments I received, which went on for about a year. Nothing was required of me, but I was extended every possible kindness. There was a lot of healing in that. I'd come to the Yoga Society a withered flower, and they'd given me unconditional, loving care. Sarasvati was easy to talk to, gentle, and graciously non-specific when I asked for advice. But though I tried to learn their path, I never seemed able to follow it.

Then again, it probably didn't help that even as Dr. Mishra and Sarasvati were putting me on the road to wholeness, the Piano Player was still in my life.

For as bad as it was, I didn't know who I'd be without him.

Where Did Our Love Go?

That February day in 1977 started out ordinary enough. I took AC Transit to the terminal in San Francisco, and then got on a Muni bus to Japantown to go to work. Sometimes I'd walk, but this morning I felt a little tired so I rode, stopping at a sandwich shop on the way to get a cup of coffee. I stepped into BCA and was taking off my jacket when suddenly a violent, sharp pain shot across my abdomen, causing me to double over in cramps.

It had to be the coffee. What a stupid idiot I was to drink coffee, which I knew was poison. I was such a jerk. The pain was unbearable; I stumbled to the women's bathroom where there was a small resting bench. But the pain didn't subside. One of my coworkers came in and saw me, pale and knotted up. What could she do to help, she asked.

My friend Nancy was a nurse at the nearby San Francisco Presbyterian Hospital. I gave my coworker the number.

"Please, call her and ask what she thinks I should do."

Nurse Nancy's answer was swift and clear: Get her to the emergency room. *Right now.*

Ever since I'd been with the Piano Player, I had worried about becoming pregnant. He was dead set against using protection, and in the throes of my aversion to food, I'd also stopped taking the Pill. The twisted little paper clip doctors called an IUD had given me one horrendous pelvic infection after another, so apart from some wacky plan I'd read about to chart your ovulation by the moon, there wasn't much I could do. The idea of getting pregnant by the Piano Player was terrifying. But since being wanted for sex was the only way I could feel wanted at all, I went along with the demands of love.

Now my period was late.

In the emergency room, there was a lot of bustling, starched white activity, but the physician on duty who was gently poking my abdomen didn't seem able to find the trouble. After explaining my theory about the coffee, I thought perhaps I ought to mention something else. My voice came out sounding like the reluctant confession of a four-year-old.

"I might be a little bit pregnant."

And then the high drama kicked in. The doctor determined I was hemorrhaging internally from a ruptured ectopic pregnancy. My fertilized egg hadn't dropped into my uterus like it was supposed to. Most likely hindered by scar tissue from all the infections I'd had, it'd gotten stuck in my fallopian tube, where it continued to grow anyway. This morning, the narrow passageway finally burst.

The deadly explosion of something stuck in a place it didn't belong and getting bigger by the minute may well have been a metaphor for my toxic relationship with the Piano Player. Despite all the physical and emotional healing that Dr. Mishra and Sarasvati had invested in me, I was still blind when it came to dealing with what had caused me to get sick in the first place. Now all hell had literally broken loose.

The physician said it was urgent that they get me into an operating room.

Wait a minute, I thought. *This is impossible! It can't be happening. I was just at my job an hour ago. I have work waiting to be completed.*

I wasn't about to let a doctor I didn't know slice me open. I peeked under the sheet and tried to sit up. I didn't see any blood. How could I be sure that he was telling me the truth? This was the same Western medicine that had told me, a vegetarian, to eat liver when I was anorexic.

"I have to speak with my spiritual adviser first," I said to the doctor.

I may as well have told him I needed to go home and water my Coleus.

The doctor shook his head. "There isn't time."

"Well at least go and get my friend Nancy. She's a nurse here."

He sent someone to track her down, and Nancy arrived like an angel from heaven.

"It's okay," she said. "Really. Just go. You need to let them do this." She went to the nurse's station to call Sarasvati.

The room was beginning to swirl, and the Piranhas were in a frenzy.

A surgeon came in and brought with him an anesthesiologist. As attendants loaded me onto a gurney, the anesthesiologist took my hand and put his face right in front of mine, wanting me to focus and understand what was about to happen.

"There are five levels to consciousness," he said. "Level One is when you're awake, like you and I are right now. Level Five is when you're dead."

He squeezed my hand as the gurney began rolling.

"I have to take you to Level Four."

The doors flew open, and they wheeled me out of the ER toward the operating room. In the hallway I saw the shawl-draped figure of Sarasvati, prayer beads in hand. She touched my arm as I rolled by.

"Don't have any anxieties, dear. I'll be here the whole time."

When they got me into the operating room, I wondered about going to Level Four, and then they put a heavy oxygen mask over my face. It hurt the bridge of my nose and made me feel as if I were being suffocated. A few minutes passed and I put my hand to my face: *What's taking that doctor so long? I have to get this thing off of me.* As I reached up, a flurry of tubes went on about my head. When I opened my eyes I saw the wide face of a nurse, inches from mine, staring at me.

"When is the doctor coming?" I asked.

She pointed to the clock. It was seven hours later.

"It's all over honey. You're in recovery now. You're gonna be fine."

I couldn't believe it. The nurse said amnesia comes with the territory, and all things considered, maybe that wasn't such a bad thing. I found out later that by the time they finally cut me open, more than half my blood was in my stomach. Fifteen minutes more of trying to find my spiritual connection would have speed-dialed me directly to Level Five. *Do not pass 'Go.' Do not collect two hundred dollars.*

My chest felt like I'd just smoked a carton of Camel cigarettes.

"It hurts to breathe," I said to the nurse.

"You were on a ventilator. They had to stop everything but your heart. You'll be sore for a couple of days."

She called for two hospital attendants to roll me out of recovery and into a room. Waiting for me there were Rose, Nancy, Sarasvati, and two other women from the Yoga Society. One of them held a little pot with an African violet. As the attendants put me into my bed, the telephone rang. Still groggy from the anesthetic, I picked up the receiver and put it to my ear.

"You bitch," said the Piano Player. "You didn't tell me you were pregnant. I'm going to burn down your house, and then I'm going to come over there and kill you."

"I . . . I . . . Can you please call later?"

I fumbled with the receiver and the surgeon, who'd just walked into the room, took it from me.

"She can't talk now," he said, and hung up.

CHAPTER NINE

Purple Haze

The capacity of human beings to turn even the most spectacularly death-dealing moment into something positive and life-affirming is often referred to as *faith*. But in 1977, I still had no idea what "spirit" made you spiritual or what God was really about, apart from the kindness of friends. My propensity for plastering over bad stuff with "cosmic consciousness" was, in truth, just the delusional effect of living on the River Denial and repeatedly being bitten by the love bug. Not only wasn't I of this world, I barely knew how to live in it.

Just as when my life had been so rudely interrupted by the shakedown at Wally's drug emporium and my sudden relocation to jail, in the hospital I was abruptly forced to abandon concern for my day-to-day agenda, responsibilities, and material possessions. (Though I did feel relatively safe there from the Piano Player's threats; in a sense, he'd already nearly killed me.) I concluded that, as always, it was my fault. I'd been too attached to "things," and I convinced myself that gratitude for my predicament was in order. This experience of near-death and loss would be my initiation into a higher realm of devotion and selflessness, and I prayed to be worthy of the trial I'd just gone through.

So the hospital became my ashram, my bed the clean white altar. A window filled with blue sky and seagulls and the tops of concrete buildings was my bird's eye view from an island in the Mediterranean, as I imagined what was below to be sparkling blue water and white foamy surf. At night a lone star sat in the sky above the billowing fog, winking and blinking at me: *Enlightenment! Enlightenment!*

Maybe it was from being taken to Level Four by the anesthesiologist. Maybe it was because of the Piano Player's phone call. Whatever the case, I was now supremely out of my mind.

A few days into my recovery, another patient, an older black woman, was wheeled into my room for the night. Mrs. Willie Mae Hayes was scheduled for surgery the next day. Ailing from cataracts, hearing loss, heart trouble, smoker's cough, high blood pressure, and a lifetime of bad memories, Mrs. Hayes decided, without any inquiry on my part, to tell her story to me. Perhaps it was just time for somebody to hear it.

When she was fifteen years old, Mrs. Hayes said, she'd given birth to a baby girl but was told there were complications, and after delivery the doctor removed her uterus and ovaries. Tragically, her daughter got sick with a brain tumor and died. Then, thirty-two years ago, she'd married Mr. Hayes who at first seemed like a good man but soon began to cheat on her with other women.

"He had himself a Filipina gal. Shameless, I tell you; one time she left her panties in my bed. Then she got pregnant, but she didn't want no baby, so I told her I'd raise it, on account of losing my daughter and not being able to have any more children of my own. So one day the woman comes over and gives me the baby, and then she left. I don't know where she went, but I was so happy to have that little baby and raise her as my own. But my husband, he went and got himself somebody new and left me and the baby by ourselves. On Christmas my brother had to come over and bring us a little tree because my husband didn't buy nothin' for us, and we didn't have no presents to put underneath it. And it was cold, too, 'cause my husband didn't pay the gas bill neither."

Still not having asked her a question or even told her my name, Mrs. Hayes continue to unfold her travelogue of trouble.

"After a while, my husband just got mean, really mean. Cut me bad."

She poked one thin brown leg like a broomstick out from under the sheet.

"See? I still got the scar. Broke my glasses all up in my face. Never did nothin' for the baby or for me. I cried a lotta nights and I been sick a lotta days."

I felt bad for her but couldn't help wondering why she was talking to me. As her story came to a close, Mrs. Hayes, who after thirty-two years was still married to the mean, no-count, cheatin' dog of a husband Mr. Hayes, provided a clue to what I'd been searching for since my Anaïs Nin days: an explanation for Why Things Were The Way They Were. Finally, here was something that I could write down in my journal and memorize for all time, but it wasn't cosmic, poetic, or encouraging.

"Well," she said, adjusting her glasses, which were held together by a small strip of white medical tape. "I guess I been stayin' all these years 'cause I just didn't think I could do no better."

I just didn't think I could do no better.

Her confession echoed in my head and cast a glaring spotlight on what I'd been telling myself: *I just don't think I can do any better. So I keep on staying with the misery and fear. . . .*

I turned to face the wall, unable to listen any longer to Mrs. Hayes, and wondered if I was even capable of doing better. Maybe things would have turned out differently if my parents had taken the school counselor's advice and let them advance me from fifth grade to seventh. Maybe my once-brilliant mind wouldn't have become a burnt sacrifice that I had to lay on the altar in exchange for friends. Maybe I wouldn't have become a liar and gotten pregnant if my parents had let me invite my friends from the Teen Center to our house.

Whatever. None of that mattered anymore. Those coulda-woulda-shoulda options, like so many things that turned out to be wrong, were phantom limbs haunting me about people and circumstances from the past. Here I was now—twenty-six years old, broken down by an abusive man, and nearly dead. The demented, pitiful conclusion reached by this tragedy-ridden woman forty years older than me was the same one by which I'd been living my life.

The next morning a nurse came to take Mrs. Hayes to surgery, and I never saw her again. Our encounter was not a conversation; it was as if she'd appeared in my room to deliver her testimony and then exited stage left. Perhaps, I thought, she was just another one of my hallucinations, sent to administer a hypodermic needle full of head-spinning truth.

Alone again, I saw myself outside my body, the same way I had seen myself when I was on LSD, but this time the image was not inspiring: I lay mortally wounded on a reeking garbage heap, clinging to hurtful people and destructive dead-end situations because it was impossible to imagine a life of my own, apart from them, or that I ever could grow to being strong, healthy, and whole.

I closed my eyes and forced myself back into the clean white light of my delusion.

Try A Little Tenderness

I've heard it said that many of the patients in hospitals are there because they want to be. In the hospital, you get a lot of attention. Someone's always checking to see if you're okay, if you need anything. They all want to know what they can do to make you feel better. You have no responsibilities; other people bring your food and keep you clean. It's safe, your needs are met, and people are nice to you.

On my last night in the blissful Mediterranean ashram of San Francisco Presbyterian Hospital, I thought about Frankie, the soft-spoken sister I met in jail who vowed that no matter how many times they let her out, she'd do another crime so she could come back, because jail was a place where people cared about her and she had everything she needed. In the morning, watching my bed stripped for the next patient, my meager belongings stuffed into a red plastic ER bag, and a crowded Muni bus waiting for me outside, I understood.

It was tough being so vulnerable and out on the street again, having to do things for myself, make decisions, and deal with living life rather than almost losing it. I was shocked to find out I didn't qualify for State Disability Insurance. Since the Buddhist Churches of America was a non-profit organization, California didn't require them to pay into the system. I thought that was weird, as if the government assumed that working for a religious organization gave you the edge of a Higher Power that would keep you immune to sickness or debt collectors. But BCA gave me a little money to help me out till I could come back to work, and I was grateful for that.

As far as I knew, the Piano Player hadn't followed through on his threat to burn down my house; James, Medina, Clarence, and Louis had probably stood in the way of that. Still I wasn't ready to face whatever was going on in Oakland.

Nancy offered to take me in, which was very kind as she had a family and plenty else to do. I stayed a couple of nights but didn't fit in with the household routine, so Rose, who'd left the Napa Valley and moved into a cute studio in the Castro, offered to let me stay with her. As well as a goddess and a warrior, Rose was a nurturer, and she went into high gear to make me comfortable in her place on Diamond Street. She gave me a new yellow journal to write in, put a small vase of fresh flowers next to the couch where I slept, and made sure her kitchen was well-stocked. But after a week of pampering, neither of us was sure what I ought to do next. She was working a marketing job for the Dunhill company and, unlike my hospital caretakers, Rose needed to get back to living her own life. Bracelets clanging, she challenged me to do the same.

"What do you want to do with your life? You have to do something; you can't just sit on your butt forever. Think about it."

So I thought about it.

I started writing in my new journal and tried to resurrect for myself what it meant to be an artist. The previous summer, in 1976, I'd been captivated by an idea for a screenplay and had spent many nights as The Quiet rolled in typing away on the Olivetti, convinced that mine was the most important movie script ever written. Inspired by the Viking mission to Mars, I wrote a surrealistic story about evolution and the origin of the different races on Earth. The news and images transmitted from the Red Planet seemed to confirm my fictional premise, keeping me motivated and intent. Not even the Piano Player's dramas had deterred me from writing that summer.

In December of 1976, I'd heard that Gordon Parks, the legendary *Life* magazine photojournalist and author, was going to be at the Oakland Museum to promote his new film, *Leadbelly*. During my father's stint at Columbia Pictures, he'd designed the title sequences for both Melvin Van Peebles' *Watermelon Man* and Sidney Poitier's *Buck and the Preacher* and was a fan of the new wave of black film directors, including Parks, whom he'd met once. When I told him about *Leadbelly*, he said I should go to the screening and that Gordon Parks would probably be interested in my screenplay. I worked like mad until the day of the event to finish my treatment.

I arrived at the Oakland Museum feeling excited, a copy of my screenplay treatment in hand, certain it would be a life-changing evening. Gordon Parks got up to speak, and after presenting his film, made himself accessible without vanity or artifice. He reminded me of my dad. Skin color aside, both men were remarkably similar in sensitivity, stature, and demeanor. They'd also both been born in 1912. I could see why my father liked him. Parks interacted with his admirers in the same kindly manner I'd seen my father do with his students, and I felt an instant bond with him.

I stuck close by as he and the crowd of admirers moved along like a crab on the beach. I think he saw me staring at him, and I think it amused him but in a kind way. I was sure that he winked at me, just like my father did. When he stepped into the corridor to go upstairs to a cocktail reception, I pushed my way to his side.

"Mr. Parks, I have a treatment for a movie script that I believe you should read."

"Thank you, dear," he said, "but please forgive me. I don't like to accept manuscripts by hand because I travel all over the place and things get lost. I would hate to be responsible for your work falling into the wrong hands."

Just then, a barrel-chested man in a three-piece suit got in between us and tried to shoo me away.

"Mr. Parks is an extremely busy man," said the Suit, his arms folded across his chest like a sentry.

"But I . . ."

"Weren't you listening?" he barked. "Mr. Parks just told you that he doesn't accept scripts."

Gordon Parks and I looked at each other. Was he a little sorry at seeing me so roughly treated? My father would have been. Thinking that the Suit was his handler, I let it go, but I followed the two men upstairs, where they disappeared into the crowded reception. Meanwhile a bearded, bright-eyed brother holding a manuscript of his own had been watching and followed me up the stairs.

"You tried to give him your story?" he asked.

"Yeah, but then that guy stepped in," I said, pointing to the Suit. "The whole reason I came tonight was to hand it to Gordon Parks myself. Still, I guess if that's his right hand man, then that's the way he wants it."

The bright-eyed brother laughed. He had a stunning gap between his front teeth, just like my high school chum Antoinette.

"That guy isn't Gordon Parks' right hand man. He's the curator of the museum."

"You mean he doesn't have anything to do with Parks?"

"Naw, nothing at all. If you want to give your story to him, go do it. What have you got to lose?"

I looked for Gordon Parks, who was now standing across the room. *Was he smiling at me?* The bright-eyed brother nodded for me to take my chance and go. *All right then, this is why I came.* I went back to where Parks was standing; the barrel-chested bouncer had disappeared.

"Hi again, Mr. Parks. I'm sorry to keep asking, but I went through a lot to be able to give you this in person tonight, and I think it's something that will really interest you. I trust you won't lose it or anything."

He surrendered like a true gentlemen and took the folded papers from my hand.

"Okay, dear. Thank you. I'll read it. I promise."

I was elated and went back to tell my new friend.

"I did it! I gave it to him."

"Good for you!"

"Aren't you going to give him yours?"

"No," he smiled, sliding it inside his jacket. "Another time maybe."

"What's your story about?" I asked.

"It's about a black gold miner named Buster," he said, "and it takes place during the Gold Rush."

"Mine's about how the white man came from outer space."

He laughed again, and this time it sounded like rain. I liked him.

"This is the first screenplay I've ever written," I confessed. "I feel like I need to learn so much more. I'm just working in a vacuum all by myself; I don't really know what I'm doing."

"I've been writing for a long time," he said. "I'd be willing to help you. I have a lot of movie scripts you could look at. I also teach creative writing at San Francisco State University."

He handed me his card. The bright-eyed brother had a peculiar name: Buriel Clay.

But I didn't call him or go by to look at his collection of movie scripts after that night at the Oakland Museum. My screwed-up life with the Piano Player and the billowing clouds of fear he provoked were too much in the way of starting a new friendship, especially with a man.

After Rose gave me the lecture about getting off my butt, I realized I had with me the same jacket I'd worn two months earlier to the Gordon Parks' reception. I pulled it off a hanger in her closet, fished Buriel's card out of the pocket, and called him.

Two days later I was on my way to class.

If I Could Build My Whole World Around You

It was exciting in kind of a subversive way to be out on the streets of San Francisco at night minus a car. I felt far more exposed than I was accustomed to, but being on foot in the evening darkness also had an alluring mystique.

A short walk from Rose's was the Castro Muni station, where I hopped on the streetcar to San Francisco State University.

Swerving and clattering through people's backyards at twilight, the ride felt straight out of Toyland. When I stepped off at 19th Street, I was bombarded by the noise and lights and energy of cars on the busy boulevard: traffic signals blinking like Christmas and people walking hurriedly toward the campus in a stiff posture that said they meant business. Unlike the day students who gathered in leisurely clusters with their unlaced shoes and backpacks slung over one shoulder, hoping to find direction for their young lives, the night students were a determined bunch juggling families and bottom-feeder jobs, desperate for something better.

Having gone from the sterile serenity of the hospital, and then the cloistered womb room of Rose's studio, to being out and about in this cyclone of swirling, no-nonsense humanity was a shock to my system. But I welcomed it like a bracing cold shower that wakes you up.

Over the phone, Buriel had told me that my timing was great; the new semester was just starting. I didn't have money to pay the class fee, but that was no problem, he said. I could attend off the record without registering.

I was surprised that he even remembered me, but I didn't tell him everything that had happened since we'd met at the Oakland Museum. When I arrived at his classroom, it was nice to see that big, sunny smile again. If I'd had any reservations, they were allayed when I saw a giant appliqué of Tweety Bird sewn on the right leg of his jeans. I felt safe. He was an encourager, a positive force determined to funnel good energy into his students.

"Welcome to Creative Writing 101," Buriel said as we took our seats. "Here you will learn how to discipline yourselves as writers and gain the technical background necessary to give strength to what you are intuitively motivated by. In writing, just as in any other art, you must study the rules, and then you must forget the rules. And if you're really serious, you must force yourself to be disciplined about what you're doing."

He motioned to each of us in the room to give our name and background and to describe our writing aspirations. The students were from all walks of life, including office workers, a gym teacher, a waiter, and a lawyer. Everyone agreed they needed to learn discipline; most had never written anything before but wanted to try.

Then the lawyer spoke up, "We've told you about ourselves, what about you?"

"I've been a writer a long time," Buriel said, "but I didn't really know it until about ten years ago when I finally made the decision to write seriously. I was attending this school, San Francisco State, as a graduate student, and you know what the teacher said to me? 'You'll never be a writer. You should give up and do something else.' But I had the desire to become a writer, and I believed in myself. My grandfather used to tell me, 'All you have to do is pay your dues. If you get knocked down, get up and try again.' So I did, and look: here I am, teaching you writing at the same school that told me I'd never be a writer. If I can do it, so can you. In fact one of my plays, *No Left Turn*, was just produced at ACT, the American Conservatory Theatre."

The true believer in me nodded like a bubblehead doll on the dashboard. It was time to follow my dream.

Buriel explained that we were going to learn how to tell a single story three different ways: as a short story, a stage play, and a screenplay. We'd study the basics of all three kinds of writing, and then our assignment over the semester would be to create one story and write it in those three forms. Right away I knew I'd draw on my own story; perhaps turning my life into art would redeem all the pain and loss I'd been through.

The class was friendly, and I found myself engaged in intelligent, insightful discussions, seeing myself in positive ways I never had before. It made me wonder what I'd missed by getting kicked out of high school and then spending my three years of college demonstrating in the quad instead of learning in the classroom.

We ended about nine o'clock, and Buriel offered to walk me to the streetcar. His attention was surprising and welcome; he seemed like someone I could trust, so I told him about the exploding baby.

"Are you serious, you just got out of the hospital?"

"Yeah, but I'm fine," I lied.

The streetcar arrived, and he hopped on it with me.

"I want to make sure you get home safely," he said. "I can catch the bus to my place from there."

Buriel was easy to be with. He made me laugh. He knew a lot. He told me he was from Texas, liked country and western music, and was hooked on watching *60 Minutes*. Inside the streetcar, he pointed to an advertising banner above the seats that showed a sailor walking with a Polynesian beauty along the white sands of a tropical beach. The caption read, "The Navy: It's not just a job; it's an adventure."

"I wrote that," he said, grinning. "I was in the Navy and now I do some PR for them."

"Really?" I couldn't tell if he was pulling my leg.

"Absolutely," he smiled.

We got off the streetcar at Castro and Market.

"Say, are you hungry?" he said. "There's a cafe I know just up the street."

We walked a block from the Muni station to a restaurant on Market Street. The night was turning into more than I expected.

"I've eaten here before; it's great," he said, opening the door for me. Two bulky men were seated at a window table, talking loudly over cigarettes and beer.

"My bitch just doesn't listen. Don't know what the hell is wrong with her. I have to beat her ass on a regular basis," one was saying to the other.

I sucked in my breath and hoped it didn't show.

Buriel took me by the hand, and we went upstairs to a smaller dining area. He pulled the chair out for me before he took his seat.

"I just don't get how guys act like that," he said. "I will never understand a man who beats up a woman. Never."

I said nothing about the two men, but after ordering supper, we talked about writing, and he gave me a list of magazines he thought I ought to subscribe to.

"What do you really want out of your writing?" he asked.

"I don't know," I said. "I guess I'm just a dreamy poet. I write to express myself, how I feel."

"Come on, now. You've got to do better than that," he scolded. "If you only write for yourself, then why did you want to give your screenplay to Gordon Parks?"

He had a point, even if I had no answer.

"What I'm telling you is this," he said, "your art is a gift. It's life. It's your life; your destiny. You've got to write your story. The world needs to know. You've got to do something with your gift that matters. It's important. You're important."

I let out a sigh and looked down at my plate.

"Listen to me." He leaned across the table and put his hand on top of mine. "Writing changes people: It changes the people who write, and it changes the people who read."

I gathered the nerve to look at his face. He was smiling, excited, passionate.

"Think of the writers whose books changed you."

I recalled my great awakening in the fiction shelves of the North Hollywood Library and the man who gave form and voice to the deepest places of my soul; who articulated what I could not speak for myself and reignited the brilliance I'd been forced to dim.

"Like Richard Wright . . . ?"

"Yes, exactly like Richard Wright!" Buriel said. "Think of how it defined Richard Wright's life to be a writer. Art is the only way to express your truth and not go mad. That's who you are. You have to give yourself completely to the thing you love, not just play around with it. You have to apply the meaning and purpose to writing that it deserves in your life in order for you to fulfill what you're supposed to in this world. You've got to take yourself seriously if you want other people to."

Nobody had ever spoken to me this way. Like what I thought mattered. Like I mattered.

We talked until the cafe's proprietor signaled it was closing time. Stepping outside, the chilly San Francisco mist greeted us, and Buriel made a circle with his arm for me to put mine through. I felt like a butterfly with paper wings—afraid to surrender, afraid to refuse. We walked back to Castro and then down toward Rose's in perfect stride, our shoulders pressed ever so lightly into one another. Never had the City seemed so still; it was almost as if The Quiet had rolled in from Oakland.

When we reached the bus stop near Rose's, Buriel withdrew his arm just as the Muni came rumbling toward us. I wanted to thank him, but without so much as a handshake or "Hi-Yo Silver!" he hopped on the bus, backpack and all, and waved at me from the window as he found his seat, and the bus roared off toward Divisidero.

The night was over, but I would never again see myself or my talent the same way. I put my key into Rose's door; it was close to midnight, and despite everything I'd suffered, I felt happier and more hopeful than ever.

I had just met my next Teacher.

CHAPTER TEN

October, 1977

> *Sometimes I feel like a tiger in a steel cage*
> *pacing pacing from space to space,*
> *ready ready ready for the attack.*
> *Sometimes I feel like a pale little mouse*
> *scurrying scurrying back and forth,*
> *eyeing the scientist as he prepares his test tubes and syringes,*
> *looking at me from over his half-focals with calculating eyes,*
> *ready ready ready for the test.*
> *Sometimes I feel like a brass trumpet*
> *waiting for my master to pick me up and set his lips to mine*
> *and blow a nuclear explosion through my body,*
> *screaming screaming screaming at the world.*

Along with putting myself back on track as a writer, it was time to get serious about a spiritual path. Outside the hospital, I was no longer floating above the Mediterranean. The near-death catastrophe of my relationship with the Piano Player and his exploding baby had sobered me as much as any addict's intervention, and all signs pointed to sex as the substance that led to my abuse. Beyond the fact that my body and emotions desired it, sex had caused me to lose myself in mortal men who couldn't be trusted with my heart, mind, or soul—all of which were in critical need of someone who wouldn't lie, cheat, let me down, or hurt me. Wanting to believe, but not knowing in what, I wrote endless requests to God in my journals and was answered in surreal, Fellini-esque dreams.

> *It's night. I'm at shore's end. Towering above the horizon is an enormous Buddha glowing against the jet black sky. I watch, mesmerized, but then it transforms as if the hood of a sweatshirt were being pulled back. Slowly the face becomes that of the Piano Player.*
>
> *I keep seeing God above everything else and that he will shine for me in the darkest hour. But I still wind up turning my trust over to men and seeing them as God.*

But which spiritual path led to God? I was familiar now with Buddhism from having worked at BCA, and I'd spent time with my friends from the Yoga Society. While I'd received practical direction from Buddhism and unconditional love from Dr. Mishra and his followers, neither path truly registered as the door to my spiritual growth. Judaism was of no interest; I'd been bequeathed the dysfunctional inheritance of my family's persecution and prejudice, not their faith. My experience with Jews had been ethnic and tribal, not spiritual; not even religious.

My antenna was still seeking the Big Truth's signal; and now I'd come to the recognition that sex interfered with that.

So then what was I doing in a movie theater watching an erotic Japanese film, *In the Realm of the Senses*, with my teacher Buriel Clay? He must have asked himself that same question when it was over and my arm wound through his, our shoulders touching as we sat together on the bus; and then I said goodnight, running off without so much as a hug, just as he'd done to me on that first night of school.

In my mind, we'd just gone to see the film as fellow storytellers. And it wasn't that I'd blacklisted sex. Engaging in it, however, just put too much at risk. The dreadful end of the film's main characters proved that.

If I were to take myself seriously as a writer, as Buriel had told me to do, I needed to reserve my power for something greater than seduction's thrill. I assumed he would understand that, since he was the one who'd launched me in the direction I was now headed. That's what I told myself, anyway.

At the end of March 1977, I returned to the house in Oakland. Although I was growing stronger, had gone back to work for the Buddhists, was attending Buriel's class and working on my story assignment every day, the Piano Player was still coming around, stalking me like prey. I knew he was trouble, but I allowed him to linger around the periphery of my life, which made Rose furious with me. And for good reason; she knew firsthand the warning signs that I was ignoring in my supposed effort to be diplomatic. I kept saying I wanted to be finished with him, but it never seemed to be over. I tried to reason with him as to why it was best for both of us to end the relationship, but I couldn't seem to muster the courage to actually kick him out of the storefront or my life.

Bad Moon Rising

The last time I saw Boni Grove was on Sunday, April 30, 1977. I'd spent the day doing errands around Berkeley, ending at the Co-op about four o'clock, where I ran into her at the checkstand. Picking up a few last-minute items to make dinner, she seemed harried and stressed-out; her normally bright eyes were dull and ringed with dark circles. I hadn't been to her African dance class in months, and I felt guilty for not having spoken to her in so long.

"I lost the Center to Halifu," she said.

Everybody's Creative Arts Center had gone up for sale, and both my friends Boni and Halifu had made bids to purchase it. The decision had just been announced that day; Halifu would become the new owner.

"I really wanted that studio," Boni said. "I knew I could do great things with it."

"I'm so sorry," I said, giving her a hug as she paid the cashier. "I'll come dance with you soon, I promise."

"By the way," she said, turning to me as she headed toward the Co-op's glass door. The late afternoon sun shining through it unexpectedly lit up her face. All the darkness disappeared, and for a moment, she looked radiant.

"I need a really big desk. If you hear of anybody who has one, let me know."

⁂

It was late, close to midnight, two days later. The pounding of his hard shoes running up my driveway was violent and angry, shattering The Quiet like plate glass. I heard the snapping of wood as the Piano Player tore open the lattice gate at the back of my house and tossed the flimsy padlock that had once held it together to ground. He thundered his way into the mudroom and pounded on the back door.

"Open up, dammit!"

I'd refused to answer the telephone any more that night; he must have called a dozen times, yelling at me, infuriated, demanding to know what I was doing behind his back and who was I doing it with. I finally said I didn't want to see him or talk to him anymore and yanked the phone out of the wall jack. That's when he'd gotten into his car and driven around the block to my house.

"I said, open the damn door, or I'll bust it down!"

I was too terrified to do anything except stay put, thinking the back door would keep him out. It was old and heavy, and it had a deadbolt. Then the walls began to shake as the Piano Player broke the door off its hinges and stormed in.

"Where is he, dammit?"

He yanked me out of bed and forced me to go room to room with him. When he was satisfied that there was no one else in the house with me, whatever evil demon from hell had possessed him seemed to depart like a barely perceptible wind. Surprisingly, without doing any further harm, the Piano Player turned around and left.

I wrapped myself in a blanket and sat trembling in the living room with the lights on until dawn, and then I called a handyman to fix the door, packed a bag, and took flight.

Buriel told me I could come to his apartment in San Francisco. We'd taken to calling one another "Tania" and "Cinque" in joking mockery of Patty Hearst and the Symbionese Liberation Army's Field Marshal, Donald DeFreeze. Buriel made me lemon tea and tried to comfort me with cowboy songs and silly jokes.

Exhausted from the night's toll, I could barely sit up. After drinking the tea, Buriel told me to lie down on his bed, where he put a blanket over me, and then he went to his desk in a corner of the room to write. A small square of paper was thumbtacked above it. On it he'd written, "No birth is painless."

I tried to sleep, and he tried to work, but before long the feelings that had been building up between us became too powerful to resist. So much for my theory about holding out for the Higher Power; temptation has a way of making you modify your philosophy as needed.

For the next two weeks I lived out of my car, shuttling back and forth from Buriel's place to Rose's (who took the opportunity to feed me a big fat "I told you so" sandwich) until finally I felt it would be okay to go back home. Concerned for my safety once I got there, Buriel came with me to Oakland, and we spent the night in the downstairs bedroom that faced the driveway.

When morning came, we heard the Piano Player enter the storefront below and then those hard, angry footsteps thumping up the stairs to my part of the house. The door burst open, and the Piano Player finally got what he'd been looking for: He found me with another man.

I tried to get away from him, but he punched me in the gut, near where I'd had surgery, knocking the wind out of me. I struggled to breathe. Buriel tried to get in between us, but the Piano Player, who was taller and fueled by rage, pushed him to the floor. There was no way to get around him or out of the room, so I opened the window to yell, then thought better of it; grabbing a sheet to cover myself, I pushed out the screen and jumped into the driveway. Barefoot and barely covered, I ran next door into the shop run by the man who sold vacuum cleaner parts.

"Help me, please help me!" I screamed.

The Piano Player bolted through the open window and charged into the store after me, knocking vacuum parts everywhere and grabbing me by the hair. The owner, who was a devout Muslim, shouted at us both to get out, and then he called the police.

The Piano Player dragged me by the arm back up the driveway.

"See," he pointed to the open gate in the back. "He doesn't care about you! He's gone! He ran away. You're worthless, stupid. I hate you, bitch. I ought to kill you right here and now. You're a tramp, a slut."

Once inside, he pinned me against the wall, shaking me by the shoulders, yelling in my face, ridiculing and interrogating me. He demanded that I tell him Buriel wasn't as good a lover as he. I didn't know what'd happened to Buriel, but I was sure he hated me now. My dreams of being a writer and having a friend to encourage me were over. Maybe the Piano Player was my Cinque, and like the calamitous end of the Symbionese Liberation Army, we'd both go down in a blazing hail of fire and bullets.

We heard the police cruiser pull up, and then they started banging on the door of the storefront with their nightsticks. The Piano Player didn't want me to talk to them, but the cops weren't about to go away.

"I'll kill you right in front of them if you say a damn word."

We went downstairs and, shaking, I opened the door and told them there'd been a mistake. They could see the bruises starting to form on my shoulders and my arm, and that I was wearing a ripped sheet, and that the Piano Player was standing behind me with smoke coming out of his ears.

"Okay ma'am," said Oakland's Finest, and the police went on their way.

This time, before he would leave, the Piano Player wanted to make sure I knew he was better than the man he found in my bed. He raped me and hurt me, making me tell him over and over again how great he was, until finally he felt like he'd proven his truth.

I ran away again, but this time it was harder to find a sympathetic ear. Buriel hadn't left me to be brutalized as the Piano Player said; he'd gone to summon help. But there was no replay of falling innocently into his arms. If I hadn't been convinced before, I was certain now that sex was the root of all evil and more determined than ever to preserve the gift of friendship and support I'd been given by keeping him as my Teacher, not my lover.

I tried to hear what people who cared about me were saying about my situation; that I was somehow drawing all this trouble to myself, and that when I stopped wanting to be pursued I'd be free. But my ears were ringing with violence, and my dreams were full of bad karma and radioactive rain.

> *My mind is the only safe place I can go. The waters of this world are too treacherous, and I find myself meek before them. I am sinking into misty emerald fathoms, my conversations muted and abstract, my words and thoughts melting together like butter in a warm dish. I must go deeper into the refuge of myself. I want to take my Teacher with me, but I fear. I want. I fear. I am a sunken treasure buried beneath the sea. "Love yourself," he tells me. "Write your story and be what you think you are. All will come to you as you deserve, in time. You are still beautiful." But I just want to go to sleep and wake up somebody else.*

A month passed, and all I could think was that it had been so long since I danced.

Once again I returned home from exile, like folks in the Gulf coast towns of Louisiana and Florida and Texas who emerge to survey the destruction every year after hurricane season. I wasn't sure my season of disaster was over yet.

Cautiously I put my key into the new padlock on the gate and walked into the mudroom, then I unlocked the door to the kitchen, not sure what I'd find. The only sound to greet me was the incessant hum of the aging, purple-painted refrigerator left by the Hippie Mechanic and his girlfriend. It was cold in the Market Street house; far colder than it had been outside in the driveway. I walked into the living room, where ribbons of dust illuminated the sunlight that streamed in from the patio windows.

It was so quiet. So empty. So cold.

I needed the restoration of dance, to forget myself in the movement and the drums, and to sweat till I couldn't breathe or think any more. It had been five weeks since I'd seen Boni at the Co-op and promised her that I would come by and take an African dance class with her. There were so many times I'd thought about doing that but just as many times I never did.

It felt good to put on my leotard and tie the colorful African sarong called a *lapa* around my waist. But when I arrived at her studio, there was no Boni and no African class. A jazz class taught by someone whom I didn't know was in session. More surprising, however, was a sign hanging on the studio's wall:

> *In memory of Boni Grove,*
> *the staff of Full Spectrum,*
> *her friends and family*
> *ask you to Keep On Dancing.*

I didn't understand; it was as if in a foreign language. I read the sign again and again. The words "in memory" kept flashing, but it still didn't make sense. How could I be "in memory" of someone my age whom I'd just seen a month ago? That was the kind of thing you say about sick people with terminal diseases and grandmothers who pass away in nursing homes. I waited for the jazz class to end so I could ask the dance teacher what the sign meant.

"Where's Boni?"

"You don't know what happened?"

I shook my head.

She sighed and looked away, weary at having to tell the story one more time.

"Boni was trying to break it off with her boyfriend. She'd been trying to end it with him for months, but he didn't want to let her go. She just kept talking to him, trying to make him understand why it was over. Finally, he got frustrated and went to her apartment with a gun, and he shot and killed her. Then he killed himself."

How could that be, I thought, *I'd just seen her.*

"When?"

"May first," the jazz teacher said. "Monday night, May first."

Boni had been murdered the day after I saw her at the Co-op—the night before the Piano Player broke down my back door.

Before I could think about what I was saying, the pointless, demanding accusation spilled out of my mouth.

"Didn't she know he was dangerous, that he had a gun?"

It was an incredibly stupid question, as if it was Boni's fault that her boyfriend killed her. As if there were some "Ah-ha!" that would bring her back.

The teacher shrugged her straight shoulders.

"Well, you know how Boni was," she said. "She was really nice. She never wanted to hurt anyone's feelings. She just kept trying to talk to him. She wanted him to understand why they couldn't be together anymore. She was trying to be nice."

She was just trying to be nice. You know how Boni was. She was just trying to be nice.

You know how Selimah was. . . .

Suddenly I was dead, and someone was talking about me. I saw myself laying in a grave with a wretched little pile of yellow daffodils on top and all my friends gathered around, shaking their heads: "*Well, you know how Selimah was. She was just trying to be nice, trying to make him understand, but he didn't want to let her go, and so he killed her.*"

I couldn't believe it. As if just because Boni was my age, just because I'd seen her five weeks ago, she couldn't be dead. I wondered if the boyfriend drama was the undertow I'd seen behind her smile and the clouds of Marlboro smoke.

I tried to savor our last moment together that Sunday in the supermarket. I was ashamed for all the months I'd stayed away, not keeping up our friendship and preferring to wallow in my misery than to dance. I couldn't believe what happened to her, nor that it had come so close to happening to me, too.

It could have been me.

It could still be me.

Finally, I understood what everyone had been trying to tell me about how I was drawing trouble to myself. The next time the Piano Player tried to walk up my driveway, I went outside and confronted him.

"Get your stuff out of my building."

He froze in place.

I'd never spoken to him with the conviction I now held. No one was ever going to ask those dumb "didn't-she-know-he-was-dangerous" questions about me. And I wasn't going down "nice." I made sure he saw me reach into the loose pocket of my jacket.

"I want you to know that I have a GUN," I announced. "And you think I'm crazy, right? So you know how dangerous it is for a crazy person like me to have a gun, right? Right??!!"

He stared at me, his jaw open, his eyes darting around for witnesses or an object he could use to defend himself. He started to speak, but I cut him off.

"Let me tell you this, and listen up good. If you EVER set foot on my property again, I . . . WILL . . . SHOOT . . . YOU."

Carefully he walked backwards down my driveway, his eyes fixed on where I might be hiding his ticket to kingdom come. And then he ran.

I never saw the Piano Player again. Not because I had a gun (I didn't), but because I no longer wanted to be pursued. And I most definitely did not care whether anyone thought I was nice, or if he ever understood why.

CHAPTER ELEVEN

Oakland, 1978

"Art is the only way to express yourself and not go mad."

Buriel's words that first night we met, along with his mandate to take myself seriously as a writer, were my visa into that community of wounded souls who create art to keep themselves from insanity and rage. I extricated myself from the debris field of Boni's murder and the Piano Player's mayhem, and relocated into the parallel universe of *Writer*, bounded between my dreams and disappointments and the green Olivetti.

Encouraged by Buriel, who continued to mentor and befriend me, I composed a one-act play set in a women's jail in 1970. My characters were based on the women I'd met at Sybil's: the Manson girls, my entrepreneurial cellmate Liz, and the dope-ravaged Marguerite who, like me, had been secreted away in a home for unwed mothers for the crime of being teenage and pregnant. I also drew on Patty Hearst's stunning conversion from heiress to revolutionary and, for good measure, threw in a beleaguered senior citizen based on Mrs. Willie Mae Hayes from the hospital. But like the elderly woman I met in jail who'd finally had enough, my character took a pistol to her no-count, mean, old husband.

These women were the threads with which I wove my own frustrated story of wanting to believe in something bigger than myself; the insatiable longing for acceptance, love, and security; and the willingness to do (or become) just about anything for that. I called my play *The Daddies*. When I finished the first draft, Buriel read it and said it was great.

The end of the 1970s was a heady season for artists, writers, and performers in the Bay Area, and just as he tried to nurture and inspire his creative writing students at the university, Buriel worked tirelessly to grow and support the theatre community. He founded the Black Writers Workshop, served on the San Francisco Neighborhood Arts Commission, and rallied to establish the new Western Addition Cultural Center (WACC) at 762 Fulton Street, for which he was rightfully named its first Director.

In early 1978, Buriel began putting together *Three Slices of Life*, a trilogy of plays to be mounted in WACC's theatre that June. Along with his own play, *Citations: A Blues for the Theatre*, and *Rent Day*, whose writer, Salina Mobley, chose not to take an active part in the production or publicity, Buriel wanted *The Daddies* in the series. The process would be good for me, he said, and he invited actress Lee Chamberlin, whose formidable credits included *Uptown Saturday Night*, *Let's Do It Again*, and *The Electric Company*, to make her stage directorial debut with my play. To my amazement, she accepted.

In one year I had gone from being a vagabond victim scribbling poetry in two-dollar journals to a legitimate San Francisco playwright. I was thrilled. I committed myself to an artistic and spiritual journey, having seen the hell that could be conjured up when sex got in the mix.

Yet even without that, I'd fallen in love with Buriel. No one had ever been as enthusiastic or supportive about getting me to trust my intuition, respect my talent, and thrive as an artist.

When Fear and Doubt, the evil tormenters of my youth, reared their ugly heads, he was always ready to counterattack with an infusion of Texas get-up-dust-yourself-off-and-try-again grit. I needed that.

One dismal morning as a slashing rain plummeted the City, I asked him to meet me in the warm haven of a Union Street café for waffles. I'd found myself blindsided by insecurity and needed his help and guidance to set me straight. My radar had been picking up static from some of the people at WACC. Buriel had brought me in from outside the established borders of the theatre community; I was not a member of their clique. No one knew who I was or where I'd come from, and speculation was rampant about our relationship. In their eyes, he appeared to be putting an inordinate amount of attention into the success of my play, which he was presenting under his Black Writers Workshop banner.

As well, the process that Buriel had said would be so good for me had become agonizing. I'd never before had my work picked apart, and being interrogated as to why I thought or wrote the way I did pushed a lot of uncomfortable buttons. Lee's ongoing calls for revisions to my script were causing me to question my ability as a playwright.

"You studied with me, right?" Buriel said. An endearing drop of syrup clung to his moustache, nevertheless he was stern as he faced me from the other side of the table.

"And I believe in you enough to produce your play in this show. Now you've got to believe in yourself."

It was more of a scolding than a pep talk. Falling into the poor-me victim ditch was a natural response in my world, a default resignation to worthlessness and the choice to dumb down rather than rise up. I studied the Rorschach of syrup on my plate, ashamed at having told him about the doubts I was having.

"Listen to me," he persisted. "You have every reason and right to believe in what you're capable of doing. I got told I wasn't good enough, that I'd never succeed. Self-examination and rewriting are part of the process, so don't think it means you aren't a good writer. No one else knows what you know the way you know it. And the world needs to hear your story."

As he had done countless times, Buriel reached across the table and put his hand on top of mine.

"It's not important whether your audience or anyone else agrees with you, or even likes you. What counts is that they leave the theatre talking about your work."

The rain outside began to let up, and we watched people darting out of the Union Street shops where they'd gone for shelter during the worst of the storm. As cars and Muni buses flew by, tidal waves of dirty street water splashed over the curb; only the quickest and most nimble were able to avoid the disaster of soggy shoes and trouser cuffs for the rest of the day.

I pushed my plate to one side. The terror in my soul had again been abated by my Teacher and friend—a masterful magician who could tie up my troubles in his scarf of words and "Poof!" they disappeared.

Buriel always made everything okay. Our times together had been an alchemist's mix of lessons and laughter: zipping across the Bay Bridge in his teeny red sports car, swimming laps at one of San Francisco's indoor pool clubs, or digging into cupcakes at Just Desserts and talking for hours. There'd never been anyone like him in my life.

I'd always wanted someone to really know me. To nurture the good, embrace what was different, and extract the pearl from the protoplasm. Someone who wanted to see me be great at doing what I could do, not what I could do *for them*. I wanted to be loved, but even more, I wanted to be known: to be understood, even when I made no sense. To be in real relationship with others, not just alphabetic, ancestral, or social order.

Buriel didn't waiver in his warmth or his friendship, even when I told him that I needed our relationship to transcend to a higher level (translation: no sex). I struggled with my own desires, wanting to believe that being celibate would detour the disappointment and pain that I had been through.

Nevertheless my soul was in relentless conflict between the physical, which had always been my source of validation, and the spiritual, which was beckoning me in ways I didn't understand but couldn't ignore, to stop being his lover. And all of this was attended by bizarre and disturbing dreams about graveyards and twisted metal and flashing red lights outside my window, like those of an ambulance or fire truck, and the bleeding fluorescent outline of my bedroom walls.

Buriel didn't pressure me. He continued to be generous in mentoring my writing. But not being lovers anymore meant I saw less of him, until our relationship became only about writing and the play. There were no more days flying around in his little sports car or meeting at Café Flore.

When spring arrived, taunting me with the scent of romance, my teenage addiction to Motown's suffering soliloquies returned like a bad rash. *How dare you arrive at my moment of nothingness*, I thought. And when night fell on Market Street, instead of The Quiet's lavish symphony, there was only the wail of sirens and the whoosh of passing cars.

We continued to talk daily, but I missed the closeness we'd shared. Still, as much as it bruised my heart, I didn't want my life to go up in flames again; neither did I want to risk losing him as my Teacher and friend. I prayed to be satisfied with a love that stayed on simmer and began to sense a tender and reassuring answer to that prayer, clinging with hope to what Buriel kept telling me about writing my story. *I had to carry on.*

For every romantic impulse I was forced to banish, I was yet on my way to becoming a San Francisco playwright with a produced work. There were actresses to audition, lines to polish, scenes to rewrite, and personalities to deal with.

Lee got our cast in place, and in April we began a series of staged readings at the theatre. The first time I heard my words spoken out loud by actors on a stage and responded to by an audience—words I'd written in the desperation of night, alone in my room above Market Street—it was electrifying. I never imagined how it would feel to hear people laughing and applauding and genuinely responding to something I wrote. The glimmer of another kind of validation began to replace the one that'd gotten me into so much trouble.

After the reading, Buriel walked me outside to the landing in front of WACC's door; we were arm in arm, our shoulders touching as they always seemed to do in mutual defense against the night. People were passing by us, headed to the parking lot, talking animatedly about *The Daddies*. He turned to me, beaming.

"You see that?"

He pointed to the exiting audience members who were unable to stop fussing and discussing my play and its characters as they got into their cars.

"This is what I told you would happen if you took yourself seriously as a writer. Now you must believe that there is something good inside you that attracts all of this good."

The bright eyes that had captured my heart at the Oakland Museum were shining, and he was smiling his gap-toothed smile. Leaning forward, he kissed me lightly on the cheek.

"When this is over," he said, "you need to write your book."

Whatever I'd felt about losing my lover's affection was replaced with the hope that my Teacher instilled: the fulfillment that awaited me as a writer. With my journal and the Olivetti, alone in the midnight hour as I'd been, I'd become strangely and wonderfully free.

Ole Man Trouble

Opening night for *Three Slices of Life* was scheduled for Friday, June 8, 1978. Buriel made arrangements for a press luncheon with theatre critics, including Stanley Eichelbaum of the *San Francisco Examiner*, to take place on May 30th at Rosebud's, an upscale restaurant.

The closer we got to opening night, the more frantic things became: rehearsals, temper tantrums, meetings, money, and disagreements over everything artistic, administrative, and otherwise. From serious setbacks to stupid squabbles, we leaned heavily on Buriel to referee and solve our problems. As easygoing as he was, Buriel's good nature was wearing thin.

On Monday morning, May 22nd, our leader was nowhere to be found. Throughout the day, all of us involved in the performances, as well the staff at WACC, called his apartment at various hours, but no one answered the phone. I remembered him showing me how he'd pull the phone cord out of the wall jack when he got sick of talking to people, just like I did.

"See this?" He dangled the cord like a captured grass snake.

"It just rings and rings and rings, and I never hear it!" He was wearing his Tweety Bird jeans, laughing himself silly, as if it were the greatest gag on Earth.

I wondered if anyone had gone to his apartment. Word was that he had a visitor named Beverly from out of town, and that made his disappearance seem all the more cavalier and frustrating.

I was cranky and tired, having woken up with a jolt in the middle of the night before, drenched in sweat, unable to fall back asleep or get any kind of rest. By five o'clock Monday evening, when I arrived at WACC along with Lee and our cast for rehearsal, I, too, was upset with him for not calling me as he was supposed to. I parked in the lot and walked toward a group of people huddled on the WACC landing; we'd all been locked out. Gloria Weinstock, the one person at WACC with whom I'd become friends, took me in her arms and pointed to a handwritten note that had been taped to the front door. Before I could read it, John Doyle, who was co-directing *Cituations* with Gloria, drove up in his blue Citröen and rolled down the window. The words barely made it out of his mouth.

"Buriel got killed," John said.

And then he drove away.

∽

It had sounded like, "Buriel got *something* . . . and he'll be right back."

But he wouldn't be back. Not ever.

Hanging onto Gloria, I turned around to read the sign on WACC's door:

ALL ACTIVITIES ARE CANCELLED DUE TO THE DEATH OF A STAFF MEMBER.

The story, as we heard it, was that the previous night, Buriel and his writing partner Joe got the good news that after years of collaboration, they had finally sold their screenplay. Perhaps going out for a late-night dinner or to celebrate, Buriel and Beverly got into his tiny red sports car and headed into the foggy San Francisco night.

The light was green for Buriel as, just before midnight, they approached the crossroads of Fifth Avenue and Geary, a busy, fast-moving boulevard whose signals are synchronized to accommodate the City's east-west traffic. But as Buriel entered the intersection, his and Beverly's path crossed with that of an eighteen-year-old kid from Daly City—reportedly drunk and at the wheel of a vehicle twice the size of Buriel's little putt-putt—who either didn't see or didn't care that the light for him was red.

∽

I hear your name and it is glittered in gold. The sound of it brings music and laughter to my ears. I remember you waking up, singing your corny cowboy tunes, drinking lemon tea, and the sincerity in your voice when you tell me about the things which have great meaning. I am filled with your response, knowing with each word I write that you will read them and shape them and lead me through this writer's life, pruning my words to grow in the straight and good way in which you've taught me.

You are the prince who saved me from the dragon, and even though you would not let me turn you into another dragon, you have remained my friend, my Teacher, my confidante—a man I can always call and always count on. Your name rings golden in my ears, but the word which follows is beyond comprehension.

Buriel's dead.

How can the smile of your name be in the same sentence as the word "dead"? It does not compute. Nor do the TV news pictures of a mangled sports car and the battered corpse which flashes on the screen for a second—my last image of you. I try to imagine your body on a slab at the morgue; maybe if I see you dead I will believe it.

There are no more words, only vast silences filled with intermittent Morse code and giant implosions in dark spaces. Your love overflowed to each of us who asked for it; we are orphans without you. I can't believe your magnificent, beautiful life is over. And that you will never talk to me again.

∽

The memorial was held four days later at a mortuary on Third Street near Candlestick Park, after which his body would be shipped to Abilene. The funeral director invited mourners to pass by the casket and pay our respects. Buriel's face didn't look like him, and his chest appeared to have a board in it (which it probably did, a mortician told me, saying that was typical for drivers who'd been crushed by the steering column). The only thing I recognized was his hands, and I brushed them lightly with mine as I passed by. Part of me wanted to linger, but another part of me couldn't. My friend wasn't there, that much I knew.

After the service, we filed outside. As I listened to others talk and reminisce about their last encounter with him, I recalled how on that Sunday night, the night he died, I'd been jolted awake and found myself sitting straight up, soaked in sweat, my heart pounding. I'd looked at the clock: It was 11:45 P.M., the exact moment in which Buriel and Beverly had been killed.

Who would have thought that *Three Slices of Life,* which he planned as a showcase for us, would instead become a memorial tribute to him, and that as we ate the lunch he so proudly arranged for us at Rosebud's on Tuesday, May 30th, Buriel's family would at the very same hour be lowering his dead body into a grave in Texas.

None of my ruminations on the spirit world had prepared me to come this close to death. It was impossible to grasp. Unlike my friendship with Boni, Buriel and I spoke often, at all hours; we were still intimates even if we weren't lovers. From his first gentlemanly kindnesses that night he took me to the cafe and then made sure I got home safely, to the humiliating assault by the Piano Player, and finally the transit of our affair from Teacher to lover to friend and mentor, Buriel Clay had become a part of my life—a piece of who I was and the motivator for who I could become.

Buriel, where are you?

As days and weeks went by, I became morbidly obsessed with wondering what happened in that split second moment in which life changed to death.

Where did you go?

There was no answer. It haunted me day after day after day. My mind hovered apart from the earthly world's ebb and flow, longing for a glance into that terrifying last frame of his life, as if it would somehow resolve the mystery and bond us forever.

It never came; only silence.

But what was coming into focus were the bizarre dreams and premonitions I'd had about graveyards and flashing red lights and bloody rippling walls. And I knew that whatever had been pulling at my soul to withdraw from him as my lover, even though it broke my heart, had probably saved my life. I was not the woman he chose to be with that night.

Predictably, like bickering children after their parents die, the volatile negativity that erupted after Buriel's death pitted those of us who believed in going on with the show, which we feared might be the last performance of his work, against those who wanted to cancel it out of grief. With our third playwright in absentia, I was accused of wanting all the recognition for myself and told to take my "white ass back to Oakland."

In the end, we honored his memory by presenting *Three Slices of Life* as he'd planned. But I can't say it was what he would have wanted.

What Buriel would have wanted was to have been there.

Slippin' Into Darkness

All my life I've dreamed of a light so bright I could not open my eyes. Of desperately trying to call someone on the phone in an emergency but not being able to dial the numbers correctly. Of driving over a cliff and thinking, "This isn't a dream. It's really happening."

When my dream ends, I lumber toward Earth from the netherworld and all is blank. In that first moment of wakefulness, even today, I do not know where I am. Are these walls in Los Angeles? Oakland? San Francisco?

When the lights dimmed on *Three Slices of Life*, and the actors, directors, lovers, fighters, and critics all went home, I wondered if Death was in the shadows, silently waiting for me as he did for Buriel. I wondered, *If I die will the pain go away?* If I died, would I no longer be responsible for becoming the success he wanted me to be?

Partly I wished I was dead so I could be with him. Partly I wished I was dead so I wouldn't have to figure out how to go on without him. A psychic told me she saw a bright white light when I said his name, and that he wanted me to know he was okay. Weeks, months later, I still couldn't reconcile what had happened.

And still I kept asking, *Buriel, where are you?*

Possessed by melancholy, I wandered between two worlds, the living and the dead, belonging to neither and needing to step ever so carefully in the ruins left behind, because there was no arm to grasp, no shoulder to lean on anymore.

"Love yourself," he'd told me.

But how could I do that now, without him?

CHAPTER TWELVE

1978-1979

What Becomes Of The Broken Hearted?

Summer arrived, and I rode the tailwinds of my illustrious, if brief, career as a playwright. I applied to theatre companies in San Francisco and Berkeley that were looking for new scripts. None of them wanted to produce *The Daddies*, but I was invited to present it at San Quentin State Prison's 1978 Sapphire Day— a messy, raucous affair in which my literary skills were less the main attraction than a stage full of eight sexy women talkin' trash.

The warden seated me barely arm's distance from a cluster of burly, tattooed inmates. The men hollered cat calls at my actresses and scared the heck out of me. Halfway through the play, I called a halt to the performance, seeing my cast in confusion, unable to hear one another's lines above the inmates' ear-splitting, testosterone-driven howls. As far as the play's story, no one in the audience knew the difference anyway.

After that, several writers and directors I'd met at WACC came to me with offers of freelance publicity jobs for projects of their own. Apparently, now that my "white ass" had gone back to Oakland, it was acceptable for them to enlist my services. I took on the jobs, thinking they might be a way to forge peace between us; perhaps even open a fresh door to the San Francisco arts community. But in the end, I never got paid for my work. The reasoning of those who hired me was that while they had to pay bills like rent and PG&E, it was optional to pay me because we were "friends."

I felt like an idiot; suckered like Charlie Brown who agrees to let Lucy hold the football for him in spite of knowing she will yank it out from under him at the very last minute.

Yet even in death, Buriel's words came to comfort me. I rediscovered them in my journal when I'd gone with pen in hand to mull things over at the Ashby Avenue fishing place, where the afternoon sun danced like diamonds on the water. Now the gleaming diamonds were Buriel's spirit, shattered into a million pieces.

"Love yourself," he'd said to me so many times.

Why was that still so hard to do?

"Have faith in your motivations that are truly selfless," he told me. "You aren't stupid for loving people, even if they don't treat you back with love."

There was talk around San Francisco that Mayor George Moscone had been lobbied to dedicate WACC's theatre to Buriel, but by the end of summer, I no longer had it in me to care. With all the vitriol spewed after his death, the gesture felt as empty and unsatisfying as paying tribute to my friend's corpse at the funeral home.

I put my attention back on my job with the Buddhists, but I knew in my heart that after working there for six years, I was only staying because I didn't know what I was supposed to do next.

And then Rose called.

On what was supposed to be a stopover from Japan, where she'd gone with her then-boyfriend, a jazz musician, Rose landed in Hawaii and contracted an incurable case of "Aloha Spirit." She broke up with the jazz musician and decided to stay on Oahu to build the business of her dreams: a bed-and-breakfast where she could welcome guests and live out her mission to celebrate life as one grand party.

"Get on a plane and come help me!" Rose demanded. "I've got the most incredible beach house you ever saw. Right on the water! Get over here now. What else are you doing with your life anyway?"

It was time. I was ready to leave the Bay Area and all of its darkness, death, and drama. I said goodbye to the nice people at BCA, sublet the Market Street house, and headed across the Pacific to Paradise.

Man, Oh Man

The tropical air, lush with the fragrances of plumeria and tuberose, and the welcome lunatic madness of my friend were healing to my battered soul.

Rose and I recreated our Calistoga days on the beaches of Kailua: riding the bus back and forth from Honolulu across the emerald green mountains of the Pali, talkin' story till our jaws wore out. We went disco dancing late into the night and woke up in our bikinis for an early morning swim. We splurged on the two-dollar plate at Patty's Chinese Kitchen in the Ala Moana Shopping Center and flaunted our Hawaiian Tropic suntans in halter tops and sarongs. At night, we ate dinner on the sand with linen tablecloths and candles, watching the flash of fishermen's lights, and in the morning, we scrambled to retrieve the escaped green glass balls they used to buoy their nets.

Rose had scored a beachfront house on Mokulua Drive in the exclusive Kailua horseshoe called Lanikai, or "Heavenly Water." She named her bread-and-breakfast Lokelani, meaning

"Heavenly Rose." By day, the ocean behind us was mint jelly and creamy surf. At night, the moon made a glossy transit across shimmering black water, while blinking crystal stars tried to outdo one another for our attention.

I wrote every day in my journal, but my poetry had vanished. I must have left it in San Francisco, though the City had lost its right to my heart. Lanikai's incoming and outgoing tides seemed a metaphor for my own never-reconciled cycles of purpose and insignificance. There were days when I felt gratified and full, and days when I was pulled into an abyss of darkness by forces I could not control. Fortunately, because of Rose and her six-foot goddess-warrior perseverance, I was yanked out of those depths as quickly as I fell into them. We were too busy trying to make money for rent and food to *la-de-dah* around on the astral plane.

I'd brought two hundred dollars with me, and in a week, it'd been spent getting the house ready for guests. I wasn't worried; our backyard was a sandy white beach and the Mokulua Islands, two rock pyramids in the clear, turquoise water—guaranteed to attract cash-paying travelers.

After we fixed up the house, we set about schmoozing tourists in Honolulu to stay with us. When we succeeded, we gave them our rooms, and Rose slept in the garage while I relocated to a tent outside on the lawn. But our efforts were not as fruitful as we hoped, and we spent the winter dodging downpours and the landlord, struggling for money, and eating beans. Living in Hawaii, I found out, was expensive and hard work, not nearly as glamorous as just visiting the place.

Love The One You're With

The Blues Man arrived in Honolulu in December to play a gig at the University of Hawaii. But it was different with us this time. While I remained the hippie girl of the Mystic who had church with Van Morrison and Otis Redding on the moon-viewing platform of my house in Mount Washington, things were different now between the Blues Man and me. Our afternoon under Gaudi's pavilion and our nights at the Ash Grove were the past. The blindfold of fake naiveté I'd worn when he was my lover had decomposed, gone to its watery grave in the River.

Yet I would always love the Blues Man. He had, after all, been my first Teacher. And while there was no chance of reviving our Mount Washington affair, I remained in awe of him and the truth that poured from his guitar. I still wanted to become the person he'd inspired me to be.

I might have been on my way to learning how sometimes the thing you're most attracted to isn't life-giving or progressive when it comes to one's long-range destiny. Sometimes that thing you want so badly is really just a truck stop, not the destination. Pursued in spite of all the warning signs, it becomes a forty-car pileup on the Interstate that leaves you crippled for life.

Or dead.

When all you wanted to do was have some fun.

In Barcelona, the Blues Man had given me my first look at a realm that was "more than the physical." I took that to heart as only a true believer could and spent the next eight years trying to find out what it meant. Now, having witnessed so much since that psychedelic day in La Floresta, I saw this great big man, who'd played such a great big part in my life, for who he was—a wise Teacher, an artist of incomparable gifting, and an unabashed lover of women.

Perhaps it had never really been about him. Maybe he and the other men I'd loved were just instruments of that *something* I'd been drawn to in the Music. Something that went deeper than the chords and notes and wails; something that moved my soul to tears and brought forth a hunger in me that couldn't be satisfied. It was gruff and determined, yet broken and desperate. The Blues Man's guitar sought to transcend it, while Otis Redding and James Brown had taken it raw, busted, and filthy to the floor with no hope of getting back up. In Oakland, there'd been Al Green, and then The Persuasions, who raised it like an offering to heaven. And along the way, my Motown mentors had me believing that to suffer on love's behalf was glamorous and cool.

I watched Rose and the Blues Man talking and laughing. Having been friends over the years, never lovers, there was an openness and liberty they shared that hadn't been possible between him and me. Yet as the evening went on, I realized that for this man whom I'd loved, and who had altered the course of my life, "more than the physical" seemed related more to the cosmic or philosophical, and so far, that hadn't led me to the spiritual world I was searching for.

So I kept looking.

I met a woman in Kahala, a devotee, and tried to follow the path she was on. Its teachings were like the Yoga Society's and seemed to make sense: "Honor yourself. God dwells in you. See God in each other." I went with her to meetings, retreats, and *satsang*, but like Buddhism and yoga, it didn't awaken the power that turned those precepts into more than just good advice. Finding the truth was frustrating, even in Paradise.

So, after all of that, I decided to go back to being a heathen.

It was familiar, if not pathetic, territory. But honestly, what else could be expected? I was twenty-eight years old, living at the beach, and walking around half-naked most of the time. The only requirement for my next lover was that he had to be someone with whom I had no previous history. So, I headed straight into a forty-car pileup on the Interstate with a fun-loving, *pakololo*-smoking baby daddy from Kahaluu who had already fathered eight kids by eight different women. The outcome was as depressing and emotionally miserable as it was predictable, although I did manage to leave him before becoming Number Nine.

I may have thought everything was different, but I hadn't changed that much. I wasn't going back, but I wasn't moving forward either. Whatever vows I'd made in the hope of getting on a positive track with my life, I continued to be sucked into the hurricane of high drama by the irresistible (and implausible) music and lyrics of songs embedded in my soul and promising what no man could deliver.

Like a dormant virus, the damage of my childhood still lingered with outbreaks as sure as sunrise. Loneliness, as the song, "Superstar," had pointed out, is a sorry affair. It messes with your head, cranking out the toxic by-product of terrible ideas: from trying to understand why you've been left out of the good times everyone else seems to be having, to trying to figure out ways to insert yourself into them. No one who worships at its shrine, like I did as a Motown-addicted teenager, escapes the haunting obsession for something they believe will make them feel whole. Even if you do manage to snag a few iconic tokens, like a lover or a family or a career, the implanted soundtrack of your misguided youth keeps coming back to taunt you as an adult: *Is that all there is?*

Or as Rose used to say, "Okay, I'm satisfied. Now what?"

By January, I was fed up with being broke and weary of island fever: going round and round and winding up in the same place. I was ready to return to the mainland and try being a writer again. Maybe I needed the friction of a place like Oakland to make me fight back and get strong enough to bear fruit.

On the day of my flight, Rose invited our friends over for a send-off party. She barbecued some chickens and fixed me a sandwich to take on the plane. Like other compromises, I was calling myself a vegetarian but eating dead birds and fish.

At the Honolulu airport, the agricultural inspector pulled the sandwich out of my bag, unwrapped it, and peeled the lettuce leaf from between the bread and the sauce-soaked meat, waving it in my face like a little flag.

"You can't take this with you," he said.

He dropped the lettuce leaf in a trash can and handed me back the remains of my now dismembered sandwich. Then he smiled.

"But this part okay."

Knockin' On Heaven's Door

We'd barely heard about it in Hawaii. In November 1978, just days before Thanksgiving, the *Honolulu Star-Bulletin* arrived, and we opened it to the headline story about nine hundred souls from Reverend Jim Jones' Peoples Temple who'd taken their own lives in the South American jungle of Guyana by drinking cyanide-laced Kool-Aid. A photo of bodies sprawled face down, some laying side by side in a grotesque pinwheel, could have come from the archives of Auschwitz or Treblinka had they not been wearing colorful shorts and tee shirts.

And then the story was gone.

A week later, Rose was on the phone with someone in San Francisco who began screaming that Mayor George Moscone had just been shot to death in his office at City Hall and so had Harvey Milk, the City's first openly gay supervisor. That was as much as we could find out. In Hawaii, news from the mainland came and went in a single day, if it came at all.

The intertwining of so many San Francisco destinies at the end of 1978 was mind-boggling. Mayor Moscone had been a colleague of Jim Jones; he had even appointed Jones to the Housing Authority Commission. Just as the mayor had extended his condolences to the San Francisco arts community after Buriel got killed, he reached out to the loved ones of the hundreds who'd perished in Guyana, including the family of California Congressman Leo Ryan who'd been ambushed and shot to death as he tried to investigate Jones' faux-topia.

And then, like those he grieved over, Moscone was killed.

I arrived back on the mainland a couple of months later. I can't say I felt it when my flight from Honolulu began its descent into San Francisco. But after getting off the plane, I caught an airport bus bound for the East Bay, and when it turned the curve into downtown San Francisco, the pall of death that hung over the City was as stunning as the fallout of an atomic bomb—a toxic cloud blotting out the air, the sun, and the very life force of a population in which nearly everyone had lost someone to Death: grandparents or a neighbor and her kids at Jonestown, plus the beloved mayor and trailblazing supervisor. The gloom was like stench, and I held my breath as we passed through it, until the bus barreled into the mesh underbelly of the Oakland Bay Bridge and the City began to shrink behind us.

The darkness lasted for months.

Invisible to the eye, it mushroomed into a life of its own. San Francisco's grief became a dumping ground, a communal soup where mourning for any loss—including the pain still lodged in me from Buriel's death—could be shared in weeping and hugs with strangers; a bucket of sorrow from your life spilled into the great reservoir of other people's tragedies. Personal heartbreak was no longer a private burden you had to carry by yourself.

Under the umbrella of Jonestown and the assassinations, we clung together as a population unified in anguish and horror, whether it was for the victims of that awful season or something else. It didn't matter. It was a phenomenon I would observe again when other Big Moments came tearing into history: the opportunity those Moments give to our individual moments to pool together our pain—or as in my college years, our collective anger and rage—and give it a home outside of ourselves.

But there was an unsavory ingredient to our grief stew that year: the lack of someone to hold accountable or punish for it all. With the Bad Reverend Jones gone to his inglorious doom in the jungle, there was no one whom authorities could put their hands on to blame for what had happened at Jonestown.

Yet there was one man, former Supervisor Dan White, who would stand trial for killing Mayor Moscone and Supervisor Milk.

Sympathy For The Devil

I settled back in the Market Street house and went to work for a temp agency that sent me on short-term secretary jobs at corporations in San Francisco's Financial District, crossing the Bay Bridge with other business commuters on the AC Transit bus. Going from a halter top and sarong to polyester and pantyhose was a challenge, but the money was good, and as a temp, I assumed I was beholden to no one.

Exactly one year after Buriel's death, on May 21, 1979, a San Francisco jury convicted Dan White of two counts of voluntary manslaughter for his assassinations of George Moscone and Harvey Milk. That verdict, rather than two counts of first-degree murder, was reached due to what came to be known as the "Twinkie Defense." Dan White's attorney successfully argued that the former Supervisor had acted of out of diminished capacity, a mental state caused by depression, stress, and eating sugary junk food in the weeks prior to the killings.

Angry demonstrations and rioting followed, turning San Francisco upside down. The news media called the protests "White Night" and tried to blame the gay community for storming City Hall. But there were plenty of upset heteros too, from corporate types in the Financial District to PTA parents. On our commute back to Oakland the evening of the verdict, the secretaries and suits who rode the bus with me across the Bay Bridge were in an uproar. Still tending the wounds of Jonestown, as well as whatever private troubles had surfaced and been cast into the communal pot, everyone was outraged that Dan White hadn't been convicted of first-degree murder.

Like the waves of a sonic boom, a profound sense of collective betrayal resonated across the Bay Area that year, as the justice system failed to provide any measure of payback or reconciliation in the midst of a horrific and irresolvable season of Death.

CHAPTER THIRTEEN

Los Angeles, 1979

Don't Look Back

The Pacific Ocean along Santa Barbara's coastline was as sparkling and heavenly as the waters of Lanikai had been. Its dancing sunlit diamonds bore none of the brooding conjured up by those at the Ashby Avenue fishing place.

I could not have been happier to get away.

After the Dan White verdict, going into the City felt like being sucked into a toxic vortex. There was no question that it was time to re-establish what my life was about. Then, in one of the magazines that Buriel had encouraged me read, I saw an ad for the 1979 Santa Barbara Writers Conference and felt it was just where I needed to be. And there was enough money in my savings account for the registration and to take a week off from being the temp agency's polyester, pantyhose puppet.

I drove the Beetle to Santa Barbara's Miramar Hotel, a picturesque collection of white bungalows topped with blue tile roofs and surrounded by manicured flower gardens and expanses of green lawn. On the other side of the tennis courts, I was delighted to find a whistle-blowing train that came through several times a day. Just beyond its tracks was the Miramar's private sun deck and white sand beach. The hotel grounds reminded me of Hawaii, and every morning I picked a Hibiscus flower off one of its plentiful bushes, pinning it into my hair as I had in Lanikai.

Opening night was exciting. Established screenwriters, authors, and literary agents were on hand to mingle with hopefuls like myself seeking to grab the brass ring of success and not fall into a chasm along the way. I promptly learned the most laughed-at reason anyone could give for why they were there was, "My life has been so interesting, everyone says I should write a book." I made a note to myself never to say those words, even though they are why I'm writing this book.

The conference was populated by recognized writers who genuinely wanted to mentor those of us beginning the journey, and by lecherous old drunks who fancied themselves Hemingway (or his muse), at least in behavior if not talent. Famous or not, I despised the alcoholic men and sloppy women who stumbled their way through the gardens at night trying to find their room, or someone else's. Drinks at the bar and clandestine trysts in the bungalows seemed to be why they came, not because they cared about writing. I made it clear to the boozy old men who tried to hit on me that I hated drunks because a drunk driver killed someone I loved.

During the day, aspiring and seasoned writers came together in workshops, and in the evenings, we assembled in the Miramar's auditorium to glean from a famous author or publishing icon, such as *Los Angeles Times* book editor, Robert Kirsch, or superagent "Swifty" Lazar. Whispers abounded when one hopeful writer, a lovely but shy woman named Priscilla, arrived with her eleven-year-old daughter, Lisa Marie.

The list of literary lions that year was impressive: Arthur Hailey, Ray Bradbury, Rita Mae Brown, Fannie Flagg, Shane Stevens, Barry Hannah, and Bill Downey. The writer I most wanted to meet was Curt Gentry, co-author of *Helter Skelter*, the best-selling true crime book about the Manson murders. We shared a lively conversation about my week in jail with Susan, Leslie, and Patricia, as well as rumors each of us had heard about the post-Tate-La Bianca activities of Manson's extended "family."

Still obsessed with the Music, I'd begun writing a novel about a 1960s soul singer whom I named Clayton Willow. Having heard it was best to start your book at a high-pitched moment, my novel opened in August 1965, as Clayton arrives in Los Angeles for a performance at the Shrine Auditorium. But the night is about to become historic for something other than a concert.

> *The ear-splitting thunder of Clayton Willow's jet approaching LAX went unnoticed on the ground below. South Central Avenue was roaring with tanks and troops; the LAPD mobilized, the National Guard called in by Governor Pat Brown. From his air-conditioned Spring Street office, Mayor Sam Yorty struggled to make sense of what was happening to his city. Chaos filled the streets while gasoline filled empty pop bottles, stuffed with rags and hurled flaming through plate glass windows into stores to which they had once been returned for a three-cent deposit. No one in Watts cared about the three cents today.*

Along with daily sessions in which we presented our works-in-progress for feedback or listened to an insider about how to get an agent, a beloved tradition of the Santa Barbara Writers Conference was its Short Story Contest based on a one-word theme. That year the theme was "Goodbye." So instead of slobnobbing at night with the drunks, I worked on my story, packing in all the mega-melodrama one might expect from an amateur. It was about a young man named Justin who comes to San Francisco with the great dreams all young men have but winds up in a "nightmare-by-day ballet of metropolitan survival." Ashamed and discouraged, Justin decides to leap to his death, but he mistakenly goes to the Oakland-Bay Bridge, which has no walkway, instead of the Golden Gate.

Some people just can't do anything right.

In the final scene, Justin is standing near the tracks as a train's glowing white eye emerges into view, "its monstrous engine barreling, sparks flying, ten thousand tons of steel and salvation." But instead of hurtling himself in front of the locomotive, Justin enters a passenger car and takes a seat. When he hands his ticket to the porter, the destination is a sweaty blur.

It didn't matter. He wasn't going anywhere; he was simply leaving.

On the last day of the conference, we gathered together in the Miramar's auditorium for farewells and to learn the winner of the 1979 Short Story Contest. I could hardly believe it when the director of the conference, Barnaby Conrad, announced my name, and applause rang out. I walked to the podium and read my story aloud, a stolen Miramar flower pinned behind my ear. When I finished, everyone in the auditorium cheered, even the drunks.

The Long And Winding Road

It was dark in our house at night when I was a kid. There weren't any street lamps to shine through the windows or night lights in the hallway. Instead, my mother taught me to find my way to the bathroom by putting out my right arm and keeping my right hand to the wall until I found the opening that was the door. One night my father intercepted me preparing to go out the front door to the street at two o'clock in the morning.

"Where are you going, sweetie?"

"Baffrumm."

I had mistakenly put out my left hand and gone on an entirely different journey.

As my twenties drew to a close, it might have seemed that I was on track and knew where I was going. I believed I was about to become a best-selling author. But nobody really knows what's ahead. We're all trying to make our way through the dark with whatever advice or maps we've been given, and sometimes a simple thing, like not knowing right from left, can take you to a place you never expect. Or thinking you'll find something in one place, and then discovering it in another.

Notwithstanding all the good that Buriel had instilled in me or the recent flow of accolades for my writing, what remained at stake wasn't so much whether other people liked me, but whether I could ever love myself. One out-of-body LSD trip in the forest ten years ago, a few moments in the limelight, and a devoted but dead teacher had not been enough to heal my chronically hemorrhaging self-esteem.

So I concluded that since Radio had been my schoolhouse and Motown the headmaster, it was time to hold them accountable for all the lies I'd been told and for all the trouble I'd seen. I wanted someone to blame for falling in love. For being sent to the home for unwed mothers. For going to jail. For the men who broke my heart. For all those losses I'd endured, including my baby, and for the anger and bewilderment I'd walked around in my whole life because nothing ever matched up to what I'd been told.

Despite the nugget handed to me in the hospital by Mrs. Hayes, I was still looking for The Answer.

Then one day, just minding my own business on the Sunset Strip, I met someone who knew someone who took me to meet somebody else. That somebody else into whose orbit I was about to transit was the Great Poet, the author and finisher of the mixed-up ideas in which I'd put my faith, and editor-in-chief of the Encyclopedia of Misunderstanding that I'd believed in and lived by since 1964. Being introduced to him might have been one of those circle-of-life things, like being led to the Mount Washington house by a someone I never saw again. Like going to Barcelona with Marvin and meeting the Blues Man who introduced me to Rose. Or like thinking my dream would be realized in Gordon Parks and instead finding Buriel.

You get it, a left-handed walk in the dark.

Boogie Wonderland

Whenever I came to visit them, my parents were glad to see me. They never knew how bad things had been, like with Buriel getting killed. Or my life-or-death drama with the Piano Player. Back when I was being wheeled into surgery with his exploding baby, the hospital had called them, and my mother asked the nurse if I wanted her to come. On my way to Level Four, I told the nurse to tell her no. Just like how I said no to seeing her or my father when I was a teenager in labor, giving birth to their unacknowledged granddaughter. We never spoke about that or the exploding baby. It wasn't because I was afraid they'd be angry with me, but because I'd have to look into their sad faces and be responsible for their pain.

Still, the warmth and love with which my parents always received their prodigal daughter was overwhelming. It was as if they'd spent every day since the last time I was there thinking about me and planning for my return. There were phone calls to be made to aunts and uncles, and projects that my father wanted to share. My mother cooked piles of food and took me outside to show me what was flourishing in the yard. My habit of wearing a flower in my hair hadn't started in Hawaii; I'd been plucking orchids and camellias out of my mother's garden since I was a teenager. I'm sure it made her happy to see her errant daughter wearing the bloom of something she'd cultivated more successfully than me.

It felt good to be so welcomed, but with our amputated history and the clutter of detritus piled up by our encampment on the River, it was also hard to receive. I guess when you shut out difficult things, you also close down to incoming good stuff. I wanted to match their enthusiasm for our reunions. My parents had only tried to do what they thought was right, and even in our worst times, I knew they loved me. With that, I'd come to realize one truth: People are who they are. You can accept them, you can reject them, or you can put your relationship with them into some kind of demilitarized zone, where you respect who they are, and stay as far away as you can from who they are not.

"You're my heart," my dad would say. The etching on his face had become as detailed as scrimshaw, and with each passing year, my mother's dark eyes were set farther back into their sockets, the fragile skin around them translucent and red. The plumpness of middle age had turned to empty, sagging folds over bony arms and crooked bodies. My parents were growing old, and as I observed them now, I knew that someday they were going to die. I didn't want to wind up on the other side of that River bereft of their lavish attention and filled with guilt, hearing the wail of Otis Redding's "You Don't Miss Your Water" in my head. So I gave back as much as any crippled and broken daughter could, and they gave to me everything they had left.

Nevertheless, after a few hours together, the dense silence of my parents' house began to weigh on me, threatening to undermine the liberty of my new identity in Oakland with the bondage of my unhappy childhood in North Hollywood. No matter how I tried to recast it, the residue of those years still reverberated in the house I'd grown up in, like the dissonance of bad plumbing.

So I took breaks, driving around to cruise my old haunts: the apartment I'd lived in on La Mirada Avenue; the Ash Grove, where so many nights had been spent under the Blues Man's spell. I drove to Mount Washington, passed the Southwest Museum, and turned up Crane Boulevard for a glance at my old house. Then I circled the flatlands of Griffin Boulevard and slowly rolled by the Florence Crittenton Home—unsure what I was looking for, but unable to stop chasing the scent of it.

On one of my outings, I went to Sunset Boulevard, where I decided to park the Beetle and walk the length of the Strip. I passed an old burlesque club called the Body Shop and what was once a soul food restaurant, Players' Choice, owned by Douglas' stepfather. Just before the yellow railroad car that had been turned into a hot dog stand, I came to The Source, an offbeat cafe that I'd frequented on late-night runs from Mount Washington to pick up leftover avocado and sprout sandwiches, wrapped in plastic, and piled neatly at the back door after closing. And then there was the Hyatt, where I'd waited in the lobby to get an autograph from James Brown before dashing back to school on the bus.

Though I'd missed the 1966 uprisings at Pandora's Box, I did have my share of riotous, mini-skirted nights later that decade at the Whiskey a Go Go. Sunset Boulevard's next generation looked a lot like we had: lanky girls with long hair, short skirts, and determined gaits; chins down to protect their warpaint, and headed to find their love connection.

At Sunset Plaza, I caught a glimpse of my reflection in a plate glass window: army surplus camouflage pants and a dancer's white tank top. Hair as big as Chaka Khan's, a collar of tribal beads around my neck. Shades. Wandering around, looking for a glass of cold carrot juice, and maybe the sound of Teddy Pendergrass.

At the end of my stroll down memory lane, I found myself in front of an import shop whose window displayed a colorful array of African fabrics, clothing, and jewelry. Happiness filled my soul, like meeting a familiar friend in a foreign land. I went inside and was heartily greeted by the owner, a tall, dark man beautifully dressed in a traditional West African grand boubou over matching pants and kufi cap. His outfit was made of sky blue damask; intricate white embroidery festooned the neckline of his flowing robe and cap. His smile was bright when he saw me come through the door.

"Hello, hello. Welcome! I have wonderful new dresses that just arrived. You will look like a queen in them!" His accent was British, but his cadence strictly West African, stretching his words with a funny lilt. I knew that accent from the Nigerians and Ghanaians I'd met at Everybody's.

The shopkeeper and I talked for about thirty minutes. I told him I took African dance classes in Oakland, and his eyes lit up. From the back room, he brought out several fabulous outfits for me to try on, some crusted with gold embroidery and heavy as armor. The clothes were handmade and very expensive. They looked great on me.

"I'm sorry, I don't have money to buy anything like this right now."

"Don't worry, queen. I want you to try these on because I'm having a fashion show this week. Would you like to be a model in it?"

And so it went. The following weekend, I went to a ritzy house on the Westside and walked a runway of sorts that had been fashioned around the homeowner's swimming pool/grotto. It was crazy, and it was fun. And there I met somebody, another model, with whom I got to talking about how much the music of Motown had influenced me, and about the soul singer novel I was writing. Right down the street from her mid-city apartment, she said, lived a singer named Patti, whom the model thought might like to hear my story and maybe introduce me to her boss.

Which is how I got to meet Smokey Robinson.

You Really Got A Hold On Me

Coming face-to-face with the person you expect to give you The Answer you've searched for your whole life is a lot like the approach of your first kiss: tempting, terrifying, and once you see it coming, there's no turning back. Will it live up to my expectations? Or will it be more than I can handle? And if I find what I've been looking for, what do I do with it?

He may have been a legend, but I made up my mind to confront the Great Poet, whose smooth lyrics and sweet seduction had coaxed me out onto the firing range, where raspy-voiced desperados like David Ruffin had shot me down and taken my soul captive. I'd nearly died for believing in the words they sang.

Maybe it was the "warped perception" I'd been diagnosed with as a teenager, but to my mind, lurking in soul music's most gut-wrenching songs seemed to be an unspoken threat: *If I can't have you, no one will.* So in addition to the soundtrack of that sunny six sixty-six school's-out afternoon—when Smokey serenaded, and Douglas told me to trust him, and then I got pregnant and sent away—the lyrics I fed on had also provided the how-to guide for my no-self-respect, violence-ridden relationship with the Piano Player, as well as the deadly confrontation between my friend Boni and her ex-lover.

True, there was desperation in Smokey Robinson's songs, but unlike David Ruffin or James Brown, Smokey made himself the vulnerable one. It was easy to believe that no matter what he got you into, he'd take the misery hit if it went wrong. Smokey Robinson promised that whatever tears were shed, they'd leave their tracks on his face, not yours. He was the tender, sensitive, wounded lover; not the hysterical madman falling to his knees screaming, "Please! Please! Please!" and backing you into the corner with a do-or-die ultimatum.

Or showing up at your house in the middle of the night with a bad attitude and a loaded gun.

If ever I'd doubted, I was certain now that love was indeed the thing that saved you *and* the thing that sent you to hell. And that no human being could ever live up to what the Music promised. So I prepared to hand Smokey Robinson an indictment for all the wrongs I'd been done in the name of what it had taught me.

I made up my mind I wasn't going to meet him as a starstruck fan and let him get away with it again. No, the Great Poet and I would have to come face-to-face, mind-to-mind as creative artists. What I wasn't prepared for was how he would respond to my demand for The Answer. Or those green eyes.

Everything happened quickly after the fashion show. The next time I visited Los Angeles, the model walked me a few doors down the street from her flat on South Orange Drive and deposited me at the apartment of her neighbor, Patti Henley. *Circle-of-life. Left-handed journey. Whatever.* Without hesitation Patti welcomed me into her world. A brown velvet beauty with a voice as rich as Rockefeller, she was a transplanted Chicago native with musical roots in church, now singing backup with Smokey Robinson.

We spent the afternoon in her sunny dining room talking about the Music and what it meant to each of us. She told me she'd grown up in a family committed to love, community service, and Jesus; and she shared her experience in the 1960s singing with three other Chicago sisters as the musical voices for Jesse Jackson's Operation Breadbasket and the civil rights movement. I could tell that Patti was a spiritual person and seeker of truth, and I wondered how she managed to have a life infused with God and still pursue her worldly dreams as an artist. The spiritual paths I'd tried to follow weren't wide enough for both.

After getting to know one another, Patti popped the question.

"So, are you ready to meet him?"

The next day, we were at the door of Smokey Robinson's house in Beverly Hills. When he opened it, I almost forgot why I was there.

"Hey baby, come on in."

The Great Poet's home was beautiful but not pretentious; a Pac-Man video game sat in the foyer. He took Patti and me into the den, where he'd been watching sports on TV with some friends. His wife, Claudette, for whom he'd written "My Girl," came in and introduced herself. She was gracious and lovely; I recognized her strong, clear voice from the Miracles.

And here I was, in their house.

I'm not just a fan; I'm a writer and an artist, I reminded myself as I took a seat on the couch next to him. I'd brought my credentials: laudatory reviews of *The Daddies* and a self-published volume of my poetry, giving the Great Poet a rundown of the confusion and drama that Motown had wrought in my life. I showed him the poems I'd written about that and told him I was writing a novel about a soul singer and the Music.

It seemed like he was paying attention, but his easygoing friendliness was disarming. By this time, he was into his lyrical *Quiet Storm* years, and perhaps the statute of limitations on what the 1960s did to impressionable true believers like me had expired.

With the TV going and other people chatting in the room, I studied that remarkable face, as gentle and unassuming in person as he looked on the album covers. I tried to find in it a key to the magic with which the lyrics of Motown had captivated my soul. How could they have led me so far astray, into a world which glorified pain and put heartbreak on the throne?

Finally I blurted the profound truth I'd brought to confront him with: the conclusion at which I'd arrived after fifteen years of trying to live out what I learned from the masters of Motown.

"I don't mean to be disrespectful," I said, "but if the Motown songwriters would have changed the word 'you' to the word 'God,' those songs might have made sense. And then I wouldn't have gotten into so much trouble."

He burst into surprised laughter, and yet I suspect he knew what I meant.

"You give me too much credit," he said.

"Well, you're the one who wrote those songs. How can you not take the credit?"

"The thing is," he said, "artists don't always understand the implications of what they're creating until it's completed and out of their hands."

"So then, where does it come from, that creativity and magic to be an artist?"

"There isn't any magic, baby" he shrugged. "It's just work. Artists are merely vessels of something greater than themselves."

I wondered if he was talking about "more than the physical realm." Maybe we were getting somewhere after all.

"But if that 'something greater' really is so great," I said, "how could it also be so cold-blooded to make me believe things like, 'My World Is Empty Without You'?"

He laughed again, and then I knew. If the Great Poet did possess The Answer, he wasn't giving it to me. I sighed and asked him my last question.

"Well, at least can you tell me if you've creatively achieved what you set out to do?"

"It's not like that, baby," he said, a smile appearing below his fuzzy moustache. "No creative person ever achieves what they set out to do, because they really don't know what they're doing."

Okay, now, that was it! Was he for real, or was he just taking the Fifth?

How could Smokey Robinson not know what the words that he and other Motown songwriters wrote would mean to a true believer like me? I'd come to his house on a quest for truth; to indict the Great Poet for filling my head with fantasies and falsehoods about love. But he'd been maddeningly friendly and humble; claiming he couldn't possibly hold that kind of power over anyone.

I wondered if I would ever find what I was looking for. Apparently the circle-of-life did not come to an end here. Maybe this encounter, promising as it had seemed, was like meeting Gordon Parks with my load of chutzpah and a crumpled screenplay that I thought would change the world.

I didn't know what else to say. He just sat there pleasantly amused; maybe thinking I was a nut case and wondering when would I leave so he could get back to his music and his family and his friends and the sports game on TV and his Pac Man game in the foyer. With my safety net of meeting him as a fellow artist yanked away, I felt myself falling into the mosh pit of starstruck territory. The reason I thought I'd come there—to hold someone accountable for what the Music had led me to believe and all the trouble that had caused—no longer seemed important.

Patti motioned that it was time for us to leave. I took a deep breath and tossed my demand for The Answer, like a bag of trash, into the River. I was being offered acceptance and camaraderie in its place; there was no debate over which to choose.

We all stood up to say goodbye.

"I'm glad you came," he said.

I think he meant it, in spite of my badgering. He walked us to the door and gave us each a farewell hug. It was then I noticed a gold charm hanging from a slender chain around his neck.

"Try God," it said.

Then again, maybe he did know something.

PART THREE

SIGNED, SEALED, DELIVERED, I'M YOURS

CHAPTER FOURTEEN

Oakland, 1980

Reach Out I'll Be There

The new decade began with a rainy night. Glistening and wet, Market Street put on a psychedelic light show of red and orange, the reflections of cars and streetlamps bouncing off the drenched asphalt and onto the glass of my upstairs windows. Out in the driveway, the rain played a calypso rhythm against landlord Louis' beat-up metal trash cans.

I'd been working all New Year's day on a calligraphy project for Halifu after a night of celebration, and evening had come again. Life felt good for a change. There was art and dance, and I was writing. Mornings I headed to the running trails in Berkeley's sleepy hills, still tucked in beneath low clouds at dawn and nearly as green as Oahu's Pali. I looked forward to starting the day with quiet stillness broken only by the thumping of my shoes and my heart.

If there was anything I'd gained from living in Oakland, it was the value of simplicity. For better or worse, the men and women who lived in my modest neighborhood, where the buses rolled along by day and The Quiet rolled in at night, had provided my first opportunity to take people at their word. It was a far cry from Los Angeles and the enforced fakery that defined life on the River.

Still, it was different now than when I'd arrived in 1973 with the Hippie Mechanic and his girlfriend. One by one, my neighbors across the driveway had all moved away. So had the devout gentleman who sold vacuum cleaner parts and whose store the Piano Player and I had terrorized during the big dust-up of 1977. There was no more "Hey, hey, hey!" or Johnnie Taylor music coming from Clarence's place. "Disco Lady" had been replaced by a Church Lady who swaddled herself in white like Lawrence of Arabia and went to her house of worship every weeknight, twice on Sunday. After James and Medina left, their apartments also saw a turnover of tenants, including a couple of belly dancers from Halifu's studio and a New Age sister with matted dreadlocks who left at four every morning to go to Habiba's Bakery, where she made carrot juice and whole wheat donuts. Despite counsel against it, she moved on to become the newest wife of an Afro-cult polygamist. Or so I heard.

Then there were the concerts. Becoming a Smokey Robinson fan hadn't turned out to be so bad after all. Patti invited me to their shows at the Greek Theatre and the Roxy in Los Angeles, and the Circle Star Theatre and Concord Pavilion in the Bay Area. Both on stage and off, the Great Poet genuinely enjoyed what he gave to people and showed his gratitude for the love they poured out to him in return. All these years later, he still had fun with "Mickey's Monkey," and when he sang "Ooh, Baby, Baby," the audience went as easily under his spell as I had in my teens. He was masterful at making each person think his song was just for them, begging for affection in that sweet high voice: eyes closed, knees bent, elbows close to his body, and arms waving with emotion, until all their applause and screaming became harmonic, like it was part of the music itself.

A few Sundays into the New Year, I was dawdling around in the morning before writing, and I turned on the radio, which I usually only listened to at night. Out of it rolled syncopation as pulsating and infectious as James Brown, satisfaction as smokin' as Otis Redding, and groups as smooth as the Isley Brothers and the O'Jays. But the lyrics of these songs were totally different. Whooping and howling, these soul men weren't begging, "Please! Please! Please!" They were calling out to Jesus.

I sat down by the radio, a bit shaken.

Why have I never heard this music before? The bold voices pouring out of my radio wouldn't let go of me. The program I had stumbled upon was a six-hour, commercial-free gospel showcase that pre-empted the usual tracks on my favorite station every Sunday morning. It was hosted by a local woman named Sheila Robinson.

Another S. Robinson. Now that's left-handed, circle-of-life funny.

The chords and beats of this soul music got to me in the same deep way that rhythm and blues had, but its lyrics weren't degrading or self-destructive. These singers were emotional and passionate about the happiness that God could bring, not crying over rejection or a failed romance. Everyone I heard on the radio—Shirley Caesar, the Clark Sisters, the Williams Brothers, the O'Neal Twins, and Reverend James Cleveland—was singing about being lifted up when you're down, hope against all odds, and how God's love could and would solve every problem. Unlike the Temptations' gloomy forecast on "I Wish It Would Rain," Rance Allen welcomed the sunshine with "Ain't No Need of Crying."

What I'd seen a glimpse of in James Brown sixteen years earlier came into full view when I heard gospel music. Nobody who sang it was afraid to tell the truth, to get raw, to let you know, "I've been in the storm, just like you, brother. But Jesus rules the clouds, he rules the waves and, hallelujah, he owns the boat! And if you fall overboard, he'll have you walking on water, if you'll let him."

There was no River Denial, no pretending the bad stuff never happened (and no putting up with it anymore, either). However messed up your life had been, gospel music proclaimed that God would make a way, not what the ministers of Motown had preached: "My Whole World Ended The Moment You Left Me."

What a revelation! The profound truth I'd handed the Great Poet in my indictment (and then tossed when he offered me friendship instead of The Answer) was, after all, true. In gospel songs, the word "God" replaced the word "you."

And so with the same true-believer zeal as when I discovered KGFJ, Los Angeles's soul music station, I plunged into Oakland's rockin' radio gospel service with Sheila Robinson every Sunday morning.

On my next trip to L.A., I told Patti what happened, and she invited me to come with her to a recital at Neighborhood Community Church, just south of downtown. Patti always seemed to understand and take seriously the things we talked about. That meant a lot. The longer I knew her, the more her openness, warmth, and faith became qualities I wanted in myself. However misguided my search for the Big Truth may have been, Patti was willing to partner with me on the journey, and I admired that her faith didn't require her to renounce being an artist. As she saw it, the various threads of God's plan all came together in the same tapestry, whether she was singing in a church or a night club.

At the recital, she sang a gospel song, "Peace Be Still," that nearly made my heart stop. People around me got emotional, waving their hands, almost in desperation. I didn't understand what was happening, but I felt it, wanting to go where that song was going; to touch the place where Patti's singing came from.

Where does it come from? What does it mean? Those two questions were still unanswered.

We left the church and went to Patti's apartment, where I told my new friend how deeply moved I'd been listening to her sing.

A knowing smile lit up her face.

"That's the spirit of the Lord," she said. "The Holy Spirit is touching your heart." She began to sing, *"Jesus, Jesus . . ."*

I stiffened; hearing the word "Jesus" was different face-to-face in her living room than it had been on the radio, but that seemed to make no sense. I'd just been with her in a Christian church and was telling Patti about my discovery of gospel music, yet I was still a Jew who'd been taught that "Jesus," like "Hitler," was a curse word that would get you a mouthful of Dial soap.

That contradiction brought to mind how, a few days earlier, I'd been fascinated with a silver and abalone necklace in the jewelry case of Cost Plus, an import store near the Oakland waterfront. I couldn't stop staring at it, and I wondered why. It was a cross.

In the household of my childhood, the cross, the swastika, and the Easter bunny were interchangeable symbols of the evil that had been perpetrated on Jews by *goyim*. So it was odd that I would be attracted to this icon which my mother had drilled into me ought to be despised. And yet there I was, nose to the glass. Intrigued by my own dilemma, I'd gone ahead and bought the necklace. Listening to Patti sing about Jesus, I experienced the same fascination. It was peculiar, but I wanted more.

"What makes Jesus so special?" I asked her. "How is he different from Buddha or any other spiritual teacher?"

Patti thought for a moment, wanting to provide an answer that would make sense to me. She stood up, using the back of her chair as a pulpit, and transformed herself into a preacher.

"Well, you see, chile, it's like this. God gave man the law, and man said to God, 'Hah! That's easy for you to say. You hand out commandments: *Do this. Don't do that.* But you're up there in heaven. You don't have to live down here in this world and put up with all the stuff that I have to deal with every day.'"

She came around and sat down on the chair, facing me.

"So God told him, 'Okay, man, I'll come where you live and show you. I'll go through not only the tough stuff you've got to live through, but also more terrible stuff than you can imagine. And I still won't fail or break the rules. But even though I'm gonna do all of that, I'm giving you an escape clause, and that escape clause's name is Jesus. Jesus is gonna take all the punishment that you deserve: for every mistake you make, and for every failure that dogs you—past, present, and future. All you have to do is let him into your heart."

She stood up and went to her bookshelf, pulling out a white leather volume.

"Have you ever read the Bible?" she asked, holding it up. "The Old Testament, maybe?"

I had once bought a used King James Version at a yard sale but could not get past the first few pages. Having only read as far Adam and Eve getting kicked out of the Garden, I told Patti that if God were as mean as he sounded in the Bible, I didn't think I could follow him.

After I returned to Oakland, Patti sent me a copy of *The Living Bible*, a much easier-to-read version. The next Sunday morning, I tuned in to my radio gospel program and pulled out my new Bible; it seemed to fall open of its own accord to these words:

> "I don't understand myself at all, for I really want to do what is right, but I can't. I know perfectly well that what I am doing is wrong. But I can't help myself." [1]

A few lines down, these words stood out to me, as if they'd been highlighted:

> "For the power of the life-giving Spirit—and this power is mine through Christ Jesus—has freed me from the vicious circle of sin and death." [2]

And then I heard a voice, not audible but speaking to me as clearly as my own thoughts:

"It's not that you don't know what to do; the problem is, you don't have the power to live up to what you know."

POWER. That got my attention.

It was true; I had none. I thought of all the things I wanted to change in myself but couldn't. No matter how much encouragement and affirmation I received, when it came to breaking bad habits and living out the positive things I saw in others, I made it look as if I were growing, but I was still failing. Underneath the exotic identity I'd garbed myself in—dancer, writer, artist—when I was alone, stripped of artifice and achievements, the Piranhas laid waste to my soul as viciously as they always had. Only now I was better at disguising that tumult.

Never had I considered power to be something I could have without another person giving it to me. All my chanting, "Power to the people!" when I was in college didn't make up for the powerlessness of being an outcast in elementary school; a potential casualty of atomic war on the playground; a pregnant teenager in exile, forced to relinquish my baby and told to go home and pretend it never happened; a prisoner locked up with convicted murderers who looked just like me; a lover to men who were scoundrels.

"You don't have the power to live up to what you know."

The words were frightening, but they also held the key to what had been missing in my search for the Big Truth. I'd never had the power to overcome a lifetime of hurt and rejection or the smoldering anger it produced, which I'd tried to pass off as my creative fire. Most of all, I didn't have the power to stand up to the River and lay claim to who I really was.

Whatever there was yet to learn about Jesus, I couldn't deny the reality of this moment resonating in my soul: an experience with *Something* that was indeed more than the physical and greater than myself.

A great swelling tide (was it love?) began to pour into me. Tears filled my eyes, but I wasn't sad. Then, out of the radio came the towering voices of a local church choir whose worship service was being broadcast that Sunday on my gospel show:

> "I love the Lord, he heard my cries, and pitied every groan; long as I live, and troubles rise, I'll hasten to his throne...."[3]

And I knew, finally, I found what I'd been looking for.

---

[1] Romans 7:15, 16, 17, TLB

[2] Romans 8:2, TLB. Verses marked TLB are taken from The Living Bible, copyright @ 1971. Used by permission of Tyndale House Publishers, Inc., Wheaton, Illinois 60189. All rights reserved.

[3] Isaac Watts – Public domain

CHAPTER FIFTEEN

Oakland, 1980

Can I Get A Witness

The great spiritual revelation I had that Sunday morning marked me as permanently as a tattoo, but as Diana Ross said, "You Can't Hurry Love." It was going to take time for change to set in. I was still finding my way but now with a fragile sense of being plugged into something wonderful that I couldn't define. The lyrics of gospel songs began taking hold in my mind, just as those of Motown had, though I doubted I'd ever be free of the irresistible force, like gravity itself, with which the music I'd listened to as a teenager still tugged at my soul.

 I turned my attention back to writing, encouraged by authors Curt Gentry and Barry Hannah with whom I stayed in touch after the Santa Barbara Writers Conference. And a novel-writing class at UC Berkeley Extension looked like just the ticket. The instructor was Leonard Bishop, a broad-shouldered, silver-haired shout of a man. At first I couldn't stand him. He was gruff and coarse, too earthy and blunt even for my taste. I complained to my parents in one of our weekly telephone calls about how awful he was. My mother offered a nugget of insight.

"When you were little," she said, "every semester you'd come home from the first day of school and tell me you hated your new teacher. But by the time it was over, he was your favorite."

We'll see about that.

Leonard Bishop was from the mean streets of New York, author of a dozen novels, and a contemporary of Mario Puzo, William Styron, and Norman Mailer. His writing wasn't unlike the hard-boiled style of Richard Wright, and in time I began to see past the crust of his personality to a mind that was sharp and darkly funny; underneath his tough-guy exterior, he'd given his Jewish heart to Jesus.

Leonard was determined to aggravate, provoke, and dare his students to become great writers, and I was ready. I told the temp agency I was no longer available for work assignments on Mondays which, along with Sundays, became my writing days. On Saturday, I speed-dialed life's domestic details: laundry, errands, and housework; and took at least one African dance class with Malonga or Halifu at the studio. Then on Sunday, with my world clean, my body refreshed, and my soul on fire after listening to Sheila Robinson's radio gospel fest, I could go down the rabbit hole and devote two full days in the wonderland of writing my novel about soul singer, Clayton Willow.

Being on the Berkeley campus every Wednesday night was reminiscent of going to UCLA with my father, and of the semester I'd spent with Buriel at San Francisco State. Two years after his death, I was still having bizarre dreams and florid nightmares that seemed like real encounters with him. I could feel his shoulder touching mine, even smell him. In that strange, parallel universe I would ask, "How are you doing?" and his answer was always the same: "Moving, moving . . ."

Listening to gospel music and reading the Bible that Patti sent me opened up a new dimension to my story about Clayton

Willow. I became fascinated with the rise and fall of Sam Cooke: how he'd crossed over from being a gospel singer to an international pop superstar, only to wind up shot to death in a sleazy Los Angeles motel in 1964. The unsavory circumstances of his death were suspicious (there was talk he'd been tricked into going to the motel, and rumors of a police cover-up), but the fallen-star legend that lived on after he died was epic.

When I read the story of Jesus's temptation in the wilderness, in which the devil offers him all the kingdoms of the world, I decided my novel would be an allegory of what it means to achieve everything you ever wanted but lose who you are in the exchange. (Jesus and the devil aside, it was a transaction I was more than familiar with.)

So I added the component of church and gospel music to my soul singer's background and set my story in Chicago, hometown to both Sam Cooke and Patti. Clayton Willow grows up a decade behind Sam, idolizing him and dreaming of following in his hero's footsteps. Like Sam, Clayton starts out singing in church and then heads for the pop singer path, positive in that arrogant way of young men that the tragic ending which happened to Sam will not happen to him.

Though a story like Clayton Willow's might not appear to fit the write-what-you-know maxim, I felt connected to my characters from living in the ebb and flow of a city like Oakland, with its night train and weedy fishing place, its neighborhood griots in their skull caps and dashikis, its music stores out of which the sounds of John Coltrane and Pharaoh Saunders floated to the sidewalk, and its old bearded hipsters chanting their mantra, "Everything is everything." Just as when I was a teenager discovering James Brown and Richard Wright, it didn't occur to me that I wasn't entitled to be so deeply moved in the ways that I was; or that I didn't have the right to write about what I hadn't personally lived. If that were true, how could a historical novel or any work of fiction be written?

To my relief, Leonard told our class that it was more important to believe in what we were doing than to know what we were doing. That suited me just fine. Every week I submitted a new chapter to him, hoping he'd pick my work to read aloud for discussion. When the university semester ended, Leonard invited me to join a private workshop he convened on Monday nights at the home of one of his students. I was happy to continue receiving his guidance.

And this time, I had to admit that everything had turned out just like my mom said it would.

Light My Fire

At least twice a week, I could be found pounding the floor over at Everybody's Creative Arts Center. No matter how weary, cranky, or stressed I was, moving my body to the rhythm of African drums took me to a place where I experienced myself as liberated, beautiful, and on intimate terms without becoming a victim.

And after months of listening to Sheila Robinson's six-hour Sunday gospel show, it occurred to me that the way the African drummers played off one another, almost in competition, was akin to the call-and-response of gospel singers. Like Clara Ward and her sisters who delivered the Good News like machine guns; or the gruff squall of men like Ira Tucker and the Dixie Hummingbirds. Or like Joe Ligon and the Mighty Clouds of Joy whose syncopated madness would escalate until the words became unintelligible; burned up like cosmic debris in a cataclysmic battle-to-the-death of holy hollers, whoops, and growls. Then there were the gentlemen singers, like the Jackson Southernaires, and the sweet harmony of the Clark Sisters, with their cascading, jazzy riffs and Twinkie burning up the organ.

Like African dance, gospel was an unself-conscious, unedited, irresistible explosion: nothing held back. In the same cathartic way that dance released life's pressure and kept my body fit, my Sunday romance with gospel music gave me strength for the week, and kept a lid on the unfulfilled yearning and emotional turmoil which that other Music had bred in my soul.

I also discovered that not only Sam Cooke but most of the soul singers whose music I'd been listening to for years had started out in church and then crossed over to rhythm and blues, Motown, or pop. That included Johnnie Taylor who'd stepped in as Sam's replacement to sing gospel with the Soul Stirrers before recording songs like "Who's Making Love?" "It's Cheaper to Keep Her" and "Disco Lady."

Well, well, well. I didn't know what she had in her record collection, but the Church Lady who'd moved into Clarence's apartment across the driveway might yet have something in common with my former neighbor. One day I ran into her as she was leaving for her nightly meeting. She was swathed in white from head to foot and could have been mistaken for a sister in the Nation of Islam. I told her I was just starting to read the Bible and wanted to understand it better. I asked if they had Bible study at her church.

"Praise the Lawd! Our church has Bible study every Wednesday night," she said. "You can come with me on tomorrow."

It was a cordial, if not surprising, invitation. But I was about to leave for a trip to Chicago. I needed to see Clayton Willow's hometown for myself, and Patti's parents had invited me to come stay with them. I think her mom was also interested in helping along what she called my "conversion experience." I was still having a fine old time on Sundays listening to the radio and hadn't felt ready to attend church. Plus I didn't know which one to go to; there were probably a dozen within four blocks of my house.

I thanked the Church Lady for inviting me and said I was getting ready to go away on a trip and didn't want to start the Bible study and then have to stop. I promised I would go with her when I came back from Chicago.

Her face crumpled up in anger.

"That's the devil talkin'!" she hollered, shaking her Bible at me. Her thin white shawl came loose and fluttered behind her like an apparition. "That's the devil makin' you not want to go to church. Nothin' but the devil! You hear me? It's the devil!"

Taken aback by her outburst, I turned away and left her yelling in the driveway by herself. Inside my house I tried to breathe and remember who I was, and Who I was falling in love with. I locked the door and pulled the curtains together to block her out. That was exactly why I hadn't gone to church.

Sweet Home Chicago

My trip to Chicago turned out better than expected, for the sake of my novel and my eternal soul. Patti enlisted a friend of hers to pick me up from O'Hare, providing instructions that he'd recognize me when I got off the plane, because I looked "like a flower." He dropped me off at her family's house on South Rhodes, and the Henleys welcomed me as enthusiastically as my own parents did when I came home for a visit. I was loved, fed, and counseled about my budding walk with Jesus by Patti's mother, Marion, her father, Robert, and her grandmother, Dawn, whom everyone called Great-Great. Marion even arranged for her friends to help me find my way around Chicago so I could set straight the details of Clayton Willow's life. With my camera and a notebook, I did my best to soak up Chicago's images and impressions, relying on my guides to fill in the gaps for me about how it was back in Clayton's day.

Before I left, Patti's mother said that she believed I'd received Jesus in my heart and pronounced her blessing on me as having had a conversion experience. I was now certifiably a Christian, though it would be an uphill struggle to explain to my parents that no conversion on Earth could turn me into a *goy*. I promised Patti's family that I would start going to church when I got back to Oakland. I didn't want to let them down after all they'd done for me, but I was still nervous about running into any more saints like the Church Lady.

The first Sunday morning after returning to Oakland from Chicago, I decided to attend service at a small brick church in my neighborhood because it looked nice. I had no idea what the different denominations were, so I can't tell you which of those it might have been. I just made sure, by watching from my window upstairs which way she caught the bus, that I wasn't going to the same church as my zealous neighbor across the driveway.

At first it was thrilling when the choir came two-stepping down the aisle, their colorful robes swishing as they belted out "Walking Up The King's Highway" at full throttle. But then it got a little weird. I never stopped to consider what it might mean to a small black congregation for a Jewish hippie to show up in their house of worship, and the curiosity it aroused was more than I could handle. Plus, when the pastor did his invitation to be born again, it came with automatic church membership, tithing on the spot, and a sign-up for what task you would be doing at the church next week. I was polite and stayed until the end of service, but I never went back.

The rest of my Market Street Sunday mornings were spent worshipping at Our Lady of the Radio and reading *The Living Bible*, hoping that God (and the Henleys, if they ever found out) would forgive me.

Gotta Serve Somebody

After my trip to Chicago, I decided to no longer hold it against Smokey Robinson for telling me that he was ordinary. In fact, I came to agree that no creative person ever really does know what he or she is doing. Bob Dylan, for example, seemed to leave it to other people to make careers out of explaining his art, while he just went on creating it. Even Leonard Bishop said, "Critics or time are what promote writing into art; the writer isn't thinking about that. The writer is just writing."

I guess when the artist steps outside his art to look at it, the art is no longer his. He becomes an observer of it rather than the vessel for it, which is probably the reason why so many artists hit the dead end of their own mythology.

I had always believed that getting close to the artist would bring me closer to the magic, and that would ignite the magic in me. The compulsion to find that had driven my life since the TAMI show. But the more I watched how audiences acted at Smokey Robinson's concerts, the clearer it became that the hysterical fans who jumped up and did the most hollering at the stage weren't trying to express their appreciation; they were trying to get *him* to notice *them*. As if interrupting the artist to make themselves more important than his art would bequeath to them his status. I now realized that the Great Poet had done me a favor by turning my attention away from the pedestal on which I'd put him.

Thinking about how Clayton Willow wanted to follow in the footsteps of his idol, Sam Cooke, but didn't believe he'd make the same mistakes, got me wondering if being on a pedestal might actually be more like teetering on an overturned crate with a rope around your neck. One wrong move and the bottom drops out.

Every man who's reached the top wonders, Where can I go from here? Unlike the victorious mountain climber who stakes his flag atop Mount Everest, arrival is more often a bloody survivor's crawl toward a treacherous pinnacle. At the top, footing is unstable. At the top, your next move is always down.

Like others before him, Clayton Willow wondered about the failure of success. Why hadn't it been what he expected? Sometimes our last shred of wisdom only sends us seeking a wiser man. But who could he talk to now? He'd walked away from those who tried to warn him, never considering what it meant to trade obscurity for fame. He was no longer in charge of even his own perception of himself. The press, the fans, the record company had all reduced his identity to its lowest common denominators: sex, race, and money. He now found himself having it all but having nothing. He'd reached his goal, but Clayton Willow no longer knew who he was.

Then he had the dream . . .

Ragged shreds of moonlight hung from a weary sky. The street groaned as an "L" train rumbled overhead. The sign above the Chicago storefront spelled out the words "Appearing To-night" in red plastic letters, and a line of people waiting to get in stretched for miles and miles down the street. Knee-deep by fours and fives they huddled behind one another, forming a wide human ribbon that twisted around the block, disappearing into black oblivion.

Clayton took his place in the line and waited, a sense of anticipation and a little bit of fear, just like when he was getting ready to go on stage. Only the clattering rumble of the train could be heard in between vast pauses of emptiness. Though they numbered in the thousands, the crowd was strangely silent. He wondered who he was waiting to see. "Appearing To-night" *was all the sign said. Without a sound, the throng inched closer to the door.*

Where was his manager? The band? Where was anybody he knew? The mob of people around him wore blank faces that seemed to melt into a blur of brown, black, and gray. The wicked smile of a Cheshire cat danced in flickering broken shadows, but he could not place it on anyone's lips.

Up ahead at the door, a dapper brown-skinned man in white greeted the people as they entered. White tux, white trimmings, even white shoes against his rich cocoa color made him look razor sharp. He flashed a gleaming smile at everyone who came to the door and handed each one a white rose as they entered. The crowd squeezed through the door like cake batter, and Clayton wondered how so many people could fit into this one tiny little place. Maybe it wasn't a night club. He looked back up at the marquee overhead, but nothing had changed; it still said, "Appearing To-night."

A fat woman in a baggy dress with her stockings rolled down around her ankles was in front of him. Holding her hand was a little boy about six. A bent-back elder leaned on his cane as his turn came to go in, and a seductive beauty the color of rye toast followed the old man through the door. Finally it was Clayton's turn. As he stepped up to the entrance, the handsome man came forward to greet him face to face. My God, thought Clayton in shock, it's Sam Cooke!

"Man, you're a sight for a wanderin' soul," said Clayton, *marveling at the unexpected reunion. Lord, it felt good to see Sam again.*

Sam flashed the sparkling smile that had won him the world.

"Welcome, brother. I've been expecting you."

Clayton could almost hear that silky voice singing lead on "Wonderful" with the Soul Stirrers.

"Appearing To-night." The red marquee seemed to be blinking at him from inside of Sam's eyes. Clayton tried to concentrate, but he was so overwhelmed by this pleasant meeting, he couldn't think. He wanted to linger in Sam's presence and reminisce how good it had all been—the gospel highway, the sweet inspiration of Jesus that had first compelled him to stand in front of people and sing. Now here he was with the man whose path he'd sought to follow.

A white rose was pressed into his hand, and Clayton glided effortlessly with the crowd toward something at the front that everyone was gently pushing forward to see. He squinted, trying to adjust to the darkened change of light inside. Glancing back, he saw Sam standing by the door, the glow from outside shining around him like an aura. Sam smiled again and waved him on to the front.

When Clayton reached the stage, he saw a gleaming silver casket covered with white roses, its Dutch door open and its white satin lining crisp and clean, holding precious cargo. As the crowd pressed him toward it, Clayton thought he heard the faint rat-tat-tat of gunshots. He spun around quickly toward the door, but it was closed now, and Sam had disappeared. When he turned back to look into the shiny coffin, it struck him that he wasn't in a night club but a funeral home. A fiendish pair of hands snatched the breath from his throat as he realized that it was he, Clayton Willow, who was the center of attention, lying there in the casket, **"Appearing To-night."**

CHAPTER SIXTEEN

Oakland, 1981

A Change Is Gonna Come

Along with losing my copacetic neighbors across the driveway, not much of what I'd once loved about Market Street remained. The little boys in their shiny shoes and three-piece suits who used to walk to church with their petticoat sisters had all grown up. The midnight voices now rising from the sidewalk weren't the serenade of young men praising their last rendezvous but of schemers plotting their next rip-off. The Quiet was replaced with the roar of motorcycles and Teena Maria blasting from car radios. Even my beloved Oakland Local had finally been retired from its faithful service to the Twinkie factory, perhaps another casualty of the Dan White debacle. I mourned its demise. Like the men in my life, the train had become an old friend passing by in the night, blowing whistle kisses and loving me on the way to loving someone else.

The Wash-O-Mat up on Telegraph was also losing its charm. A white-haired black man named Eddie had been hired to take care of the machines. Eddie wore a big heavy cross that looked like it ought to have been mounted on the top of a building and always greeted me with a lot of God-bless-you's before prattling off his complaints while I folded my towels.

"I ain't got nothin.' Ain't never gonna have nothin.' Nobody understands me," Eddie would recite. Then he'd smile. "Now that I know you, can we be friends?"

Once in a while he would ask me to marry him.

Then landlord Louis came by to tell me he'd decided to sell the Market Street properties. The buyer was a black businesswoman who'd purchased both buildings for fifty thousand dollars. She had entrepreneurial plans, the first of which was to turn the storefront under my house into a boutique, and the second was to take up residence where I was living. I wanted to stay, but she said I had to go.

Having to find a new home for the first time in eight years was tough, but other things in my life were changing as well. The corporate bankers for whom I'd been working as a temp had asked me to come on board with them full time when their team moved to Oakland, and I accepted. Despite our differences, we'd managed to plant ourselves in shallow soil alongside a tributary of the River.

Now I'd be able to drive to downtown Oakland for work instead of commuting across the Bay Bridge on AC Transit. I would have to show up five days a week; no more Mondays off to work on my novel. But the lure of a regular payday and benefits like health insurance, paid holidays and vacation, and free membership at the swanky Oakland Athletic Club, one of our corporate clients, was enough to make me believe it wouldn't affect my writing about a man who sold his soul to the devil.

The bank would own my life, but in exchange they would take care of it. Seemed like a fair deal. Besides, I wasn't going to stay there forever; I was an artist after all, not a banker. And I showed up at the office accordingly, tying my big 1980s hair off my face with a purple zebra-striped scarf. I wore a black leather motorcycle jacket over a Norma Kamali ankle-length dress, footless dancer's tights, and iridescent green snakeskin hightops. The bank's corporate clients adored me, stopping by daily just to see what I was wearing. My secretarial skills were outstanding, so the bankers didn't demand that I dress, act, or think like them. That is, until the veneer of agreeability upon which we'd set up camp wore off.

But like most things, in the beginning it was all good.

Amazing Grace

I began looking for a new place to live by perusing the *Oakland Tribune's* classifieds every morning before I went to work. A one-bedroom apartment with a fireplace and hardwood floors caught my eye, and I dialed the number listed. The manager said she wasn't available to meet me there on my lunch hour, but that I should just go by and take a look. It was located in a lovely neighborhood of winding streets that branched out from upper Park Boulevard and headed straight up into the lush Oakland hills.

The rental unit was in a salmon-colored four-plex, the only apartment building on a tree-lined half circle of homes. The street itself, Dolores Avenue, sat at the crest of a hill overlooking the rustic beauty of Dimond Canyon and the pinnacle of the Mormon Temple. Down the hill was the bustling Fruitvale district with its public library, Safeway supermarket, and Cybelle's pizza parlor.

I parked the Beetle and got out to look around. The apartment building was on the terraced high side of the street, resting atop four small garages. Walking up the steps, I shielded my eyes from the sun's noonday glare and peered through the window of the empty living room of the downstairs unit that the manager had told me was for rent.

"Hi there!" I heard someone call. Next door, headed toward the landing of an enormous two-story white house, I saw a twenty-something red-haired woman lugging groceries and a baby up the concrete stairs.

"Hi," I called back. She was fumbling at the front door with her keys and bags and the child on her hip.

"I'm not a burglar," it seemed best to say. "Just checking out the apartment that's for rent here."

"You looking for a place to live?" she said, shifting the baby to her other hip as she opened the door. "We're moving out. You can have this one. Come on over and see it."

The house was huge: ten rooms, including three bedrooms upstairs that all had walk-in closets with crank-out windows. Its Craftsman touches were characteristic of homes in the Oakland hills. From the upstairs front window, you could see all the way to the Oakland Coliseum. *Another perch in the sky*, I thought, imagining my desk and typewriter facing that impressive view. Also upstairs was a large bathroom, its floor neatly tiled in white hexagons, with both a stall shower and a freestanding claw foot tub.

The downstairs front window faced a wall of liquid amber trees lining both sides of the street. Leaded glass pocket doors divided the living room from an elegant dining area; I could host sumptuous dinner parties at which my guests and I would engage in brilliant discussions about the meaning of art and life over a fabulously appointed table. It was easy to see myself living in this house; it had everything I wanted, only more of it and bigger.

"The stove and fridge are the landlady's so you'll have those," said the tenant, whose name was Holly, as we passed through the spacious kitchen to a cheerful breakfast room. On our way to the back door, we came to a washer and dryer which were also staying behind. *Perfect*, I thought. Now I could break up with Eddie and the Wash-O-Mat. I wondered about a curious little door mounted in the middle of the wall; perhaps it was a compartment for storing detergent.

"What's this?" I asked Holly.

She popped open the latch, revealing tin walls and a pile of rumpled bedding and clothes.

"It's a laundry chute," she said. "It comes down from the closet in the upstairs back bedroom."

I was ecstatic. Now I could give my dirty duds *and* Eddie the shaft!

We stepped outside to a sunny backyard with a dry fish pond and a messy red bottlebrush tree. A portly white cat, the size of a spaniel, stopped to examine me with Halloween yellow eyes and then continued lumbering along the rear fence.

There was one hitch. The rent was more than double what I'd been paying. Holly said that she and her family would be out at the end of the month, and the owner hadn't listed the house yet. She wrote down the landlady's phone number, and I hesitated for a moment; even with my full-time salary at the bank, the rent was still higher than I could afford.

Saying goodbye, I folded the slip of paper and stepped out onto the front porch. A light breeze blew the loose ends of my hair across my face, and I brushed them away. The afternoon stillness was almost a presence in itself. It was as calm on Dolores Avenue on a weekday afternoon as it had been when The Quiet rolled in at night on Market Street. All I could hear was the paper-like rustling of tree leaves and low throb of traffic a few blocks away.

What a turn of events. I'd complained about being kicked out of Market Street, and yet look at where I'd wound up. I didn't believe in coincidence; even calling it left-handed or circle-of-life seemed wrong, though it was as similar as you could get to how a lot of things had happened in my life.

Name It And Claim It

"Roommate."

The word popped into my head as soon as I got in the Beetle. The Dolores Avenue house was big enough to accommodate another person, and if we split the rent and utilities, it would be affordable. A woman I knew at the bank was also looking for a place to live, and though Jeanie was more traditional in her ways (she was a career banker who wore Macy's suits with high heels, and all of her furniture matched), I was certain we'd get along because she was a Christian.

Becoming a Christian had opened a new true-believer window of perception for me, one just as mistakenly literal-minded as when I discovered Motown. I assumed that everyone who said they were a follower of Jesus was on the same wave length as I was, and that the Bible provided universally simple resolutions to life's most complicated problems. Ordinary words like "glory" or "bless" or "praise" became imbued with profound meaning to me, as if I belonged to a special club and was being spoken to in code. Whether those words were applied to a spring sale at Capwell's department store, a social courtesy when somebody sneezed, or a brand of dog treats, in my mind, they were infused with the same awesome, Earth-shattering revelation now bearing down on my soul by the holy spirit of God.

It would be a while before I understood that human failures like betrayal, deceit, lust, greed, envy, and plain old meanness dogged the followers of Jesus just like they did those living for the world, the flesh, and the devil. After what happened to me with the Church Lady, I ought to have known that the River also runs through Christian campgrounds. But true believers are rarely willing to tote the baggage of wisdom into new terrain. We want what we believe to be true more than we want to deal with the messiness of what really is true.

But like I said, in the beginning, it was all good.

Jeanie was a great roommate, matching furniture and Macy's wardrobe aside. She was considerate, honest, and fair; and wherever she was on the church spectrum, she knew more about the Bible than I did. Her days at the bank were longer than mine, but when we met at night in the kitchen over the tea kettle, or munching leftovers standing up, she was generous in sharing what she knew with me. I appreciated that.

Jeanie took the large middle bedroom upstairs, and I settled into the one with the laundry chute, setting up my writing desk in the front room overlooking the treetops. We soon discovered we weren't alone. Dolores Avenue was overrun with squirrels whose chattering sounded like squeaky sneakers on a basketball court, and raccoons that partied in the garbage cans all night.

I learned from neighbors that the colossal white cat I'd seen trudging around was Emperor Norton, named after the nineteenth-century San Francisco eccentric who proclaimed himself Imperial Majesty of the United States. I made friends with his big fat highness by inviting him into the laundry room for a raw egg once in a while. Like my previous boyfriends, Norton decided that I belonged to him, and as I relaxed on a lounger in our backyard one afternoon, he backed up, lifted his tail, and sprayed me.

Upper Park Boulevard was a perfect neighborhood in which to jog, because the hill had several circular streets; you could start out in one direction and return home without ever having to backtrack. The sound of birds calling to one another across the canyon reminded me of Mount Washington, and the pungent smell of wild plants sparked memories of my LSD-driven adventures in the forest.

Down the hill from Dolores Avenue was a picturesque, wooded creek and a park with a swimming pool. Wearing a bikini under my sweats, I'd jog up Park Boulevard to the Leimert Bridge, cross over to Waterhouse or Lyman, then run downhill to Hanly Road, arriving at the pool hot and sweaty. After a refreshing swim, it was a quick walk up the hill on El Centro, and I was back on my street.

Nothing could have been more wonderful than to have all of that right outside my door. It was the combination of everything happy that I'd had in Calistoga and Hawaii. I loved my new home and my new neighborhood, and I never had one day in which I wasn't thankful to be living there.

Tell Me Something Good

I didn't mean to keep asking for stuff, but I needed a new car.

My parents wanted to visit me and see the Dolores Avenue house. I'd never been able to invite them anywhere else I'd lived, so I set up a sofa bed in the living room, right in the front of the fireplace, which I knew they would enjoy. But picking them up at the airport or driving them around in the Beetle was another story; it was thirteen years old and totally crapped out. The hood was banged up, and all four fenders were dented. My seat belt had been cut in half in 1974 when the lock got stuck and I had to be scissored out, and my morning start-up ritual was letting it roll down the hill in second gear, then popping the clutch. A broke-down battery had tipped over in the back and burned a hole in the floor, and the front passenger seat was missing altogether. For my sake, I didn't care if the Beetle was an embarrassing wreck, but there was no way I could put my parents and their luggage in it.

On my run through the canyon one morning I thought, *Lord, I need ten thousand dollars to buy a new car. Not to show off, but because the one I have is worn out, and I can't drive my parents in it.* It wasn't exactly a prayer; I was just talking to God, and that was that. But I had a feeling he heard me.

The next day I headed to work at the bank, parked in the lot, and then decided to go across the street to grab a cup of coffee. As I was coming back to the office, I waited for the signal to change and thought about having asked for that ten grand. It was weird, but I had the best feeling that I was going to get it. Then I panicked, remembering a super creepy TV program I'd watched as a kid about a down-and-out family who got this supposedly good luck charm—a monkey's paw—but for each thing they requested and received, something really bad happened, like a horrible accident or a member of their family died.

Immediately I thought, *Lord, whatever you're gonna do for me, I don't want it to come at anyone else's expense. I don't want my parents to die and leave it to me. I want it free and clear, no strings attached.*

The panic went away, and the good feeling came back. I was aware by then that having faith meant trusting God, but I couldn't help wondering how that windfall was going to happen.

The traffic signal turned to green, and I stepped off the curb, the cup of coffee warming my hands against the morning chill. And then I heard one word, as loud and as clear as I've ever heard anything spoken to me in my life:

"*Reno.*"

I nearly tripped in the middle of Franklin Avenue. Patti had invited me to meet her in Reno a few days before Christmas for a Smokey show. We would stay together in her hotel room and have a ball hanging out; I already had my bus ticket. I marveled at what I sensed was the answer to my prayer—Reno would be the perfect place to get ten thousand dollars free and clear without anybody getting hurt.

I couldn't wait to tell Jeanie. That night, when I heard the door unlock and her high-heeled footsteps on the wood floor, I ran downstairs.

"Guess what!" I said. "I asked God for ten thousand dollars, and he's gonna give it to me when I go to Reno!"

Jeanie shook her head till the waves in her blond hair went straight.

"No he's not," she said sternly, taking off her coat.

"What are you talking about?"

"Because that's gambling, and God doesn't work that way."

What? I shut up fast; forced to admit that besides knowing nothing about church, I didn't know anything about sin, either. Sobered by this spiritual fact, I totally dismissed the idea of getting ten thousand dollars in Reno as ridiculous, stupid, and insane; deleting the cavalier request from my mind, and looking forward solely to a weekend of winter fun with Patti.

༄

The bus ride to Reno was scenic and beautiful; snow hugged the sides of the road like big scoops of ice cream. But when I got to the hotel, no one from Los Angeles had arrived. I called Patti from a pay phone, and she told me that fog had grounded all air traffic.

"Just go on and check into the hotel room using my name," she said. "We'll be there tomorrow in time for the first show."

The next morning, with still a few hours before Patti and the band were to arrive, I decided to take a walk and see what Reno was about. It appeared to be a ratty little town, and the longer I watched men and women throwing away their money, the more stupid gambling seemed to me. Then, in the reflection of a casino's glass front, I noticed a disheveled stranger lurking behind me. So I ducked into the first open door on the street and disappeared into a noisy, smoke-filled maze.

I'd landed in Harold's Casino where, even this early in the morning, gamblers were hotly betting, and some were already drunk. The slots at Harold's were old school: banging, mechanical contraptions that reminded me of the Mount Washington train, the Oakland Local, and the bank's teletype machine. Still seduced by the sound of clanging metal, I approached a row of nickel slots; a young man with a money changer on his belt stood nearby, and I traded him two quarters for ten nickels.

I just wanted to see how the slot machines worked.

I put in one nickel, slowly pulled the handle, and watched the three carousels spin wildly until they stopped. A five. An apple. A two. I put in another nickel and pulled the handle again. A lemon, a seven, and a little guy driving a stagecoach. I did that five more times, waiting for the carousels to stop, and then studying the icons in the three windows, trying to understand what made people blow their rent money and wreck their marriages on this. The seventh time I did it, the little guy driving the stagecoach popped up in all three windows. But nothing happened. No bells, no whistles, no lights. Nothing dropped out of the machine. I signaled the change guy to take a look.

"Did I win something?" I asked.

His eyes bulged out of his head like a Looney Tunes character.

"Oh my God! Did you get that for fifty cents?" he screamed.

"No, I got it for thirty-five. What is it?"

His hands shaking, the change guy pointed to a display at the top of the machine. There were two separate dollar amounts and a lighted red arrow. The machine was a double progressive, meaning each time the arm was pulled, the total jackpot switched from one amount to the other. One of the figures read $103.

The other figure, the one that the red arrow was pointing to, was $9,106.

My request to God for ten thousand dollars had gotten the smackdown from Jeanie's religious rebuke. Now there was only one thing I could think.

God, you're a trip.

The change guy muttered into his walkie-talkie, and a security guard appeared and locked the machine. Evidently something was wrong with it. On hitting a jackpot, the slots were supposed to make a lot of noise, spit two hundred dollars, then freeze. I'm guessing my nickel machine may have hit a jackpot multiple times before I showed up, in order for its payout to swell to nearly five figures. But if you've ever watched how people gamble at machines, they mostly just stand there like machines themselves, feeding coins into the slots and pulling the lever, smoking, drinking, eating, talking; not paying attention.

I'd taken my time to watch how the machine worked, wanting only my fifty cents' worth of clanging. Whether anyone believed me or not, I wasn't gambling.

"We'll need your driver's license and Social Security card, Miss," said the guard.

I'd been wandering around with only the hotel key and a few coins in my pocket.

"I don't have those with me," I told the guard.

"Then you'll have to go back to your hotel and get them," he said. "I'll wait here for you."

Yeah, sure. I didn't believe him, nor did I believe I'd actually won anything. But what a great story I'd have to tell Patti and everybody when they arrived. I walked back to the hotel, thinking it was a hilarious mistake. When I returned to the casino, I was surprised to see the guard still posted at the slot machine. I handed him my driver's license and Social Security card, and he gave me an IRS form to fill out. Then he took me downstairs into an underground city that I never imagined was beneath the casino floor. We walked a long time, winding through hallways, until finally arriving at a teller's cage. The guard pushed my documents into the shallow well under the cage's barred window.

The teller donned a pair of rhinestone-trimmed reading glasses that hung from a chain around her neck and proceeded to read my paperwork.

And then, just like how I'd asked for it, somebody I didn't know, whom I would never see again, counted out ninety-one hundred-dollar bills, topped them with a five and a one, then pushed the whole pile of cash into the well under the bars to me.

Free and clear.

The wad of green was as big as a head of romaine lettuce and wasn't about to fit in the same pocket as my three remaining nickels.

"Could I please have a bag or something to put it in?" I asked.

The teller sighed and left for a moment, then came back with a drawstring sack, like the kind that hold liquor bottles, and pushed it under the bars. It reminded me of the denim money bag handed to me by a departing inmate in jail.

For a split second I thought about how much fun it would be to wait for Patti to show up in the room and then fling all those hundred-dollar bills all up in the air. But then I remembered the seedy stranger who'd been following me, and I asked the guard if he would escort me to the bank to get a cashier's check, which he did.

As soon as I got to my hotel room I called my parents to tell them what happened. Then I called Jeanie. I couldn't help rubbing my big moment into her theology.

"So . . . God doesn't work that way?"

Patti and everyone in the band, even the Great Poet, went nuts when they found out. That night, comedian George Wallace, who was opening the show, added a new joke to his routine.

"You know, my girlfriend's here with me in Reno, and she's a religious girl. She's got faith. She loves God. In fact, she loves

God so much, she asked him before we got here to give her ten thousand dollars to buy a new car. And you know what? She hit a jackpot on the slots for nine grand this morning. I guess that means God took his ten percent off the top."

CHAPTER SEVENTEEN

Oakland, 1982

Gimme Shelter

While I no longer had Mondays free to write, I continued to work on my novel about Clayton Willow every Sunday, after drawing inspiration from my six hours of gospel music on the radio. And as I wrote about my soul singer's loss of identity, perspective, and footing once he reached the pinnacle of success, a bizarre encounter from my 1970 European road trip with Marvin came to mind.

When we'd had our fill of Antonio Gaudi and the beaches of Costa Del Sol, Marvin and I hit the road north, intending to wind up in Paris. The two little horses of our Citröen huffed and puffed as we ascended the Italian Alps, going in and out of tunnels so many times that it became like a rhythm: entering darkness, eyes quickly adjusting; slowly a silvery disk of light beginning to emerge, growing larger as we sped toward it; finally exiting the tunnel into sunshine and a gorgeous view of the mountains.

After a while, the cadence of going in and out, circling up and down, became a pleasant journey, like being on a fun ride at Disneyland. Or a waterbed.

But then we entered one tunnel and did not come out within the time to which our psyches had grown accustomed. There was no silvery disk ahead. Just sickly yellow lights along the wall and massive roaring fans, like airplane engines, suspended from the ceiling. Marvin, who was driving, was the first to freak out.

"Look out the window, look behind us! What's back there?" he yelled, his voice cracking like a prepubescent boy's. "Can you see where we came in? Maybe we should turn around!"

He adjusted his rimless glasses, looked in the rear-view mirror, and tried to assess if it might be safe to hang a U-turn in the middle of the tunnel. It wasn't. The dot of light from the tunnel's entrance had disappeared long ago, and we didn't know whether we'd been in there for five minutes or an hour. No more fun ride. We'd been swallowed by a giant python and were never coming out. Any moment I expected Rod Serling to pop up and narrate our imminent doom: "And so they drove forever and ever in the endless tunnel, two godless hippies headed straight for . . . The Twilight Zone."

By the time a speck of light finally appeared in front of us, our minds were as blown as if we'd dropped acid. Once out of the tunnel, Marvin pulled over to the side of the road so we could read the little highway sign poking out of the dirt. We were now in Chamonix, France and had just driven more than eleven kilometers through Mont Blanc, the longest highway tunnel in the world.

It might have helped if we'd been reading the signs before we drove in. But that wasn't what counterculture cynics like us did. We believed in nothing, trusted no one. We demanded truth and freedom; and once we got them, we declared we'd rather die than get old.

When the 1970s philosophical free-for-all climaxed at Jonestown, a new expression entered the culture. To "drink the

Kool-Aid" meant to go headfirst into darkness, however untrustworthy the person telling you to do that might be, all the while wishing and hoping that the light would emerge, and that what you believed in was actually true.

It was how I'd always lived my life.

Clayton Willow, on the other hand, decided it was safer to stay in the tunnel.

> *It's been said we shall know the truth, and the truth will make us free. So how far will a man go to keep from being free—when freedom means truth, and truth means facing all the wrong he knows he's done?*
>
> *The answer is, he'll go as far as he can.*
>
> *If he's a small man, with little power, he won't be able to build a wall of defenses much bigger than a backyard fence. But if he is a man of the world, a man of great power such as Clayton Willow, he will have access to the best materials: the mortar of deceit and the brick of lies. The Prince of Darkness enthusiastically becomes architect and friend to the man of power who cannot bear the truth.*
>
> *And so the walls get built to hold on to a make-believe world. And outside that world grows the tree of life; while inside, like a cold and dark tomb, the light begins to fade, and man begins to walk as a shadow of who he once was. And he accepts this—indeed, he designed these walls—because deep in his heart, he is terrified that if he lets go, he will lose something that he desperately wants to keep.*

Just A Closer Walk With Thee

Two years after I'd sequestered my Sundays for writing and to protect my new faith from people like the Church Lady, I discovered I still had one foot in the faulty foundation of the

Music and the people who brought it to me. That revelation took place one morning when I turned on the radio and my gospel show sounded awfully familiar. Evidently Sheila Robinson was not sitting down with a cup of herb tea at the radio station every Sunday at six A.M. I was listening to a pre-recorded tape, the same one that had been broadcast the previous week.

Then I got a phone call from Patti's friend in Chicago. He was visiting California and had heard about a place in East Oakland that was, in his words, "on fire for the Lord."

Maybe it was time to give church another try.

The facade of the storefront church on East 14th Street was flat and plain; a few squinty windows faced the treeless boulevard. We parked in front, between a soul food cafe and a barber shop with its twirling red-white-and-blue candy cane sign.

Inside the church, rows of wooden pews were divided by a center aisle leading to a platform furnished with two throne-like chairs on the left. To the right was a drum set, in front of which stood a sturdy piano. The piano's bench was occupied by a box-shaped woman who was singing "It Will Be Worth It All" and pounding the keys like a *conguero* when we walked in.

With everybody standing for worship, we entered unnoticed except by a female usher wearing a navy blue suit, nylon stockings, and sensible shoes. The lapel of her jacket displayed a gold badge with her name, Sister Harris, and she had on white cotton gloves. Sister Harris greeted us with a polite, welcoming nod and walked us to the fourth row, one gloved hand behind her back, just like Michael Jackson. With the other, she pointed to two empty seats. I nudged Patti's friend, trying to get him to look at the usher's gloved hand, but he'd already started singing along with the congregation.

A statuesque, dark-skinned woman with a mane of silver hair and a nattily dressed man slightly shorter than she stepped up to the platform and took their seats in the two thrones. His striped necktie and pocket square matched the color of her dress.

"He's the preacher," Patti's friend whispered. "And that's his wife."

Almost as quickly as he sat down, the preacher got up and started singing. On cue, the woman at the piano began playing what sounded to me like a rock and roll song. Raising one hand to the sky, the other on his hip, the preacher waved to the rhythm of the music. Everybody in the church began clapping and singing "Can't Nobody Do Me Like Jesus."

Then the preacher laughed, almost to himself, and did a little quickstep which turned into a one-foot skate across the platform.

James Brown's signature move!

My eyes must have been as big as biscuits. Bit by bit, all the soul music I'd ever heard, all the shticks I'd ever seen on stage, were taking place on the platform of this little church. *Now wait a minute...* I wanted to say, but the excitement was overwhelming, and I couldn't keep from joining in. A lady in the front row picked up a tambourine and turned that Motown rattlesnake-shake into something sacred. People were dancing in the aisle, rejoicing to music and the beat of the drums.

"All right, now!"

"Praise the Lawd!"

"Hallelujah, Jesus!"

"Wonderful Savior!"

After a while, things settled down, and the music shifted to a slow-tempo worship song led by a brother in a three-piece suit who looked like Eddie Kendricks. Overcome by emotion halfway through the song, he stopped singing, shook his head, and raised his hands in the air. He might have been crying.

"That's all right, now" somebody hollered from the front row, waving a handkerchief.

But then a different kind of song erupted out of the people, rising and falling in captivating cadence; it was melodic and strange and beautiful, even though I couldn't make sense of the words. When it subsided, the preacher's wife lifted up her right hand. It got pin-dropping quiet in the church, and then she began to speak. The words tumbled out, sounding as if she'd memorized the Bible; I couldn't imagine how she was able to remember it all. She went on for about five minutes, and then she said, "Thus saith the Lord," and everybody started shouting and clapping again.

"Can you give the Lord a praise offering?" said the preacher, jumping to his feet and clapping his hands. The whole place broke out in singing and dancing till everybody's Sunday best clung to them with sweat, and the ushers handed out paper fans donated by a nearby funeral home. When the congregation recovered enough to be seated, the preacher began pacing back and forth across the platform. Then he made his way up the aisle, directly toward us.

"You!" he shouted, pointing at Patti's friend.

What had he *done?* I was terrified.

Almost like he knew what came next, Patti's friend got up and walked to the platform. The preacher shook his wrists out of his coat cuffs as if he were a surgeon preparing to operate and put one large palm on the man's forehead, spewing out a jumble of syllables in a loud voice, spit flying. Two serious-looking brothers took their places on either side of Patti's friend, and the one who'd been singing stood behind him. I watched in horror as the preacher's hand came flying off his forehead, and

Patti's friend fell stiffly backwards into the arms of the three men who gently laid him down on the floor.

"Hallelujah, Jesus!" exclaimed the preacher. The unintelligible murmur began again, as loud as a chorus of cicadas, punctuated by hollers of "Great God-a-mighty!"

What the heck just happened? Was he dead?

From the floor, Patti's friend began to stir.

"Rest in the Lord, brother," said Eddie Kendricks, putting his hand on the fallen man's shoulder. The three men helped him to his feet and walked him back to where we were sitting. I slunk down as far as I could in the pew and checked the sanctuary for the nearest exit, in case the preacher came to get me next. Thankfully, he did not.

Before Patti's friend left to go back to Chicago, he tried to break down for me what had happened that Sunday in church. The beautiful, strange words that I didn't understand were spiritual language: speaking in "unknown tongues." It was a gift from God, he said, a way to worship and communicate with him, nothing to be afraid of. The oratory spoken by the preacher's wife and ending with, "Thus saith the Lord," was what God was saying to the congregation. The preacher putting his hand on a person's forehead was a blessing that could set them free from sickness or a troubled mind, and when he fell backwards, Patti's friend said, the spirit of God had entered him, and it was more than his body could contain. Again, he tried to tell me, it was nothing to be afraid of.

I wasn't so sure about that.

Yet in the same peculiar way I'd been drawn before, I kept going back to the little church in East Oakland, even after Patti's friend left. And the day the preacher called me out, I surprised myself by not running for the door. With his big hand on my forehead, the brothers surrounding me, and Sister Harris holding a neat square of purple polyester trimmed with gold braid to modestly cover my knees in case I went down, the preacher rattled on in his unknown tongue until I opened my mouth and began to utter strange sounds, too. I didn't fall backwards, and I wasn't really sure what had happened, but everyone in the pews cheered.

After that, I decided to become a member of the church and was welcomed with the right hand of fellowship: a hearty handshake from the preacher and his wife in front of the congregation.

Still, even after I got to know them, I never told the preacher or his wife about how God had answered my prayer for ten thousand dollars with a windfall at the nickel slot machine in Reno. I was afraid they wouldn't believe I hadn't been there gambling and sinning around, and the last thing I wanted was to be misunderstood or rejected.

Los Angeles, 1982

Give Peace A Chance

"How could you do this to us?"

My mother was stretched out across her bed, a cold washrag on her forehead, just like when she'd found out I was pregnant. This time I was trying to explain my decision to join a church.

"How could you abandon the Jews?" she wailed.

It was an odd question since none of us had ever read the Jewish Bible, nor had anyone taught me what it meant to be a Jew except for the prejudices I'd been handed and my mother's list of forbidden *goy* foods.

"Mom, I didn't abandon the Jews," I said. "Jesus was Jewish, and so were all his followers. In fact you couldn't be a Christian in those days unless you were a Jew."

This bit of irony caught her and my father off guard. Their professed reason for our family not attending a synagogue was because they wanted me to choose for myself. *Really?* We saw how that played out when I chose to make friends with kids who weren't Jewish. Or white.

And anyway, how could I be expected to choose wisely when I had no idea what the choices were? That lack of information, plus the all-you-can-eat smorgasbord of cosmic, cultish belief systems spread out before my generation were what had sent me on my quest for the Big Truth in the first place—a pursuit that had taken me through the wildernesses of teen pregnancy, jail, psychedelic drugs, Eastern religions; and providentially detoured me from the likes of Charles Manson, Jim Jones, a murderous boyfriend, death by exploding baby, and a fatal car crash—all culminating at the doorstep of a tongue-talking, African-American, holy roller church.

I suspect that my parents' real reason for not telling me anything about God or faith was my mother's fear of seeing her American family persecuted and destroyed for being Jews like her family in Poland had been. We never denied we were Jewish; our family just didn't practice Judaism. Like other fixations that divided "us" from "them," it was one of my mother's irrational distinctions spawned from the River. If we weren't practicing Judaism, maybe "they" wouldn't notice we were Jews.

"I can't explain it," I said to my parents. "All I know is that since I started going to church, I'm becoming a better person." That seemed to dial back the conflict.

I'd flown to Los Angeles not only to let them know I'd found religion but also to celebrate my parents' forty-sixth wedding anniversary. During the Depression, my father had been employed as a brush lettering artist, producing marquee banners for movie theaters and show cards for clothing stores. He asked my mother to marry him but then, just before the wedding, he got laid off.

"Let's get married anyway," she'd told him. And so in 1936, they did.

We celebrated with pizza and spumoni at my parents' favorite Italian restaurant, and when it came time for me to leave, my father drove me to the Burbank airport in his Toyota Corolla, which had replaced the red Mercury.

"You're my heart," he said, reaching across the seat for us to hug before I stepped out of the car. His shoulders were bony and thin under his long-sleeved, plaid shirt. I kissed him goodbye and got out of the car, watching with a mix of sadness and relief as he pulled away from the curb and drove off. I hurried into the terminal for my flight back to Oakland.

Sixty-five minutes later, the plane landed in the middle of a ferocious rainstorm. It was forty degrees colder in Oakland than it had been in Los Angeles, and unrelenting sheets of rain were hammering the airport sideways. There was no umbrella, no hat, no nothing that could have protected me. I lugged my suitcase into the flooded parking lot, searching for the Beetle; it seemed to take forever to find it. Soaked all the way through my clothes, I threw my saturated belongings into my car and drove home.

Two days later I could not get out of bed. I was intermittently burning up with fever and chattering with bone-chilling cold, hearing the roar of crowds shouting at a football game in my head. Jeanie was away on month-long assignment for the bank, so I drove myself to the emergency room of Kaiser Permanente on West MacArthur. Sweating and disoriented, I waited for a long time to see the doctor. He diagnosed me with a severe case of pneumonia and admitted me into the hospital, where I stayed for a week.

The preacher and his wife sent over two sisters from the church to take care of me when I got home. The sisters set me up in the living room's sofa bed so I wouldn't have to walk up and down the stairs, and showed up twice a day to fix my meals. And, oh yes, it was total *goy* food: chicken fried steak with gravy, squishy white bread and butter, canned corn, and homemade banana pudding. I'd never expected to be cared for like that. They refused to let me give them money for groceries, saying the preacher wanted to take care of everything while I was sick, including my prescriptions.

This act of kindness on the part of Christians toward their daughter transformed my parents' opinion of the church. It might have even made a favorable impression on them about Jesus. When I got well, I went to the local Honda dealer and traded in the Beetle for a shiny new silver Accord, paying for it with the money I got in Reno. The first thing I did in my new car was to drive to North Hollywood so I could show it off to my parents. They were happy. My dad sent me back to Oakland with a framed piece of his calligraphy as a gift to thank the preacher and his wife for taking care of me.

That year it seemed like everything that went on between my parents and me was weighted with meaning and intent; all of us trying so hard to show our love and appreciation to one another. Things were different now than they had been in 1969, when I'd handed them an ultimatum to accept my decisions or never see me again and moved out of their house to go live with Marvin.

I don't think I can ever fathom how much my parents loved me, how deeply I hurt them, or how little I truly understood their sacrifices for me, even taking into account the terrible mistakes they made: never allowing open, truthful discussion; leaving me to wither in the fifth grade; and forcing me, like Jochebed and Moses, to send my baby down the River. As I grew up and they grew old, we tried to fill with love the places that each of us had broken in one another's hearts, but the closer we got, the harder it was for me to appreciate their hopes and dreams without feeling that I'd destroyed them.

The Society for Calligraphy, which my father founded, and over which he'd been bestowed the title of Mentor, honored his seventieth birthday in October of 1982 with an elegant dinner gala at the Los Angeles Music Center. It was a rare opportunity for our whole family to come together under purely joyous circumstances, celebrating with people who admired and loved my parents, and who knew nothing of our fractured history.

I bought my mother a purple silk dress to wear for the occasion, and for myself, I chose a slinky gown from the vintage store in Berkeley. My dad got a sharp new suit. The party was magnificent, with guests flying in from all over the country to honor my dad. I was grateful that the calligraphers for whom he'd done so much did that for him. Seeing the outpouring of love extended to my parents, and hearing my father lauded in a grand public setting by his students and colleagues, made it a really happy night.

Perhaps the last really happy night we would ever have.

CHAPTER EIGHTEEN

1983-1985

Many Rivers To Cross

My mother's bouts with illness were not limited to a cold rag on the forehead. When I was a child, there had been unexplained late night trips to the emergency room and hushed conversations in Yiddish from behind my parents' closed bedroom door. The row of medicine bottles on her nightstand looked like a city skyline.

But no one would ever tell me what was actually wrong with her.

"Your mother's not feeling well" was the sum of it from my dad. The word "leukemia" got tossed around, but after a while nobody mentioned that anymore. When we spoke on the phone, my mother gushed about how wonderful her doctors were and tried to reassure me that everything was fine and not to worry. I was never sure what I wasn't supposed to worry about. While the prospect of my mother's death loomed over every conversation I had with my family, corralling all her mysteries into an identifiable, perhaps solvable, problem was impossible. No one, not even Aunt Mary, was willing to break the River's code of silence.

In 1983 I was summoned to what might be called a family meeting and told that my mother's spleen was enlarged, and the doctor said it had to be removed.

Was that really the problem? I wondered.

Prepared for the worst, I drove to Los Angeles and sat anxiously in the hospital waiting room with my dad, Aunt Mary, and my brothers, making small talk about nothing while she went under the knife. When the surgeon emerged to announce she'd made it through, we hugged one another, rejoicing as if that were the end of the trouble.

As soon as she recovered from that, her wonderful doctor told my mother that she had breast cancer; before I could get back to L.A., they sliced off her left one without any plan for reconstruction. She was devastated. When I visited her after that surgery, a frightened look hung over her face like a veil. Her once round cheeks were deflated, and purple circles framed her eyes. She wept as she told me what they'd done to her body. My mother had been a beautiful, shapely woman. Even into middle age, she didn't have wrinkles or appear old. Her suffering wore heavily on my father, too. He'd shared the burden of her afflictions, as he'd shared everything with her since they were married.

I drove back and forth to see my parents so many times that year I knew every tumbleweed on Interstate 5. It became hard to maintain traction in Oakland. My job at the bank and my shaky relationship with the bankers were decomposing. Emergencies became the norm. Just as I'd begin a new work week, or sit down to write, or meet somebody and sense the budding of a relationship, there'd be an urgent phone call regarding some awful thing I wasn't supposed to worry about, and I'd be forced to drop everything and rush to Los Angeles. After months of this, like Pavlov's dog, every time I heard the phone ring, even before I answered it, adrenaline shot through my body like a roller coaster. It felt like I was being injected with battery acid.

When my circuits were blown from frantic alarms and the absence of facts that might have put them into perspective—when my body, mind, and soul couldn't take any more—I got in my car and headed to the Napa Valley, where I could decompress and write in my journal.

Triple S Ranch, Calistoga

How many times have I sped through Napa and St. Helena in the Beetle, madness on my tail; demons, Motown, and Jesus all masterblasting in my head at the same time. How many mornings have I woken up here feeling worthless and crazy. Walking until my boots give me blisters, until the sun burns my shoulders, until the mixtape of citified hammering yammering in my mind runs out.

Sunrise.

Dew from my cabin's eaves drips on me like the anointing of holy oil as I open the door and step outside. A rooster crows; shiny black birds with crimson shoulder pads and little blue ones with hats talk story in the cool, misty air. The smell is fresh: of hay and horses. I inhale as deeply as if it were a joint. Later it will become the heady, dry perfume of dust on a hot afternoon.

A husky dog I've never seen before makes himself my pal and comes along to walk. We pass the plowed-over sod that used to be a vegetable garden; the walnut trees, now wild and unattended. The orchards, once lush with apples and plums, stand naked and stoic. We arrive at the pond, where the husky dog roots around in the marshes and then looks up, his nose muddy, waiting for me to applaud his antics.

> *The Triple S Ranch. With its yellow hot pot, Styrofoam cups, and tiny envelopes of coffee, sugar, and cream. But there's one thing missing: Rose. Big and blond. Standing in front of her kitchen window with its view of the trees and the mountains. Shelling peas or making tempura with shrimp I've brought her from Spengler's. She asks me what's the matter, and then I start crying, and then she tells me a story, and then I tell her a story, and then we are both laughing so hard we wet our pants.*
>
> *At night we drink Mateus by the fire while the cat, Poontang, saunters around like she owns the damn place. And still, we talk story. Till our glasses are empty, the fire's gone out, and both of us have fallen asleep.*

As thankful as I was to have found Jesus, it's hard to believe that I lived through the 1980s without Rose. Never quite able to draw the *haoles* to Lokelani as she'd planned, Rose left the island a few months after I did and returned to San Francisco carrying something under her *muu-muu* that the Hawaiian agricultural inspector couldn't do anything about: a baby. After giving birth to her son, Joe, in the fall of 1979, she left the Bay Area for good and went back to her family's cattle ranch in Grass Lake, Michigan.

I visited her there during a brief lull between crises, and we trekked through the Michigan woods, acting as goofy as we'd done everywhere else. She showed me a cobweb-covered shack buried deep in the forest, where I decided I would live out my days with a dog and a shotgun if nothing better came up. We played with Joe on the bear skin rug in the den; he was a beautiful little boy with sparkling blue eyes. Rose was Rose, as always, in her kick-ass hiking boots, golden hair flying, bracelets clanging; forever cooking, laughing, and eating; surrounded by her parents, her sister, and her brothers and their wives, all of whom lived on the ranch.

It was times like these when I felt hitched to that otherwise elusive apparatus called humanity-relationship-family. Simple things like preparing a meal together, joking around, sharing with one another what happened that day, and feeling safe to speak what was on your mind without fear that someone would get angry about it seemed like the best moments anyone could ever have.

I wondered why it had never been that way in my family. We were blood relatives, but in our household, there always seemed to be a lot more bleeding than relating.

Blowin' In The Wind

My relationship with my two older brothers was, as they say, complicated.

Arriving eight and ten years respectively ahead of me, they enjoyed a private four-way lovefest with my parents until I was born. During World War II, they had all lived happily on Catalina Island, where my father served as a Merchant Marine. My mother wore pretty dresses that my Aunt Mary made for her and outfitted my brothers in little blue sailor suits that matched their daddy's uniform. My eldest brother, who was the firstborn among his cousins, had a sweet, passive nature that was eventually crushed by the high expectations placed on him. My other brother was charismatic and good-looking, but his charming traits morphed into rage and resentment when I arrived and replaced him as the doted-upon baby of the family.

Our problems weren't only due to natural order. When I was born, an expansion needed to be made to our family's two-bedroom house, so my father had a two-story structure built in the back. The downstairs was customized for my brothers, all the way to their 1950s cowboy drapes. Each of them had his own room, desk, closet, even his own sink in the bathroom; the upstairs was my father's art studio. Buzzers from the front house were connected to both floors so that my mother could summon everyone to meals.

I envied my brothers' freedom to stay up late at night and talk or read without our parents' nagging oversight. Every little peep that came out of my bedroom brought them in to scold me and demand I be a good girl and go to sleep. What I didn't know until I was older was that rather than being happy and liberated in their private quarters, my brothers were angry: convinced they'd been kicked out of the family nest to make room for me. They took it out on me with cruel remarks and mean-spirited teasing about how fat, ugly, stupid, and worthless I was; at the same time, lavishing me with big-brotherly love.

Wounded and confused, I sought help from my mother, who told me I was just being silly and amputated my antenna.

By the time I was ten years old both my brothers had left home, but the damage to my mind, heart, and soul was done: their mixed-up signals of love and abuse had given me a childhood of hopelessness and set me up for the harmful relationships that followed.

And since my family lived on the River, we never talked about it.

Good Lovin' Ain't Easy

Despite George Orwell's forecast, the clock did not strike thirteen when 1984 arrived. But my father did receive an offer from a book packager to write a calligraphy how-to manual for the Macmillan publishing company. He had already created an elaborate teaching guide for his UCLA students and asked if I would help him write the text. The publisher also wanted the book written out in calligraphy instead of being typeset.

I welcomed the diversion of getting back into an art groove with my dad, but the constant worry about my mother had been tough on him. Once an avid reader and master scribe, he'd begun to falter in his thought processes and ability to speak. At times he was so overwhelmed with anxiety and exhaustion, my father could barely complete a sentence.

The book packager asked for a proposal, so I drafted five pages of the first chapter and mailed them to my dad to write out in calligraphy. The next time I visited him, I could barely hide my shock when I saw how unsteady his hand had become. The pen strokes of the Mentor—who'd been commissioned by tycoons, kings, and presidents; whose calligraphy graced museums, movie titles, and Frank Sinatra album covers—were now as wobbly as the scratchings of a seismic monitor during an earthquake. With alarm bells going off in my soul, and disaster directly ahead, there was only one thing I could say.

"That's great, Daddy."

And we pushed on.

My mother was happy about our collaboration; the book project was a bright note in an otherwise grim season. But on October 1, 1984, she unexpectedly went into a coma and was rushed by paramedics to the hospital. The early morning telephone call came to me in Oakland as I was getting ready for work. The doctor said she wasn't going to recover and suggested my father make arrangements for her to receive the last rites. I had no idea if Jews even did that.

I called my supervisor at the bank to tell her I wasn't coming in and caught a flight to Burbank. My father picked me up, and we went to the hospital where Aunt Mary and my brothers were waiting. My mom was hooked up to a heart monitor, feeding tube, catheter, and IV. Like mourners hanging over a casket, each of us leaned over the metal rail of her bed, holding her hand, touching her face, and saying goodbye.

Two weeks later my mother woke up.

We would have celebrated if it weren't for what happened next. The moment she opened her eyes, Medicare set a fixed number of days that my mother could continue to stay in the hospital. Her actual condition didn't matter; it came down to a formula. And money. The hospital gave us one week to find a nursing home.

And, for whatever reason, that task fell to me.

Piece Of My Heart

My neck was killing me from holding the telephone receiver to my shoulder. An open copy of the local *Yellow Pages* phone book sat on my parents' kitchen table, scarred with the graffiti of my notes beside every listing in the Nursing Home and Mortuary categories. I ripped out a page, threw on my jacket, and headed for the first of three convalescent homes approved by the gods of Medicare who'd given us the ultimatum to get my mother out of the hospital.

An administrator walked me through the linoleum hallway of the first place. Like a filthy woman covered up with perfume, it reeked of disinfectant and death. Withered old bodies were collapsed into wheelchairs or tied to beds. I staggered out, nauseous, and took refuge in a pay telephone booth outside. From my purse, I pulled out some coins and the torn page of listings to call the next place; then pressed my face into the cold glass of the phone booth, sobbing. I couldn't do this to my mother. I shoved everything back into my purse and returned to my parents' house, where I fell into an exhausted, restless sleep.

> *I am on the top floor of a burning building with an old woman. I tell her we ought to try to get out, but she says, Let's eat dinner first and deal with it later. By the time we finish,*

there's no way out. I keep saying to myself in the dream, this doesn't have to happen.

It wasn't much better, but the last nursing home on Medicare's list—the one on Sepulveda Boulevard, next to the Jehovah's Witness Kingdom Hall—was the one we chose. My mother was brought in by ambu-van, bundled and helpless. She hated it. She couldn't talk because of sores in her mouth from the feeding tube. Two weeks in a coma without her bridge had caused her gums to shift, and she wasn't able to chew. She had bedsores and an infection from the catheter. Though she could still see us, the medicine she'd faithfully taken—for what, nobody really knew—had rendered her legally blind.

As soon as I got my mother into the nursing home, I was back on the phone trying to get her out. She was desperate to go home, and my father was utterly lost without her. I set about looking for a live-in caregiver, hoping that some of my parents' friends would volunteer to grocery shop or fill in for a couple of hours when needed. But despite forty years of holiday get-togethers at our house, no one offered to help. Maybe it was for the best, since instead of bringing her comfort and cheer, those who did visit my dying mother came wanting her to reassure them that everything was going to be okay.

I hired an LVN named Maxine to live at the house, cleared out my old bedroom for her, ordered hospital furniture for my mom, and set up my parents' double bed in a corner of the living room for my dad. Since the coma, I'd been flying to Los Angeles every fourth or fifth day, thanks to the bank's personal leave policy and twenty-dollar bills to help with plane fare pressed into my hand by Aunt Mary, my dad, and his brother, my Uncle Charley.

After three weeks at the convalescent hospital, everything was in place. On Friday, November 16th, six weeks after she'd gone into the coma, an ambu-van brought my mother home. I was told she sat happily at her kitchen table with my father, Maxine, and my eldest brother for dinner that night. I spoke to everyone on the phone, grateful that, for the first weekend in nearly two months, I could stay home in Oakland. The next morning I arose and leisurely filled my bathtub with lavender-scented suds, trying to regain a sense of my own life.

Then the phone rang. It was my eldest brother.

"Come home. Dad died."

"What? You mean Mom, right?"

"No, *Dad.*"

"What are you talking about?"

"Just get on a plane and get here now. We're waiting for you."

The battery acid began pumping through my veins. I hurried to get dressed in jeans and a sweater, leaving the lavender suds in the bathtub, and headed out to the Oakland airport. Again.

My father and I had just spoken the night before. He was happy. He hadn't been sick when I'd seen him five days earlier, though both of us were stressed to the max. After visiting my mom at the nursing home, we'd sat in a booth at Burger King, where I was hoping he would eat a meal; he'd gotten so thin. Instead he wanted to keep talking about my mother and how worried he was about everything. I was burned out and couldn't bear to listen anymore, so I went to the ladies room, just to get away, and left him sitting by himself—an unforgiveable act of treason that now tormented me. When I came out of the restroom, he stood up, leaving his half-eaten sandwich on the table, and then, as we'd done so many times, my father drove me to the Burbank airport in his Toyota Corolla.

"Mom's coming home Friday, Daddy. The nurse will be there with you. Everything's gonna be fine now," I said, not really sure it would.

A smile crossed his very tired face. "You're my heart, my life."

I opened the car door. "Bye, Daddy. I love you."

We hugged, and I headed to the terminal without looking back.

Maxine told us she'd seen a light in the kitchen about midnight and gone in there to find my dad sitting at the table, holding a glass of water, saying he wasn't feeling well. Probably indigestion, he said. He'd gone back to his bed in the living room, and in the morning she found him. Stiff, cold, blue. Sometime before I got there, his body was taken away without my mother being told what had happened. When throughout the day she asked where he was, my brothers told her he had the sniffles and didn't want her to catch anything.

They were waiting for me.

My mother didn't seem surprised when I walked into her bedroom late that afternoon. She was propped up with pillows in the hospital bed. It was then my brothers gave her a pill—they didn't tell her it was Valium—followed by a swallow of water, and we made small talk with her until we were reasonably sure it had kicked in. Then they told her. My mother's body jerked forward and then, eyes closed, she fell back against the pillow. I don't remember if she cried, but she said she'd known that something was going on. After forty-eight years together, my father would never have been apart from her all day.

I stayed until my dad's funeral, and the day I returned to Oakland, I learned that Macmillan had accepted our proposal for *Calligraphy: The Study of Letterforms*. After explaining that my father had died suddenly, I lied and told the book packager the manuscript was finished and that I'd hire another calligrapher to prepare the camera-ready text.

As a playwright and his daughter, I believed I could write the book in my father's voice. But it was a massive project in the midst of a chaotic season. My world was now little more than a sweep of go-here-do-that scented with airplane exhaust, juggling the bankers and trips to L.A. I hadn't danced, gone to church, or written about Clayton Willow for months. Yet I was compelled to see my father's calligraphy book to completion as a tribute to his legacy. Sort of like wanting the show to go on when Buriel died.

Stand By Me

It was on New Year's Eve, heading into 1985, that I got the call I'd known was coming but tried not to anticipate. My mother had again slipped into a coma, reportedly crying out, "Take me, God," before her eyes rolled back in her head and she went under. An ambulance had taken her to the nearby North Hollywood Medical Center.

I thought about those words, "Take me, God." Did she really mean them? Had they also been on my father's lips when he left this world? He must have been happy when my mother came home, but maybe his fear of being left behind after she died was greater than his joy. Perhaps, given the opportunity, he decided to check out first. I don't think it's unreasonable to believe that sometimes we're given the choice to stay or go. People fight to stay alive. Or they don't.

This time was different; I didn't rush down there to be at her side, sensing the need to pull myself together for what was likely to come next. Five days into January, at about four o'clock in the afternoon, I arrived at the Medical Center. With my mother still in a coma, I held her warm hand and told her how much I loved her, and how sorry I was for all the trouble I'd put her and my father through over the years; giving her the farewell I hadn't been able to give to him. I stayed about two hours.

Back at my parents' house, I ate a can of something I found in the cupboard and then tried to rest. But I couldn't bring myself to sleep in any of the beds: certainly not my mother's, nor the one my father died in. My old room, now tinged with the odor of Maxine's perfume, was out of the question.

I lay down on the floor of the living room in my street clothes and pulled a cushion from the sofa for my head. I left the light on. It felt right to be uncomfortable, and I drifted in and out of an uneasy sleep. About ten o'clock the hospital called. *Your mother is gone.* I had no proof, but I felt certain that she had held on until I could get there, and then, like my father, she let go.

A few days later, for the second time in less than two months, I stood in front of wet, rolled-back earth waiting to swallow one of my parents. My father apparently rested in peace as my mother's casket was lowered into the double grave atop his. The soil was muddy, and the January clouds that shadowed the cemetery were appropriately somber and gray.

But something was different now; I was an orphan. Without a mother or father between myself and eternity, my position on the planet had changed. People tried to console me, but there was little anyone could say that hadn't been said six weeks earlier. Instead, the words of Jesus came to me. "Be faithful until death, and I will give you the crown of life."[4]

I had been faithful unto two deaths; I hoped that meant that something good would happen next.

---

[4] Revelation 2:10. Scripture taken from the New King James Version. Copyright © 1982 by Thomas Nelson, Inc. Used by permission. All rights reserved.

PART FOUR

MY GIRL

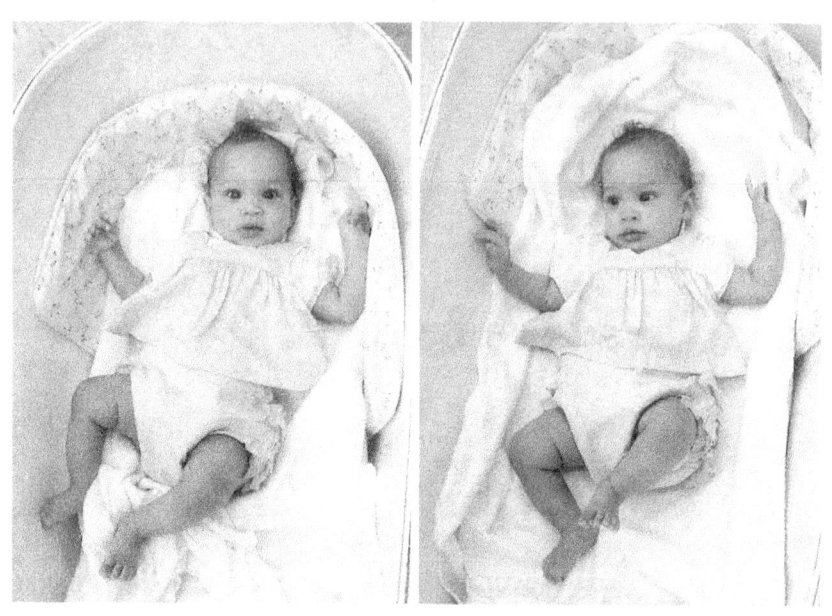

CHAPTER NINETEEN

Oakland, 1985-1987

I've Been Loving You Too Long

> *My precious daughter, I have treasured you since the day your life began—in the face of all who opposed me, through obstacles and pain, beyond distance and time. They took you from me, but they can never take away my love for you. I am your mother. I will never give up. (Journal Entry, 1976)*

It wasn't as if I never thought about her.

Every year on my daughter's birthday, I wrote to her in my journal, giving myself permission to peep into the padlocked place in my heart labeled "birthmother." That led to wondering, but wondering led nowhere since I'd signed away my parental rights for a closed adoption, the only kind I was told could be done in 1967.

The day after she was born, my daughter was taken from the hospital and placed into foster care. Four weeks later, my parents drove me to the Los Angeles County Department of Adoptions where, under their watchful eyes, I signed a relinquishment form terminating all rights to my child. The case worker said that when my baby was adopted, her birth certificate would be amended: my name would be removed and her original birth record sealed by a court order.

"No one will ever know," the case worker promised.

At seventeen years old, I summoned the forces of the River to make what I thought would be a lifetime vow never to second-guess having given up my baby for adoption. I wanted to believe what the adults who ruled my life told me: that it was the right and only thing to do.

While there was no way I could "pretend it never happened," I did manage to bury it deep enough to allow my daughter to grow up without interference, feeling paralyzed each year as her birthday approached, and not knowing why I had to look away from young moms pushing strollers around the park. I became pregnant with the loss of my child, and over the years, that loss grew into a pain in my heart so big I didn't even know I was carrying it.

They say that time heals all wounds, but it doesn't. Time is just a subcontractor to the River, doling out a benevolent humanitarian service in order for damaged people to continue on with our lives even after the worst, most unimaginable and inhumane things happen to us. We remember that horrible things happened, but we don't remember the horror itself; that's the part Time buries on our behalf. Otherwise we would go mad.

But the horror is still there, and when it becomes an obstacle to our future, an excavation team arrives and begins to tear off all the neat work that Time has done and expose the festering wound so it can be healed. The process is as agonizing and brutal as it was when we were damaged in the first place, so we intermittently open up or shut down, depending on which is causing the worse pain.

In 1979 I began a correspondence with the Los Angeles County Department of Adoptions. My daughter was only twelve years old then; I knew she'd have to wait another six years before she could legally search for me. But after losing as much as I had in the 1970s and coming so close to death, it seemed important to create a paper trail in case she ever did come looking and I was no longer around. My vow not to disrupt her life didn't exclude the possibility that someday my daughter might want to find me.

A case worker whose name was Bonnie sent me what she was allowed to share about my child: a summary of the adoption report, minus identifying details about her or her adoptive parents. I had given my daughter the name Rachel, but Bonnie said it was changed when her birth certificate was amended.

The report stated that she'd been four months old when she was adopted by a black couple in their early thirties. A year later they adopted a boy who was one year older than Rachel, giving her a big brother. The father was in the military, stationed in California during the adoption, and the mother was an actress and a singer. I hoped that meant my daughter would grow up with a love for music and art, as I had. The last worker to visit them before the family moved out of state described Rachel as exceptional in her abilities and a well-adjusted toddler. This was all I could be told, but it was far more than I'd known before.

Included with the summary were two Polaroid photographs of my baby, presumably taken when she was in foster care. She lay on her back looking up at the camera with enormous eyes, arms raised, dressed in a tiny outfit with puffy sleeves and a diaper. I put the photos in a hinged double frame, intermittently displaying them on my dresser and hiding them from sight in a drawer.

Corresponding with Bonnie provided me with the first safe haven, apart from my journal, for the thoughts, feelings, and questions I had about the child I'd been told to pretend I'd never given birth to. I was allowed to send letters and birthday cards for placement in my daughter's file, as long as they did not contain identifying information. I began doing so in the hope that if she ever decided to contact the Department of Adoptions, my daughter would know that her birthmother loved her and had not given her up willingly; that she would understand, and perhaps she would love me, too.

When my daughter turned eighteen years old in 1985, the same year in which I became an orphan, I registered with Adoptees Liberty Movement Association, or ALMA, who put my name and contact info into a computer database with the date, time, and place of my child's birth.

And then I waited.

Neutron Dance

No way was I ever moving back to North Hollywood.

Notwithstanding my new faith and the circle of artists and singers I'd become friends with in Los Angeles, the ghosts of my childhood had only been minimized, not driven out. My visits with Patti and others when I was there ended not unlike Cinderella's return home after the ball: back to the house I grew up in, where I'd felt so alone, misunderstood, and worthless.

Three hundred and fifty miles away I was in control. With its predictable people, its grit, and its bountiful trees and lakes, Oakland was now my home and Dolores Avenue my sanctuary.

So when I learned that in their Last Will and Testament my parents had left me their property in North Hollywood, I cleared out their belongings from front house and turned it into a rental in order to help pay for the new expenses I also inherited, like taxes and insurance. The legacy of my father's artwork, books, calligraphy, and equipment would remain in his studio until I could get down there to sort it out. So would decades of accumulated junk in the garage, including cans of dried-up paint, a conked-out lawn mower, rusty tools, reels of home movies, and a collection of taped-up boxes, suitcases, and a steamer trunk belonging to vagabond souls who'd imposed on my parents to let them store their possessions in our garage but never came back to retrieve them.

With my parents gone, I had no interest in their house and anticipated that someday, if the one on Dolores Avenue went up for sale, I would trade the one in North Hollywood for it. That was my long-range plan.

Now, however, after two years of traveling back and forth to Los Angeles, I was anxious to resume my routine of African dance, morning runs in the misty hills, going to the holy roller church in East Oakland, and finishing my novel about Clayton Willow.

But before I could do any of those things, I had to complete my father's calligraphy book and deliver it camera-ready to the publisher, return to my full-time job at the bank, and settle whatever was possible to settle of my parents' estate with my brothers—none of which was simple or easy.

Nearly a year later, with the help of a local calligrapher and a probate attorney whose firm was one of the bank's corporate clients, everything finally got done. But instead of a victory lap at the finish line, I collapsed in the middle of disco aerobics at the Oakland Athletic Club, stricken with a paralyzing headache and nausea. Without so much as a blood test, the nurse at Kaiser said I had meningitis ("It's going around"). When that didn't turn out to be the case, I was sent for a CAT scan and told I might have a brain aneurysm, but they weren't sure, and I should come back in a month.

I languished in bed for weeks, drugged on pain meds, unable to stand up without blacking out, and terrified that at thirty-five years old I was going to spend the rest of my life in a bleak, smelly nursing home, like the one my mom had been in.

When all hope seemed lost, a friend stopped by with a book she'd been reading about the physiology of stress and its assault on the endocrine system. Each page of *Mind As Healer, Mind As Slayer* was an eye-opener as to the cause of my mystery illness: an overload of stress hormones from the toxic fight-or-flight adrenaline cocktail I'd been living on for two years—that push-button jolt of battery acid coursing through my veins at every twist and turn of my family's drama.

At last I knew what had made me sick: I'd continued to move at warp speed after my parents died, unaware of the disaster building up inside my body. When the drama settled, and there was no more high-dose adrenaline to keep me up, I broke down. I did not have an aneurysm; I wasn't doomed to become an invalid. I'd been poisoned by my own body's jump-to-it reaction to every alarm bell that rang.

Discovering this was a life-changing moment of clarity, one that prompted me to claim ownership of my health. Instead of more tests, more drugs, or another CAT scan, I began going to holistic doctors who put me on a program of physical, mental, and emotional therapies that brought me back to life.

By January 1986 I was well enough to return to my job at the bank, just in time to share the collective horror of the Challenger disaster with my coworkers. That catastrophic event, in which the space shuttle disintegrated seconds into flight, killing everyone aboard, was an appropriate preview to the end of my banking career later that year.

It's All Over Now, Baby Blue

The bank had kept their part of the bargain, taking care of my life with financial compensation and health insurance during the course of my many absences. I was thankful for that. But the sandy soil in which the bankers and I planted our respective concerns had eroded.

As they expected from all their employees, the bankers wanted my loyalty, and the way for me to show that was to climb the corporate ladder with them. But the dangling carrot of an increase in my job title and pay grade hadn't caused me to forget my mission as an artist. When I declined their offer, the free spirit that had once intrigued them became regarded as a mutinous, uncontrollable risk.

As 1986 dragged on, I was perpetually in trouble. Every task at which I excelled went unacknowledged, and minor infractions that were formerly overlooked, like letting my filing pile up for three or four days, became major crimes. By December I was written up for insubordination, put on probation, and dismissed from the office for the rest of the year without pay. But after dealing with my mother's illnesses, the death of both my parents, writing a book, and surviving my own medical crisis, I wasn't about to be sent home crying by bankers.

A trip to Baja seemed like a better idea.

For two weeks I ate fish tacos, swam in the ocean, and sought fresh insight about my future under Mexico's sunny skies. I was miserably off course from finishing my novel about Clayton Willow. Receiving a steady paycheck had been great. So had everything I'd learned about finances while working at the bank. But just as when I knew it was over with the Buddhists, there was little I could do to convince myself that staying in the corporate world was right for me. I needed to refocus on who I really wanted to be: a great writer.

On January 5, 1987, the two-year anniversary of my mother's death, I returned to the bank from probationary exile. The bankers likely expected me to be repentant. Instead, I handed in my resignation, thanking the team for all they'd done to support me during six of the most difficult years of my life, and telling them what a privilege it had been to work there. I was grateful, I said, but it was time to move on.

When my supervisor, an irritable, chain-smoking woman, asked where I was headed next, I told her I was going back to being a writer and an artist—what I'd been doing before I came to work at the bank.

"You mean you don't have another job?" she asked, tapping her toe.

"Nope," I said, smiling as I scooped my belongings into a Safeway bag.

I watched her shoulders stiffen and her eyebrows come together in a tight knot.

"Thanks for everything," I said, throwing the bag over my arm. Waving goodbye to the tellers, I headed out the front door into Franklin Street's gleaming winter sunshine.

It felt like the ultimate insubordination.

Take Me To The River

It's been said that everything happens for a reason. Whether that reason is good or bad is often yet to be determined. But it does seem that if we can get through what's bad without becoming bad ourselves, we will one day arrive at what's good, and perhaps by then we will also understand the reason.

Along with leaving to each one of us a property they owned—the North Hollywood house and two parcels in the California desert—my parents left my brothers and me equal portions of their remaining cash. While not an extravagant amount, I knew it would be enough for me to live on while I completed my novel, sort of like receiving a grant from the National Endowment for the Arts. With that as my plan, I prepared to become the author of a *New York Times* best seller.

Then I received a notice from the landlady that she was putting the Dolores Avenue house up for sale. The thought of another disruption to my life was unbearable; I contemplated ripping up the notice and pretending I'd never received it.

Yet, hadn't owning this house been my dream? I decided to at least look into what it would take to exchange the house in North Hollywood for the one on Dolores Avenue. Maybe I could stall the landlady and make an offer.

It wasn't that simple. Before I could sell North Hollywood, I'd have to evict my tenant and carefully sort through what was in my father's upstairs studio, as well as mountains of rat-pack miscellany downstairs and in the garage. The house itself was in bad shape; the trauma of their final years had overwhelmed my parents, who hadn't painted it or done any repairs for a decade. Even if I could get all that done before someone else made an offer on the Oakland house, it would be impossible for me to pursue my writing at the same time.

Then again, spending the time and money I had set aside for finishing my novel on looking for a new place to live in Oakland was not what I wanted either.

Uncertain about what to do next, I took to sitting outside on my front porch with a cup of coffee at sunrise, looking for inspiration in the flocks of birds soaring over Dimond Canyon while the sky changed from orange to blue, and listening to the rising hum of busy-bee commuters on Park Boulevard. At least one thing was simple: the decision I would make about the Dolores Avenue house was mine alone. Jeanie had gotten a promotion and moved to Palo Alto.

I thought about how many times circumstances had pushed me away from something I wanted toward something that was so unimaginably better. Like not wanting to leave Market Street and winding up here. Was this now another left-handed journey?

Day after day I listened for an answer in the rustle of the wind and the resonance of my heart. Eventually I came to accept the idea which repeatedly emerged out of the bewildering whirlpool of my thoughts, though it utterly defied reason, sentiment, and history: Put all my belongings into a nearby storage unit, go back to Los Angeles, and live in the two rooms of my father's kitchenless art studio while I finished writing my novel.

Starving artist.

Yes, I knew how to live that kind of life. And it would be temporary, just until I sold my novel and could afford to move back to Oakland.

I mailed the landlady a certified letter and told her I'd be out by September.

Then I began the process of saying goodbye to my friends and everything I loved in Oakland: the writers in Leonard's Monday night workshop; my fellow African dancers; Aeeshah, whose love and lessons about attitudinal healing continued to inform my life; and the two women who had become my best friends in the Bay Area: Halifu Osumare, my dance mentor, and Gloria Weinstock, with whom I shared an everlasting bond following Buriel's death.

I took a farewell run through the Berkeley hills and my neighborhood. I drove to Lake Temescal, where I sat on the beach for an afternoon remembering Boni and her two kids. Finally, I went for one last tour of the winding backroads of the Napa Valley, tooling along the marshes of San Pablo Bay, turning north at Sears Point Raceway, and making a quick stop at the Cherry Cider Stand. I waved to the cows at Stornetta's Dairy, cruised along Highway 29's majestic canopy of trees in St. Helena, and ended up in Calistoga for the last time.

I knew there was a reason for what I was about to do. I told everyone it was to devote myself to the life of an artist, making it sound like a romantic, sacrificial act of courage. Yet under that colorful narrative, another motive was churning in my soul.

Going back to the River wasn't about being an artist; it had to do with recovering a part of my life that had been buried and left for dead.

∾

Goodbye . . . So long . . .
Sunset.
Ashby Avenue fishing place: where it all began, fifteen years ago with the Blues Man. Sitting in my car watching the waves undulate: gray, green, blue; rolling toward me under extravagant twilight skies that no one's brush can paint. This is where I come to find myself, staring at the lapping water and San Francisco sparkling on the other side of the Bay Bridge like a pot of gold at the end of a rainbow.
"Higher Love," sings Steve Winwood on the radio.
Then, it's moving day.
*Seventy miles an hour down Interstate 5. At two o'clock I pass the Sylmar Aqueduct and cross into the San Fernando Valley. Without warning, a ferocious pain rips across my chest. Reduced to sobs, I can barely keep driving as I recall the happiness and relief I always felt when going in the opposite direction—*away *from this wretched Valley. Back to Oakland. Back to MY life, MY house, MY freedom, MY world.*
After all I've been through, why do I have to give up so much more?
It's a complaint, not a question, but then God answers; in that way of his that dries my tears, mends my heart, and makes me willing to bunk up with the lions.
"MY, MY, MY, Selimah. Don't you know your life isn't yours anymore?
"You belong to me now."

CHAPTER TWENTY

Los Angeles, 1987-1988

My arrival in Los Angeles, just after Labor Day 1987, was welcomed with a massive earthquake in nearby Whittier, collapse of the stock market, and a letter from the Macmillan publishing company informing me that after barely a year on the shelf, *Calligraphy: The Study of Letterforms* was being remaindered. That meant the book I'd worked so hard on to honor my father's legacy would likely be shredded unless buyers for thousands of unsold copies could be found. Hoping I could sell some books to members of the Society for Calligraphy, I purchased six cases on my credit card and rearranged the garage to make room for them, as well as for the things that had to be taken out of my father's studio so I could move my bed, desk, and clothes into it.

It was strange sleeping upstairs in the space where my father had worked, but better than if I'd tried to occupy the front house which still teemed with sorrow and bad memories. Night after night I was haunted by dreams in which my parents were still alive, smiling and waving at me as they puttered around in the front yard, and sending me into a panic over why had I given away their clothes.

You Can Make It If You Try

I hadn't expected finances to be such a problem. Even with rental income from the front house, living on the property I now owned hadn't turned out to be "free" after all. Whenever something went haywire with the electricity, the plumbing backed up, the roof leaked, or if a family of possums decided to make their home in the attic, I couldn't just call the landlord like I was used to doing. I *was* the landlord. That plus thousands of dollars I now had to pay for property taxes and insurance surpassed my simple definition of starving artist.

So when one of my father's calligraphy clients offered me a part-time job at her fancy public relations office in Beverly Hills, I accepted. Wanda was a lovely, sophisticated person, and the crown jewel of her business was an exclusive women's club whose members were married to wealthy, powerful bigwigs. My job was to help organize their charity events: glamorous fashion shows at Neiman Marcus, private luncheons at Beverly Hills restaurants, and black-tie galas at the city's most fashionable hotels. I got to know the venue managers, helped secure the arrangements, and wrote out all the invitations and place cards in calligraphy.

This was my first exposure to the rarified world of super-rich, Beverly Hills WASPs. My ethnic-hippie roots and shabby wardrobe were something of a novelty to the well-heeled society matrons I served, but they were always kind to me, and our relationship never became stale. I had fun working for Wanda.

I also made a few new friends who, like Patti, became my sisters in the spirit. One of them was Akosua Busia. Akosua was from a prestigious family in Ghana, and her father, like mine, had been a beloved professor who transformed the lives of his students. He was also one of Ghana's most distinguished political leaders.

Akosua was expressive, funny, always garbed in exotic African outfits, overflowing with sisterly compassion, and ready to pray with me at any hour. Educated in Britain, she had an elegant and proper way about her, but her soul was humble and salt-of-the-earth. She lived less than a mile from my house and was an artist, writer, and actress; most recognized for her role as Nettie in the Stephen Spielberg movie, *The Color Purple*. Of great delight to me was that she'd also played Bigger Thomas's girlfriend, Bessie, in the 1986 film of Richard Wright's novel, *Native Son*.

I was thankful to have Akosua for a friend. Besides our fathers and our faith, our love of art and Africana, our friendship was intertwined in so many ways. Yet never could we imagine what lie ahead.

Something About You

One good thing about moving to Southern California was that it was closer to the beauty and beaches of Santa Barbara, which I'd fallen in love with at the Writers Conference. As Calistoga had been my runaway go-to from Oakland, when life in L.A.'s fast lane got crazy, I'd drive ninety miles up the coast to spend the weekend in Santa Barbara with my friend Joye and her family.

Joye and I met in a workshop at the conference in which she'd read a hilarious first-person account of life in the margins with her trailer-trash husband. After the conference ended, she invited me to her house for dinner, but Joye didn't live in a trailer park, nor was her husband a slouch. Their home was in the tony Santa Barbara enclave of Montecito, and her family looked like they just stepped out of the pages of *Town & Country.*

Joye and I were watching *Star Search* on a Saturday night in 1988 as competition for Best Female Vocalist narrowed down to two finalists. After a hearty introduction by host Ed McMahon, a dazzling young woman wearing chandelier earrings took the stage. Her name was Dee Dee, and she sang "Since I Fell For You," an old torch song with lyrics as long-suffering as anything that ever came out of Motown.

Dee Dee had a powerful, bluesy voice just right for that song, but it was her looks that grabbed my attention. From shape of her nose and her mocha skin tone, she appeared to be maybe part Jewish, part black; and her long, dark, curly hair was exactly like mine. When she turned to the side and I saw her face in profile, I gasped; the fleeting image was the same one I saw in the mirror. It was a stunning moment; the first time I'd ever put an adult face on the abstraction labeled "my daughter." Shaken, I walked outside alone and tried to make sense what just happened. It felt as if I'd been shoved in front of an open doorway and now stood there, tantalized and terrified by what might be on the other side.

When I got home the next day, the excavation team—the one subcontracted by Time and the River—rolled in to begin demolition.

It's Alright Ma (I'm Only Bleeding)

I'm not sure how I wound up at the cemetery the following Saturday. Maybe it was a full moon, or maybe I drank too much coffee. Maybe it was because I'd read in their newsletter that ALMA was holding a meeting that day near my house. My emotions were on edge; my body felt anxious. I wanted to jump out of my skin. I wanted to hide. I wanted to escape. *I didn't know what I wanted.* So I decided to drive up to Mount Washington and walk the familiar hills of my old neighborhood listening to Van Morrison's *Astral Weeks* on my Walkman.

But on the way there I impulsively turned off the freeway near Burbank and headed for the tall iron gates of Forest Lawn, where acres of dead bodies lay under a blanket of lush grass.

More golf course than graveyard, it wasn't what I needed. What I was looking for was a place that was breathtaking in its awfulness and overwhelmed with the enormity and sorrow of Death: a horrid repository of broken dreams and interrupted lives. A house of grief.

And then I remembered.

I know a place like that.

I got back on the freeway, and where the Golden State merged with the Pasadena, I could see what I was looking for nestled into the mountain, bathed in jaundiced, yellow light. I exited at Avenue 43, but instead of going left and toward Mount Washington, I turned right, up to Griffin, past La Fortuna Market and the next generation of brown-skinned men standing in front of it.

My heart stopped as I rounded the curve and turned onto Avenue 33. Like the Great Pyramid of Giza, it still towered monstrously over everything else on the street. I stopped the car in front of the Florence Crittenton Home for Unwed Mothers and pulled out a crumpled Kleenex, a pen, and my journal.

> *I used to live here.*
>
> *Twenty-one years ago I lived here.*
>
> *I was your prisoner.*
>
> *I was glad to get away from my parents. How unbearable could my life at home have been that I considered this hateful cuckoo's nest a refuge? Here I was forced to fight everyone: smug administrators, lying adoption workers, manipulating psychologists, bitchy girls. When you're busy fighting, there's no time to be wounded. You just stop the bleeding with rags and keep slugging away.*
>
> *I sit here in front of this awful place, shaking, nauseous. For the first time in twenty-one years I let myself cry gasping, snotty sobs about what I lost. So much betrayal and pain was inflicted on me here.*

> "You hurt me," I say to the horrible building and everyone in it who took their turn punching down my sense of self and destroying the bond between me and the baby in my womb. Five months of psychological sabotage; told every day that something was wrong with me, that I didn't fit in, that I was different from everyone else, and that difference wasn't unique—it was bad. Made to feel so worthless that it was easy to agree I couldn't possibly be anyone's mother.
>
> I've finally awoken from the bad dream. Spit out the poisoned apple. Barfed up the Kool-Aid. Been pulled from the River.
>
> No longer is it enough to leave a paper trail. I have been robbed. I am hurt. I am angry, and it's time to find my daughter.

∽

The playground of Valley Plaza Recreation Center was filled with children running madly, throwing sand, laughing, screaming, playing, fighting, and crying. *Look what you missed.* I didn't know if I ought to feel remorse or gratitude. I made my way across the noisy park to the building where the ALMA meeting was nearly over and took a seat on one of the folding chairs. Although I'd been registered in their database for three years, I'd never before gone to a meeting.

A shaggy blond man in his forties was telling the group about how he'd lost track of his pregnant girlfriend when he went to Vietnam. The deep crevices in his face and the shriveled arm that hung limply by his side told the rest of his story about what happened there. After searching for fifteen years, he'd finally found his daughter. I hadn't expected to learn that birth fathers also search.

When he finished, everyone clapped, and then the ALMA leader stood up and began talking about how to search. Although adoption records are supposed to be sealed, she said, sometimes mistakes are made. That was the needle in the bureaucratic haystack that we were looking for: *mistakes*. I tried to scribble down what she was telling us to do, beginning with contacting the Bureau of Vital Statistics and asking for a copy of my daughter's birth certificate under the name I gave her.

A woman about my age watched me struggling to take notes. She put her hand on my arm and quietly motioned for me to come with her outside. She was a birthmother who had found her son. I told her about seeing the singer on TV who I thought might be my daughter and how it had opened up a snake pit of emotions I didn't even know were in me. I blabbered on to this kind stranger, probably sounding incoherent, but she nodded, listening. Then she wrote down a name and phone number on a slip of paper.

"Do what you have to do," she said, pressing the paper into my hand. "But one day you're going to get fed up and realize that the only way you'll ever find your child is to pay somebody."

Having just signed on as a true believer in ALMA, the birthmother's disclaimer threw me for a curve. So I put her note in a safe place: the drawer where I kept my daughter's baby photos.

I'm Gonna Make You Love Me

I decided to call the *Star Search* production office to see what I could find out about Dee Dee. Despite how well she'd done, Dee Dee had been eliminated from the competition, and perhaps, I thought, she might be looking for a gig. I told the receptionist that I worked for a company in Beverly Hills which hired singers to perform at black-tie charity galas and was looking to reach Dee Dee's representative.

I expected her agent to call, but when the phone rang a few hours later, it was Dee Dee herself. I gushed about how much I'd enjoyed her performance on *Star Search*. She was sweet; I felt like a fraud and hoped I didn't sound as nervous as I was.

"I'm calling about two things," I said. "The company I work for produces gala events, and although we're not a talent agency, we sometimes hire singers to entertain at our parties. I can't promise anything, but I'd like to get your information for our files. Can you tell me about your training and your background?"

She said she'd studied music in school, but that her real training had come from her parents.

"My mother is a singer, so I learned my craft from her," Dee Dee said.

My hopes began to rise; Rachel's adoptive mother was a singer.

". . . and my dad's a musician. Sometimes we do gigs together."

That wasn't what I'd been told about my daughter's adoptive father, but I was willing to take a leap of faith. I tried to sound casual.

"Fabulous," I said. "Do you have brothers or sisters?"

"I do. A brother. He's a year older than me."

So did Rachel. Still, I needed to confirm an important fact.

"Do you mind if I ask how old you are, Dee Dee?"

"How old do you think I am?" she asked playfully.

"Twenty, twenty-one?" It was the age Rachel would be now.

She laughed. "Thank you. I'm twenty-seven. I look younger than I am."

Hold on, wait a minute. What? This doesn't compute.

"Are you sure?" I asked. "I mean, when's your birthday?"

She gave me a date nearly seven years before my daughter was born. That was too big to be a mistake. But before I could think of what to say next, Dee Dee had something to ask me.

"You mentioned there were two things you wanted to talk to me about. What was the other one?"

I recalled the speaker at the ALMA meeting saying not to be too direct; let the adoptee draw (or not draw) her own conclusion.

"Oh, I just asked about your birthday because besides your singing, you look like someone I haven't seen in a long time, and I thought maybe we might be related."

"I'm sorry," Dee Dee said, sounding as if she really were.

There was a pause, then her voice brightened up.

"Say, my girlfriends and I are singing at the Nucleus Nuance in Hollywood next weekend. Why don't you come?"

"Absolutely. I'd love to," I said, not quite believing I hadn't found my daughter. "Thank you, Dee Dee. I'll see you there."

I hung up the phone feeling a weird mix of disappointment and hope.

The Nucleus Nuance was a trendy jazz joint on Melrose Avenue, packed with hipsters and fashion plate femmes. From a front row table, I watched Dee Dee and her two girlfriends scat their way through a terrific set of 1940s jazz tunes, lighting up the club like rockets. The women took turns being featured, and when it was Dee Dee's solo, I was rapt with the way she held her microphone, threw her head back, and sang with so much passion.

At the break, I went backstage to introduce myself. Face-to-face the similarities in our appearance were as evident to her as they had been to me, even in the manner each of us were dressed. Dee Dee excused herself from her partners, asking if we could sit together at a table and talk until the next show.

Amid the hubbub of waiters serving dinner and customers talking loudly, I praised her singing, unable to hold back the waves of affection I felt for her, inappropriate as they may have been. I wondered if that was how I was going to feel when I really did find my daughter. But I'd made up my mind not to say anything else about my search. I didn't want to come off as some desperate, pathetic birthmother; I just wanted to be friends.

We ordered two small bottles of Perrier, and then Dee Dee asked me, "When we were on the phone, you said you were looking for someone. Do you mind telling me who that was?"

She had been listening all right. I studied her cheekbones and dark soulful eyes; her long, curly hair pulled to one side, just like how I was wearing mine. No getting around it; I owed her the truth.

"Well, to be honest, I was looking for my daughter," I said. "She was born in 1967. I was just a teenager, and my parents made me give her up for adoption. I've hoped for years that she would find me, but I never searched before. When I saw you on TV, something in me just opened up."

She didn't seem surprised or upset. But I felt guilty for having misrepresented myself.

"Dee Dee, I meant what I told you about working for a company in Beverly Hills and possibly being able to hire you for a gig. We really do produce gala events like that. But it was my heart that led me to make the call. I'm sorry, I hope I haven't offended you."

"No, not at all," she said, shaking her head. "I understand. Really, I do."

She looked down at her bottle of Perrier and then up at me.

"See, the funny thing about it is, I'm adopted."

CHAPTER TWENTY-ONE

Los Angeles, 1989-1991

I Can't Get Next To You

It wasn't easy to recover from the case of mistaken identity that took place with Dee Dee. I think both of us wanted it to be true, but her birthday and my daughter's were just too many years off the mark. After dropping the bombshell that she was an adoptee, Dee Dee said she'd always dreamed that her birthmother would find her. Surprised to hear that, I asked why she didn't search, and she told me that it had been hurtful to their adoptive parents when her brother went looking for his birthmother. Dee Dee said she couldn't bear to put them through that a second time.

I wondered if that might be why Rachel hadn't searched for me.

For whatever reason, and with regret, I never saw Dee Dee again. Yet our 1988 encounter got me started doing the snoop work that I'd learned from ALMA and to regularly attend their local meetings. I also joined a group called Concerned United Birthparents and signed up with the International Soundex Reunion Registry.

Two years later, I still hadn't found the magic mistake that would tell me who my daughter was or where to find her. It had been almost five years since she turned eighteen, and while I'd assumed that a child with my DNA would surely be curious and search for me, there'd been no database match; neither had the Department of Adoptions received an inquiry.

Hitting so many dead ends on a pursuit in which I never thought I'd engage, I set aside what happened with Dee Dee and pulled out the manuscript of my novel about Clayton Willow.

The Harder They Come

Maybe I was being tough on him, but in order to make Clayton Willow's story come full circle—and since at the top, there was no where to go but down—I decided that in August 1968 my soul singer would get shot and killed by a delusional fan while on stage at the Whiskey a Go Go.

> *They call it the Devil's Dance—the hellish, swirling Santa Ana winds that descend on Los Angeles from the desert, forecast with a warning and inevitably blamed for everything from earthquakes to madness. The hot winds signal danger, like the clanging of a railroad crossing bell. Parched yellow weeds on L.A. hillsides stand erect, like kitchen matches, waiting for the spark. Waiting for the wind. It's the demon spook that unnerves everyone. What will happen next? Eighty-eight degrees at midnight, tree limbs banging against your window, the distant wail of fire engine sirens. Your favorite TV show interrupted by breaking news: a slash of red-orange flames ravenously chewing their way across the canyons. People are on the street. Looking for a breeze. Waiting for something to explode.*

That's how it'd been in August 1965, when Clayton Willow played the Shrine Auditorium while a Negro motorist named Marquette Frye got jacked up by the cops in Watts. And that's the way it was again this furnace-hot night three years later, when Clayton returned to the City of Angels to sign a record deal and sing a night of soul music at the most popular club on the Sunset Strip.

The line of fans outside the Whiskey a Go Go twisted around the corner and uphill into a narrow street of houses. The crowd was as wide as the sidewalk, spilling over the curb with mini-skirted white girls, Afro-centric soul sisters, Mack Daddy brothers, and long-haired hippies whose bare knees poked out of torn jeans. Tonight's appearance of Clayton Willow not only attracted what the record company called a crossover audience, it also brought together a metamorphosing slice of American culture.

And yet for Clayton Willow, the end had just begun.

Writing about the notorious Santa Ana winds, the setting for both the Watts riots and Clayton's death, it occurred to me that it had also been in the same month, August, in 1969, when the three women I'd ridden the elevator with at Sybil Brand Jail had stormed the Tate and LaBianca homes, carrying out the bloody mayhem ordered by Charles Manson.

But before I could muse over that mystery; or write the climactic scene of my novel, in which my hero, like his hero Sam Cooke, dies the violent, untimely death he was so arrogantly certain he'd avoid, the drama of my own life overtook that of my fictional character.

Please Mr. Postman

On her birthday in March 1990, I wrote a letter to Rachel in my journal, as I'd done for so many years. My daughter was now twenty-three years old, an adult woman the same age I was when I left Los Angeles for San Francisco. I wondered if she was married or a mother herself, if she was a seeker and wanderer like I was, or if she even thought about me. As I wrote that year's letter, I had the odd feeling that she was right around the corner. Then I was struck by a thought unlike any I'd ever had: that it was no longer enough to wait for her to find me. Next I heard these words, as distinct and unmistakable as others that had been spoken to my soul:

"Your daughter needs to be found by you."

Like the abrupt movement of tectonic plates on a fault line, a colossal shift in my perception took place. I had vowed never to interfere in my daughter's life.

So then why was I searching?

More importantly, why *wasn't* she? Until I met Dee Dee, I never considered that my daughter might be afraid or otherwise constrained from looking for me. Or that she might not even know she was adopted.

But why did she *need* to be found, and specifically *by me*?

The following afternoon, I came home early from Wanda's and turned on the TV to catch the last few minutes of *Oprah*. The talk show queen was interviewing biracial adults about the confusion they'd navigated as children. Maybe my daughter, who'd been raised by black parents, didn't know that her birthmother was white. Or maybe she did know and was hesitant to look for me out of fear she might be rejected.

I took this perplexing pile of revelations to my next ALMA meeting, hoping they could help me make sense of it and decide what to do next. But before my turn came to speak, another birthmother shared the spectacular news of her reunion. While paid searching was not endorsed by ALMA, the birthmother admitted that after years of fruitless effort, she'd hired a man who had some kind of back door to sealed public records and had obtained her child's amended birth certificate. It was the same man whose name and phone number I'd been given at my first meeting at the Recreation Center. When I got home, I pulled out the note that I'd stashed in a drawer with my daughter's baby pictures. The next day I placed the call.

Ten days and three hundred dollars later, I received a photocopy of my daughter's amended birth certificate. Trembling as I read it, the date and time were exactly when I'd given birth. But all the other information, including her name and the names of her parents, had been changed. My daughter, Rachel, had become Ellen Latrice Garner.

The searcher also provided an address for her in Oklahoma City, a place as foreign to this California girl as the moon, but likely an important piece of the twenty-three-year-old mystery that was about to be solved.

I took her baby pictures out of their frame and photocopied them onto the top of a sheet of paper to use as stationery. And I then wrote my daughter a letter.

May 15, 1990

Dear Ellen,

I've had these photos in a frame since I was seventeen years old. And I've waited all your life to write you this letter. You have been on my heart, in my prayers, and filled many pages of my diary over the years since society and circumstance forced us apart. I listed myself with every agency and would have welcomed your call at any time. But I held back from contacting you until now out of respect for your parents and your relationship with them, which I have always hoped was wonderful. It is not my intention to compete in that relationship, but rather to complete the picture for you . . . and now for myself.

This year on your birthday, something in my heart said maybe you were waiting for me to make the first move. So I am stepping out in faith and sending you this letter. Here is my telephone number; please call me collect. We have so much to talk about.

I rejoice at the hope of your call.
With love, Selimah

I mailed the letter and waited. Nothing. I called Directory Assistance in Oklahoma City, but they had no listing for her. In July I sent another letter, and it came back marked "Unclaimed." When my third letter was returned in October, it was stamped "Moved. Left No Forwarding Address." By December, I was beset with crying jags and depression. My circle-of-life treasure hunt had led nowhere, and my faith had hit a brick wall.

Precious Lord, Take My Hand

It was just supposed to be a 1991 New Year's day lunch with a friend. But when I told a legal secretary I'd recently met about how I was at a dead-end in the search for my daughter, she suggested trying a bounty hunter, like those used by attorneys to catch bail jumpers. There was a directory in the Culver City law office where she worked, she said, and the next day I received the telephone number of a fellow named Monty in Oklahoma City.

After hearing my story, Monty said that finding my daughter would be a pleasure compared to the nefarious suspects he normally tracked down, and he offered his help without charge. I was overjoyed. Three days later, he told me that Ellen had just quit her job at Hertz Worldwide Reservations. Then he tracked her to an apartment, but it was rented under someone else's name. He got a phone number, but the woman who answered his call said she wasn't Ellen Garner.

The starts and stops kept on like that until the end of March, when Monty said he couldn't devote any more time to my case, and he'd try to get somebody else to help me. I thanked him, but I felt like we'd just been grasping at the wind.

With a heavy heart, I visited a church near my house that Sunday for spiritual solace. I entered the sanctuary and took a seat next to a neatly dressed woman in her late seventies. During a break in the service, in which we introduced ourselves, the woman told me her name was Doris. I shared with her how I'd given up my baby for adoption in 1967 and that my attempts to find her had been unsuccessful. Doris said I should keep searching, and then she told me that besides having two sons of their own, she and her husband, Jim, had been foster parents to a lot of kids. Many of them were disabled, including an infant born blind and deaf whom they raised until she was twelve years old.

I had never thought about where my newborn daughter was taken to from the hospital, or about the foster parents who cared for her those first four months of her life. I hoped they'd been good people like Doris and Jim. I thanked Doris for encouraging me and gave her a hug. As we sat down, and the pastor opened his Bible to deliver the message, Doris took my hand and drew close so that no one else could hear what she wanted to say.

"You know, among all those precious children we cared for, my husband and I were also foster parents to the son of Susan Atkins, one of Charles Manson's followers."

Tears On My Pillow

"Yes ma'am, I'll find your daughter in three days," the new bounty hunter said.

It was the same thing Monty had told me. Unlike Monty, however, the new guy wanted me to overnight mail him a thousand dollars. He said he charged forty dollars an hour but guessed it would be cheaper for me to pay him up front. Plus, of course, there would also be expenses, amount unknown.

I felt utterly sick.

I told him I didn't have a thousand dollars, and after some negotiations, we agreed on three hundred and fifty; also that before I sent him any money, he'd confirm that he'd really found her. The new bounty hunter said he'd call me back the next day, but he didn't. I struggled to stay hopeful, but that became increasingly difficult as weeks passed by and Mother's Day approached.

With no way to go forward, I turned back to the Florence Crittenton Home for Unwed Mothers, which I'd heard was now providing services for teenage moms and their babies. Maybe there were some remnants from my case file in an old cabinet or the basement, I thought. The new director was surprised by my request; no other Crittenton alumna had ever contacted the Home before. Without promising anything, she invited me to come by and talk.

I drove the familiar route, circling Griffin, and turned onto Avenue 33. Jutting out of the hillside, the Home still looked like a grotesque monument, but the sight of it no longer intimidated me. I parked my car and walked up the concrete steps. Pushing open the front door, the place seemed smaller now.

The director, Pat, was a lovely Mexican-American woman with short brown hair. Her office was the former visiting room with its full box of Kleenex. She was amiable and pleasant, nothing like the old hag from when I was a resident. Gone were the horrible stacks of files; replaced by a sleek desktop computer and a box of floppy disks.

Pat said she couldn't find any files dating back to the 1960s, but when she'd mentioned to the girls who were living there that a resident from that era was coming by, they were fascinated and wanted to meet me. We headed to the dining room, no longer painted Pepto-Bismol pink, where six teenage girls with their babies were eagerly waiting to ask me questions.

"What was it like when you lived here?"

"Which was your room?"

"What happened to your baby?"

"Were you a hippie?"

I started by telling them what a nightmare my five months at Flossie's had been: living there under a fake name, writing phony letters about "boarding school," being told what a bad person I was, and having to look at that stupid, impossible sign, which thankfully no longer hung over the reception area: *To Get Along You Have To Go Along.*

The girls listened, but my story did not seem to register. Two decades and a social revolution later, the punishment I endured for being an unwed mother was ancient history. My tales about Binky, and how we used to waddle down to Five Points to buy yarn, sounded macabre, even silly, and we all wound up laughing.

"What about your baby?" asked a girl whose two-month-old infant was fast asleep in her arms. "Wasn't it hard for you to give her away?"

The room grew silent.

"I wasn't given a choice to keep her," I said. "All I could choose to do was go on."

A dark-haired girl about fifteen spoke up. "I didn't have a choice either," she said. "In my family, we're Catholic, you keep the baby. Yeah, it was a sin I got pregnant, but it would have been way worse to give my kid away or have an abortion."

The baby in her lap started crying, and the teenager's expression shifted from defiant to broken.

"I just didn't want to give up college and my dreams to do this."

I glanced toward Pat who was standing in the corner of the dining room listening to us with her arms crossed and her head down. I walked over to where the dark-haired girl was sitting and gently put my hand on her shoulder.

"There's still more for you, for all of you. Really, there is," I said. "You must take hold of that and believe it. What other people or circumstances say you can't do isn't what decides your future unless you agree to it. Hang onto your dreams. Your life can still be happy and fulfilling if you refuse to be overwhelmed or beaten down by what you're going through right now."

In a weird way, it felt like I was speaking to myself.

After more questions, some laughs, and a couple of smelly diapers, Pat emerged from the corner to say that our time was up. The teens hugged me and asked the director to let me come visit them again. Never had I imagined that all the misery and abuse I went through at Flossie's might become encouragement for someone else.

You Keep Me Hangin' On

The bounty hunter called me two days later to say he'd found my daughter. She had her own apartment, he said, and he assured me that the woman he'd spoken to was Ellen Garner, having gotten that confirmation with a ruse about calling from the Department of Motor Vehicles.

I had forbidden both him and Monty from telling her why they were calling; I wanted that first moment of recognition between me and my daughter to belong only to us. I needed her to know from my lips that I never meant to hurt her; and if she was going to reject me, I wanted it to be personal.

But now the bounty hunter wanted four hundred and fifty dollars before he would give me Ellen's phone number, a hundred dollars more than we'd agreed to. I didn't know what to do. It seemed as if at every stage of the search, he'd tried to squeeze as much money out of me as he could. All I had in my savings account was four hundred dollars, so I told him I could pay that, and he said okay.

By this time it was late afternoon; I hurriedly wrote a check and rushed to the post office to send it to him by overnight mail. When I finished doing that, the bank had closed, so I went back the next morning to transfer the money from savings to checking. But when the bounty hunter took my check to his bank in Oklahoma City, the funds hadn't yet posted, and he telephoned me, angry as hornets, saying he didn't give a rat's ass about me or my daughter and was going to rip up her number.

I pleaded with him.

"The money is there," I said. "Please. Don't do that. I just had to move it from one account to the other. Go ahead, call my bank. Or just go back to your bank and have them put it through again. It's in there now, I swear."

He mumbled something and then hung up. I tried calling him back, but got his answering machine. Frantic, I left a message, begging him not to tear up my daughter's phone number.

My hopes were demolished; I cried for hours in despair. Finally, when there nothing left in me but pain, I decided to walk it off. I laced up my Reeboks, grabbed a cassette tape from the drawer without looking at its label, and snapped it into my Walkman. When I got outside and put on my headphones, I heard the strong, clear voices of the Soul Stirrers, the mighty men of God whose music had become my rock; they were singing "By and By (We'll Understand It Better By and By)."

I played the song over and over again as I walked the streets of North Hollywood; until my feet got sore, my emotions went numb, and the sun dropped from the sky. I walked past all three schools I'd attended and the library where I met Richard Wright. As the night grew black and starless, I doubted that I would ever understand anything. Every man I'd ever loved or trusted had betrayed me in one way or another: disappointing me, disappearing, or dying.

And yet hovering over all that grief was the Spirit who had never failed or left me, who always answered my calls, whose voice assured me I was loved, and in whose abiding reality I knew I would always be safe. Unlike people, if I stepped away from Jesus, he'd still be there with open arms when I returned; ready to give me love, courage, wisdom, and direction.

I turned around and made my way back home through the dark and empty streets. By the time I put my key in the door, I felt as though I had been shot through the chest by a machine gun. Stepping inside, I flipped on the lights; my eyes landed on a framed quotation from Thomas Edison that I'd done in calligraphy and hung on the wall:

"Many of life's failures are people who did not realize how close to success they were when they gave up."

Okay then, I thought, *if I have to start over, I'll start over.*

But I wasn't about to let this Oklahoma cowboy win his evil game; I would go to the bank in the morning and put a stop payment on the check.

Then I noticed that the message light on my answering machine was blinking.

It was the bounty hunter calling to say he'd cashed my check. And leaving me Ellen Garner's telephone number.

CHAPTER TWENTY-TWO

Los Angeles, Saturday, May 18, 1991

Someday We'll Be Together

I awoke to fading moonlight spilling into my room through its west-facing window. Slipping out of bed, I went to the opposite window, pulled open the drapes, and was met by the dazzling pink glare of sunrise, precisely as the moon signed off on the other side.

Like everywhere I'd lived, my father's studio was a perch in the sky: a treehouse sanctuary where he'd worked, listened to his music, and read books on philosophy and art. After living up here for four years, I was ashamed at how little I knew about what had gone on in his private world when my father was alive.

While packing up his things to make room for mine, I found some hair-raising correspondence and books about the Soviet Union. Employed as a graphic artist at the movie studios during the anti-Communist riptide of the late 1940s, my father was a colleague of blacklisted screenwriter Dalton Trumbo, and in 1951 my parents received a letter from the INS stating their intent to deport my mother for her unofficial entry into the United States.

Reading that letter forced me to see the world for the first time through my mother's fearful eyes. A subsequent letter, paper-clipped to the first one, stated that such action would not be taken, although there was no explanation as to how the problem was resolved. It was yet one more example of the hushed and mysterious ways of my family's life on the River.

Except for when I'd gone with him to UCLA, and then been his apprentice at Columbia Pictures, most of the time my father and I spent together was at the dinner table, in the living room of our front house, or in his car. My visits popping in and out of his studio were mainly to ask for help with calligraphy or art supplies, which he was always generous to give; or for permission to do things my mother disapproved of, to which he always said no. I wondered if he'd ever felt misunderstood out here in the back, alone in his thoughts and working so hard by himself to support us.

A rustling outside caught my attention: a squirrel had leapt into the orange tree after performing a tightrope act on the power line. I watched him grab an orange bigger than his head, eat it greedily, and then toss the hollowed-out fruit shell to the ground. The camellias my mother planted when I was born were now as tall as the roof; their branches rested gently against my window like the rose vines had on Oakland's Market Street. And into this verdant Eden, hummingbirds, sparrows, and butterflies stopped by, peering at me as I watched them.

Before coming to live up here, I had never seen my parents' lives, or the property that had meant so much to them, from this point of view. Now that they were dead, it was humbling and painful.

I fixed a cup of tea and took it into the other room, where a desk had replaced my dad's drafting table, and my books filled the shelves that had once contained his. A messy sheaf of papers related to my search for Ellen was waiting for me, topped by a scrap of paper more precious than anything I'd ever possessed; on it was written the phone number left by the bounty hunter.

Carefully I set that to one side and dug through the pile for the script that my ALMA counselor had helped me write when I thought Monty was about to find her. I wasn't taking any chances blurting out something that might scare off my daughter. My script was neatly typed, double-spaced, and across the top of the paper in letters a full inch high, I wrote:

TRUST YOURSELF. LISTEN.

It was the moment I'd dreamed of, yet I sat motionless, looking at my script and the telephone. Now that I had my daughter's number in my hand, now that I could finally make the call, what was I afraid of? The truth was about to be made known, but perhaps coming face-to-face with truth and what that might require of me was more frightening than all the years I'd spent pretending things never happened.

I called Akosua and poured out my dilemma.

"Selimah," she said, "God is turning the ashes of your past into beauty. No matter what is trying to scare you away, no matter what happens, you have to keep trusting him. Make the call. It will be so very well with your soul."

I loved my friend. We prayed, and I promised we'd talk later.

The ALMA counselor had told me that before launching into my script, I should tell my daughter that I was calling long distance and having trouble with my phone, then ask her to write down my number in case we got disconnected. That way, if she freaked out and hung up, she'd know how to reach me when she was ready.

I dialed the number, and a woman with a faint twang in her voice answered the phone.

Is this Ellen Garner?" I asked.

There was a notable pause.

"Yes, it is."

Despite all my preparation, I was shocked. I strained into the telephone receiver for something more than a voice, suddenly desperate to see her face and touch her.

"Who is this?" She sounded irked.

"My name is Selimah Nemoy," I said, reciting my telephone number and that she could call me back collect if we got disconnected.

"I'm looking for someone very special in my family whom I haven't seen for a long time, and my search has led to you."

I heard a gasp at the other end of the line, but I kept talking, eyes on the ALMA script.

"Two weeks after my seventeenth birthday, in March 1967, I gave birth to a daughter whom I was forced to give up for adoption—"

Before I could say any more, she squealed and burst out crying.

"How did you get my phone number? Are you my mother? Oh God, I wanted to know you all my life, but I thought you were dead."

She thought I was dead.

I'd never considered that to be the reason my daughter didn't search.

"But I'm not dead, Ellen," I said. "I'm right here. And I've been searching for you for a very long time."

The anguish in her voice turned into a soft chuckle.

"I know you've been looking for me," she said. "Believe me, I know. I've been getting strange phone calls for months; people wanting to know who I am, where I live, where I work. I didn't know who was looking for me, so when they asked, I said I wasn't me; I never told them anything."

So, every time Monty thought he missed her, he'd actually found my daughter, but Ellen had denied who she was.

"The thing is," she continued, "I never say 'yes' on the telephone when someone whom I don't know calls looking for me. But this time, even though it makes no sense, I knew who you were from the minute you spoke. And somehow, today, I was ready. If you'd called me five weeks ago, I'd never have let you in my life."

Apparently the timing of today's phone call had been perfect, despite the dead-ends, drama, and disappointments of my three-year-journey. Two days earlier, Ellen said—on the same day I'd been bickering with the bounty hunter—she'd gone to a counselor for the first time to talk about the conflicted feelings she had about being adopted. It was her parents who told her that her birthmother was dead; perhaps a well-intentioned but misguided idea suggested by the adoption agency, like the fake stories that my parents and I were encouraged to tell.

We talked for hours; there was so much each of us wanted to share. Ellen told me about the difficulties she'd faced in her life and the good friends she had now; and I told her about being sent to the home for unwed mothers and how Buriel encouraged me to become a writer.

I called Akosua, my head spinning with excitement. She wanted to hear every detail of our conversation, and then I mentioned I'd booked a flight to Oklahoma City to meet my daughter.

"Marvelous! So what do you think about this," she said. "How would you like to have that first moment when you and Ellen meet documented on video? Maybe Oprah has a reunion show coming up, and she'd want to do your story. I could call her and ask."

Akosua and Oprah had remained friends after working together in *The Color Purple* and *Native Son*. I hadn't thought of anything except meeting my daughter, but I told Akosua to go ahead and ask. On Monday, I received a call from a man named LeGrande at Harpo Studios informing me that Oprah had a reunion show taping scheduled for June 3rd, two weeks away.

"We've already lined up another birthmother who will be introduced to her adult child on the show," he said. "We'd like you and your daughter to do the same."

"You mean wait until we are on TV to actually meet for the first time?"

"Yes, that's the way the other reunion will take place."

"But I already have a plane ticket to meet her in Oklahoma City."

The offer wasn't even tempting. I had vowed never to give that first moment to anyone else. Not the bounty hunter. Not even Oprah. It belonged to just me and my child. I thanked LeGrande and told him we couldn't handle the pressure of meeting on the show.

Later that day, he called back, offering to have an ABC news crew at the airport to film me getting off the plane and meeting Ellen in Oklahoma City. After our initial reunion, he said, Harpo would fly us to Chicago for the taping.

Ellen agreed, and so our plans were set. Thanks to Akosua and Oprah, we would have two visits instead of just one.

I sent a photo of myself to Ellen so she'd know what I looked like when I arrived. I was wearing a flowered dress and ankle-high boots, standing outside in the sunshine with my arms open wide. I didn't know what my daughter expected her forty-one-year-old mother to look like, but when she got it, she called me on the phone, shouting with glee.

"My mom's a hippie!"

Baby, It's You

Boarding pass in hand, I hurried to the United Airlines gate, laughing out loud as I heard a Motown playlist and the Temptations's "Since I Lost My Baby" broadcast through the Burbank airport's public address system, as if it were my own personal soundtrack.

After what seemed like the longest plane ride in history, delayed by bad weather and arriving hours off schedule, I stepped into the terminal at Will Rogers Airport in Oklahoma City and was met by a galaxy of flashing lights, a wall of people, and a TV news crew from the local ABC affiliate. Bolting out of the crowd like a track star, a petite, fair-skinned girl in a blue dress with shoulder-length black hair flew toward me, sobbing, and tumbled into my arms.

"I waited for you for so long my face broke out!" she cried. "I was so scared."

My daughter!

We hugged tightly, and then I cupped her face in my hands to look at her. She was beautiful, with almond-shaped eyes and gorgeous full lips.

"I love you so much," we kept saying to one another. Neither of us wanted to let go. I don't know how we made it out of the airport and to her apartment; it was a glorious, thrilling blur. On that night's local news, the ABC station broadcast our tearful reunion.

I hadn't seen a picture of Ellen before we met, but unlike the faux recognition I'd had with Dee Dee, the longer I looked at my daughter, the less I saw of my face in hers. We touched and stared at one another, comparing everything: hands, feet, faces, hair. We were the same color, but her face was full; mine was narrow, like my dad's. I tried to connect the baby photos I'd kept in a drawer all these years to this adult woman, and then, looking at old black-and-white photos of my parents that I'd brought to show her, the surprising fact emerged. With her full cheeks, that forehead and nose, Ellen was the spitting image of my mother when she was young.

I had to laugh. *That's karma*, I thought. *The mom I drove crazy came back in the form of my own child.* We talked until dawn and fell asleep in one another's arms.

The next day Ellen took me to meet her brother, Robert. He was happy for us and wanted to know about my family, but it's possible that our reunion presented its own strange adjustment for him. We talked about searching for his birthmother, and I promised to send him information about ALMA when I got home.

Then we went to the home of Ellen's parents. I couldn't know what it meant to them for their daughter's birthmother to return from the dead, and they couldn't understand why I'd been compelled to find her. We all sat politely at their kitchen table, each of us guarding our emotions and our deepest thoughts.

While still believing they had only done what they thought was best, it seemed that neither Ellen's parents nor mine understood how resonant truth is in a child's soul, even when you lie to them. Rather than bind the family together, those lies had caused confusion and pain. I'm sure that the Garners, like my mother and father, never anticipated how hurtful their deception would be, yet in the worst of ways, my daughter's childhood had been a lot like mine. We'd both grown up on the River.

I Used To Think Miracles Came From Motown

Three days after saying goodbye to Ellen in Oklahoma City, I was on a plane to Chicago. Harpo Studios had reserved a suite for us at a luxury hotel on Lakeshore Drive in the city's most trendy neighborhood, the Gold Coast, and allotted us seventy-five dollars a day for food, more than my weekly budget. Best of all, the hotel was only two blocks from where Rose and her now twelve-year-old son, Joe, were living. I hadn't seen them since my visit to Michigan eight years earlier, so I asked LeGrande to book my flight to Chicago one day early.

It was late when I got there, but after dropping off my bags at her flat, Rose and I headed into the bustling night life. It was the first day of June, seventy degrees at ten o'clock at night, the best spring weather Chicago had seen in years. Horse carriages lined up to take visitors on buggy rides near the lake. The cafés and clubs were lit and lively. People young and old filled the streets; the night seemed truly magical.

The next morning a limo came at eight-thirty to take me to meet Ellen's arrival at the airport. Joe wanted to ride along, and the two of them became instant cousins. After twenty years as friends, Rose and I were in awe at seeing our children together. She and Joe helped us get settled into the hotel, and then the four of us went for lunch and shopping.

When we got back to the hotel, I realized how tired I was. I fixed myself a candlelit bath, something I'd missed since leaving the Dolores Avenue house in Oakland. Then I put on a fluffy hotel bathrobe and ordered room service, while Ellen went back out for a night on the town with Rose and Joe. When she returned, we stayed up most of the night talking. Early the next morning, the day of the taping, we were awakened by a phone call from Florence Fisher, the founder of ALMA, wanting to congratulate us.

After breakfast, the limo came to take us to Harpo Studios. That was fun, though I barely recall what the place looked like. From the time we arrived until the taping itself, all I could focus on was my daughter and being ready to tell my story when we got in front of the camera. It was in the dressing room while getting our makeup done that we met Oprah Winfrey. She was warm and friendly to us and seemed to have been quite touched by our reunion.

The theme of the show was "Stolen Babies Reunited With Their Mothers," and there were two other stories told that day: one was a birthmother who'd been reunited with her daughter through the ALMA registry, the women that LeGrande had told me were going to meet for the first time on camera; and the other was a heartbreaking tale of middle-aged twin brothers who had been kidnapped from their cribs and sold by black market baby broker Georgia Tann and her notorious Tennessee Children's Home Society.

Our segment was introduced with footage from the Oklahoma City airport with Ellen racing into my arms. Oprah asked me to tell my story first, and I talked about being hidden away at the home for unwed mothers, told I had no choice but to give up my baby for adoption, and then how I'd registered with ALMA when my daughter turned eighteen. Five years later, when she didn't look for me, I said, I hired someone to find her.

Then Oprah asked Ellen, "Did you register, looking for her?"

"I had never registered," Ellen said. "I'd always been under the belief she was dead. I always wanted to know everything I could about her, and about three weeks ago, I considered registering but it would have been like a history search for me; I never hoped I would actually find her. . . . "

". . . Cause you thought she was dead," said Oprah.

"I thought she was dead."

Then Oprah asked me, "Did you have fears about how she would receive you when you found her?" She turned to the audience, "These are happy reunions, folks, and the reason we don't have unhappy ones on our show is because people who don't want to meet their long-lost child or mother don't want to come on our show and talk about it."

"I had fears," I said, "but my search for Ellen was really a search of faith. I didn't know where it was going to lead. In ALMA they counsel you, 'Don't look for some little kid who's been on his knees praying every night and fantasizing his mom will show up.' But I had the A-plus reunion they tell you don't dream of. When I called my daughter, she said she'd wanted to know me all her life. It was better than anything I could ever have imagined."

"Wow. A-plus reunion," said Oprah.

Beaming with joy, Ellen and I could not stop smiling or looking at one another.

"I just want to say," I added, "I had no idea what it would feel like to have a daughter. And I'm so thrilled and so happy. I didn't even realize what emptiness I had in my heart till I found her and knew what filled that place."

"That's great. Thank you," said Oprah, dabbing at a tear in her eye.

Before we left Chicago, I took Ellen to meet the Henleys, Patti's family, on South Rhodes. They were all so happy for us, especially Great-Great, Patti's grandmother, who called our reunion a miracle.

CHAPTER TWENTY-THREE

It's A Family Affair

There was still one secret to be confessed. That day my father picked me up from school in his red Mercury and took me back to our house, where my mother lay moaning in the bed about how I'd disgraced the family, both of them assumed that the young man who'd gotten me pregnant was the one I'd told them I danced with on Saturdays at the Teen Center. They didn't know anything about Douglas, whom I'd just met, and I didn't know how to tell them I had another boyfriend. Douglas was far away in New York anyway, and I hadn't heard from him since summer.

So I went along with the story that the Teen Center boy was responsible. When I told him that I was pregnant, he disappeared, and I didn't hear from him again for six months. Just days before I was due to give birth, he contacted me, pleading for us to get back together. I wasn't proud of what had happened, but by then—with neither he nor Douglas around for support, with it decided by my parents that the baby was going to be given up for adoption, and with "go home and pretend it never happened" hammered into my psyche—I'd buried the whole mixed-up fatherhood mess. With the end of my pregnancy (and my incarceration) near, I didn't have a bulldozer big enough to dig it all up for his sake.

The lie about my baby's father made its way onto my daughter's original birth certificate, which was ultimately sealed by a court order. A few years after she was born, I heard that my Teen Center boyfriend had enlisted in the military and died overseas. I couldn't help but believe that what I'd done was, in some way, to blame for the path he chose that led to his death. It was one more situation in which the lie that seemed easier to tell than the truth caused devastating and irredeemable damage.

Now that I'd found my daughter, I was determined that lie would not carry forward into her life. On the first day we met, when we got to her apartment in Oklahoma City, I told Ellen the whole shameful story.

After we taped the *Oprah* show, Ellen asked if I would try to find Douglas, and without hesitation, I said yes, though I had no idea where to look. Then I remembered that night at the Ash Grove when his mother, Ena, had shown up with her boa and her Jag, and how the Blues Man had gone home with her. Maybe he knew where Ena was, and if I could track her down, I'd find Douglas.

But it had been a long time since the Blues Man and I had seen one another. So I called Rose, thinking she might have his number. And as things go in that crazy, left-handed, circle-of-life way, the Blues Man just happened to be at Rose's house in Chicago when I called. She put him on the phone.

"Hey sister, Rose says you found your daughter. Congratulations."

It felt good to hear that deep voice, like the growl of a lion. And to know he was genuinely happy for me.

"Thank you. Been quite a journey. Did Rose tell you we were interviewed on *Oprah*?"

"Yeah, that's somethin' else."

"You know, her dad is Ena's son. She wants to meet him, but I haven't talked to him in eighteen years. Do you know where I could find Ena?"

"Man, I haven't seen Ena in I don't know how long," he said. "Last I heard, she became a real estate agent. Try calling the California Realty Board."

The Blues Man pointed me in the right direction, and I found Ena. She hadn't forgotten me, shrieking with joy when I told her that I'd searched for and found my daughter, and calling Ellen her "grandbaby," as if we'd been a family all these years. Douglas called me an hour later.

My last encounter with Douglas had been in 1973, when he mysteriously showed up at my house in Mount Washington the night before I moved to San Francisco. In the years since, he'd fathered a son and another daughter with two other women, and gotten into enough trouble to know that trouble wasn't the life he wanted. He was now married with two more sons, had given his heart to Jesus, and to our mutual astonishment, he and his family were living in an apartment just four blocks from my house. We could hardly believe that we'd never run into one another in the neighborhood.

He came over by himself, and we talked for a long time. Mischief still sparkled in his eyes, but his countenance and frame were that of a man who'd been seasoned by experience and time. Gratefully, it felt as if we had both been given a fresh start.

Love Will Find A Way

Douglas and I drove together to Los Angeles International Airport to meet our daughter on Friday, June 21, 1991. Holding flowers and a teddy bear, he nervously chewed a stick of gum as she got off the plane and dove into his arms. I was so happy for them. A TV news crew from the local ABC station and a reporter from the Valley newspaper were there to meet us, and our reunion was featured on the six o'clock news that night, as well as the front page of the *Daily News* the next morning. As we were walking out of the airport terminal to the parking lot, a woman stopped us, recognizing Ellen and me from the *Oprah* show, which had aired the day before.

We took Ellen to Venice Beach for lunch, and by the time we got back to North Hollywood, the three of us were in a harmonious groove, the likes of which I'd never felt before. We stopped at Douglas' apartment, where his wife and their two boys welcomed us with open arms. Ellen's other two half-siblings and Ena came by to meet her. Then my daughter and I made the four-block trek to my house. I fixed a bed for her on the sofa with a fluffy comforter and tucked my precious baby in with a kiss.

"I remember your smell," she said before rolling over to curl up and go to sleep. "Even if you did only hold me once."

Reunited

The next day I held a festive celebration in my backyard to introduce my daughter to the people who had supported my search for her, including the two family members who'd stood by me since my parents died: Aunt Mary and Uncle Charley. It may have been a jolt for my daughter to come to terms with having elderly Jewish relatives, but she was affectionate and loving with them, and they embraced her with warmth and acceptance. Despite my aunt and uncle being forced to endure the bogus story my parents tried to peddle when I was pregnant, the happiness of seeing us together was written all over their faces.

Akosua came to the party with her sister, Abena, as did Iva, the one member of my teenage Girlfriend pack with whom I'd stayed in touch. Joye and her husband, Roger, drove in from

Santa Barbara. Patti was on the road, but she and her family in Chicago were with us in so many other ways. My new friends in Los Angeles came, and those in Oakland sent flowers and telegrams. The celebration lasted until dark, with hugs, singing, and lots of food. It was a glorious day.

Amid our rejoicing, I thought back to the roller coaster of events that had led to this moment of redemption: how hard the journey had been to lose my baby, then to find her. And to finally know, after all these years, what real truth and love were. Our reunion had been a miracle, just like Patti's grandmother said. Behind us now was all the tragedy, confusion, and pain, and I was certain the years ahead for us would be happily ever after.

So as our guests began saying goodbye, I took Ellen by the hand, and we stood together, beaming and radiant with love, waving for them to hear one last tribute.

"Thank you for coming today," I said. "Thank you all for your support and encouragement."

And then I delivered the kind of blind-faith prophecy that only a River-raised true believer like me could come up with.

"I just want to say that I don't believe there will ever be a difficult moment that happens in our future in which God isn't going to remind my daughter and me of the miracle he's done. Everything else has got to be easy."

EPILOGUE

You're All I Need To Get By

In reality, very little of what took place after my daughter and I were reunited was easy. But like those eight-hour Sunday visits with my parents when I was pregnant, we did our best to assure one another of our love and that both of us were now complete.

If there was one thing I learned from growing up on the River, being blood-related, with its implied familiarity and expectations, does not ensure that members of a family will either live happily ever after, or fulfill the roles assigned to us by biology and circumstance to one another's satisfaction.

Despite my desire to do well by my daughter, there was no way for me to fully comprehend what her childhood had been like, much less unravel that twenty-four years later. Neither could she be expected to share the burden that I had carried since losing her.

There's no disputing we had the A-plus reunion that made Oprah Winfrey shed a tear. Or that my daughter had wanted to know me all her life. Yet when we actually laid hold of that shiny bauble of our dreams, its flaws and quickly-fading luster forced each of us to look back inside ourselves and figure out who we really were.

Just as success had been for Clayton Willow, once dreams are fulfilled, they are no longer magic. They become mere earthly circumstances to be dealt with, often requiring far more from us than we ever imagined we'd gain. In the same way that I was forced to examine my own life, it would take a personal reckoning for my daughter to sort out damage from blessing in hers. And certainly all of us who called ourselves her parents—the Garners, Douglas, and I—had registered in both those categories.

As meeting the Great Poet taught me, the things we admire and yearn for are far more beguiling from a distance. Up close, we see the pedestal for what it is: our imagination, and the person we've put on it, simply a trembling and vulnerable human being, just like us.

Soul Serenade

There was a moment in one of my African dance classes as we were moving across the floor in rows of three toward a wall of drummers when their sound eerily transcended the drums and transported me for an instant into the cosmos. Within that moment I heard these words:

"This is how I'm going to bring you home."

I had no plan to exit this world then or now, but I believe that on the day heaven calls, I will hear the drums, as well as a choir of voices like those who've taken me so near to there in this life: the Soul Stirrers, Otis Redding, Van Morrison, the Clark Sisters. I may never know what it was about the Music that so profoundly captivated my soul, but I have come to accept its prominence there as a gift, not a curse, and to take my lessons from its lyrics with the caveat that I once sought to impose on the masters of Motown: changing the word "you" in their songs to the word "God," and experiencing his love as a presence and power far surpassing the physical realm.

The Big Truth I searched for—and found—was that all my life, God's was the love I most needed and never had to beg for. Its power detoured me from the likes of Charles Manson, kept me out of Peoples Temple, and reordered my affections to make sure I wasn't in a tiny putt-putt of a car when it got plowed into by a drunk driver.

That love gave me fifteen minutes to ignorantly haggle with surgeons while I hemorrhaged nearly to death, sparing me from a one-way trip to Level Five. And at the tragic expense of my friend Boni's life, it caused me to see the dead end that lie ahead for me, too, if I didn't change my ways of thinking and behavior.

Perhaps my story ends where it began: with those words that crossed my mind in 1971 as I rode the jailhouse elevator with Manson devotees Susan Atkins, Patricia Krenwinkel, and Leslie Van Houten.

"There but for the grace of God go I."

And grace, like the Music, has ordered this remarkable journey—still rising from the River, and called My Life.

WITH LOVE

To the Blues Man
>who opened my eyes,

and to the Soul Singers
>through whom I met the Lover of my soul;

To the Playwright
>who taught me to take my writing seriously,

and to the Author
>who dared me to become a great writer;

To my Sisters in the spirit,
>and to the Spirit that holds our hearts in heavenly escrow;

To my Parents
>who loved me no matter what,

and to my Daughter
>whom I have loved all the days of her life

This book is dedicated.

AUTHOR'S NOTE

Incredible as it seems, my life is based on a true story.

- Ashleigh Brilliant

Everything in this book actually happened, though each of us involved may recall things a bit differently, and some events were condensed for smoother storytelling. It is also a faithful account of what I know, or was told, about incidents I did not witness firsthand but which dramatically impacted my life.

Today my daughter no longer goes by Ellen; she has chosen the name Kalila for herself. And because the role they played in my life was more important than who they are, some people in my story don't have names. Others were changed to protect the innocent, or perhaps the guilty.

I thank every person who encouraged me along the way.

ABOUT THE AUTHOR

Selimah Nemoy is a storyteller, journalist, dancer, calligrapher, and advocate for truth and love. Born in Los Angeles, her coming-of-age journey was shaped in the 1960s by soul music, then by the turbulent, multicultural 1970s in the San Francisco-Oakland Bay Area.

selimahnemoy.com
Facebook / Instagram

RESOURCES

FREE CULTURAL DECODER – Get a Decoder to the multicultural tapestry of music, people, and historical events referenced in *Since I Lost My Baby* at selimahnemoy.com

FREE BOOK CLUB READING GUIDE – Share your own takeaways from the author's journey to find love and the Big Truth, the losses she endured and the insights she gained, and the music that provided the soundtrack for her life (and maybe yours) at selimahnemoy.com

WATCH the *Oprah* interview at selimahnemoy.com

JOIN THE CONVERSATION at Facebook and Instagram

THE OG PRESS TEAM
Creation Designs
Purple Gem Marketing
Hocus Pocus Focus

and all the remarkable OGs of my youth
who held a light meter to my face and clicked
but never told me to smile.

www.ingramcontent.com/pod-product-compliance
Lightning Source LLC
Chambersburg PA
CBHW071220080526
44587CB00013BA/1446